LIVES IN STRESS

SAGE FOCUS EDITIONS

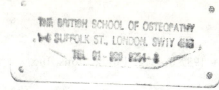
LIVES IN STRESS

Women and Depression

Edited by
DEBORAH BELLE

Foreword by JESSIE BERNARD

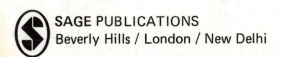

SAGE PUBLICATIONS
Beverly Hills / London / New Delhi

For information address:

SAGE Publications, Inc.
275 South Beverly Drive
Beverly Hills, California 90212

SAGE Publications India Pvt. Ltd.
C-236 Defence Colony
New Delhi 110 024, India

SAGE Publications Ltd
28 Banner Street
London EC1Y 8QE, England

Printed in the United States of America

Library of Congress Cataloging in Publication Data

Main entry under title:

Lives in stress.

    (Sage focus editions; 45)
    Presents the findings of the pilot study of the Stress and Families Project.
    "Published in cooperation with the Institute for the Study of Contemporary Social Problems."
    Includes bibliographies.
    1. Women—Mental health. 2 Depression, Mental—Social aspects. 3. Poverty—Psychological aspects. 4. Stress (Psychology) I. Belle, Deborah. II. Stress and Families Project. III. Institute for the Study of Contemporary Social Problems (U. S.)
RC451.4.W6L58   362.2′088042   81-18379

ISBN 0-8039-1768-6   AACR2
ISBN 0-8039-1769-4 (pbk.)

FIRST PRINTING

CONTENTS

FOREWORD

It has been known for some time that almost universally in the population of depressed persons women greatly outnumber men—in some places two to one, in others as much as three to one. But until recently this did not attract a great deal of research attention. In the last decade or so, however, the preponderance of women in the depressed population has challenged a considerable number of researchers. They asked what produced it. A number of cues resulted from the research. Regardless of the etiology of depression in individual cases, what did seem to stand out was that, overall, whatever the causative factors might be—learned helplessness, stressful role demands, "relational deficits," whatever—they were more prevalent in the female than in the male world.

This book on stress and families explores one small segment of that world, but a segment that contributes disproportionately to the depressed population. It documents what has been called "the feminization of poverty," but it carries no banner for any particularistic theory. It does not have to. True, it does present facts, even tables. True, it does pay obeisance to standard scientific research techniques. True, it *tells* us what depresses women. But it goes much further. It *shows* us what depresses them. It takes us behind the stereotypes. We can share the stresses that impinge on the women. Some women, reading of college students in poverty, may shudder inwardly, as John Bradford did at the thought that "there but for the grace of God walk I."

Some thoughtful readers viewing this small segment of the female world will be struck by the disproportionate part of the weight of the social system these women carry. In China there is a proverb, "women hold up half the sky," to which Mao allegedly added that the half of the sky women held up was heavier than the other half. Some of the women studied here are holding up a part of the sky that should have been held up by the father of their children. Some are helping parents, sisters, friends hold up their part. The load is made even heavier by the weight of social disparagement, discrimination, public hostility. Their part of the female world offers little support to help them maintain the self feeling that might lighten the load. A quiet "well done," for example, for the gallant copers among them. In this

7

segment of the female world the daily grind is more than a figure of speech; it does, literally, grind down the spirit.

How do you remake such a world? Where do you begin when so much needs doing? There are so many ways to be poor, so many ways to be depressed, so many ways to be put down. . . . This book does not pretend to have all the answers. It does suggest some. But perhaps equally important, it helps us—forces us—to see the questions more clearly. It becomes harder to pass by on the other side.

Jessie Bernard

PART I
INTRODUCTION

1

INTRODUCTION

DEBORAH BELLE

BACKGROUND OF THE STUDY

The decade of the 1970s held many paradoxes for women. The increasingly visible women's movement, the well-publicized entry of some women into prestigious jobs, and legislation protecting women's rights promised expanding opportunities. With much less fanfare, however, economic conditions actually deteriorated for many women over the course of the decade. Women and their children came to constitute an increasingly large proportion of America's poor, a phenomenon which has been called "the feminization of poverty" (Pearce, 1979).

Women's earnings, relative to those of men, have actually declined in recent years; and over half of the occupations women typically enter will not support a family above the poverty line (Barrett, 1979; Sawhill, 1976). Women college graduates earn less than male high school graduates and about as much as male high school dropouts (Barrett, 1979). Women full-time, year-round workers earn less than 60 percent of what male full-time, year-round workers earn in the same field (Barrett, 1979).

The escalating rate of marital separation and divorce, particularly among families with young children at home, has pushed many women into poverty (Ross & Sawhill, 1975). Few families receive regular child support payments from the noncustodial father over the years following a divorce, and even those who do typically receive only a small fraction of what it costs to feed, house, and clothe a family (Pearce, 1979). While many women must turn to government welfare payments to support their families, these benefits rarely raise families out of poverty. Three-fourths of all families receiving Aid to Families with Dependent Children (AFDC) benefits have poverty-level incomes, even after adding their legally allowed earnings or other income to their welfare checks, and virtually all families receiving AFDC payments would have incomes below the poverty line if they did not have additional income from other sources (Pearce, 1979).

Almost one in three female-headed households lives in poverty, and the chance that a woman who headed a household would end up poor was greater in 1977 than in 1967 (National Advisory Council on Economic Opportunity, 1980). If present trends continue, we may be heading toward a time in which almost all of the poor in this country will be female family heads and their dependent children (National Advisory Council on Economic Opportunity, 1980).

The social and economic trends that are throwing so many women and children into poverty also have tremendous significance for the mental health of women. It is widely recognized that women are more likely than men to suffer from depression (Weissman & Klerman, 1977; Guttentag, Salasin, & Belle, 1980). Often overlooked is the fact that not all women are at equal risk for experiencing this mental health problem. Women who live in financially strained circumstances and who have responsibility for young children are more likely than other women to become depressed (Brown, Bhrolchain, & Harris, 1975; Pearlin & Johnson, 1977; Radloff, 1975; Goldman & Ravid, 1980).

As a passing mood, depression is familiar to everyone. The sorrow, the sense of futility, and the loss of interest in accustomed pursuits form part of the human condition. When these sensations last for weeks and months on end, accompanied by crying spells, difficulty in sleeping, disinterest in eating, and a pervasive sense of life's hopelessness and one's own worthlessness, depression has become more than a passing mood. Such episodes can become unendurable, and, in fact, suicide is a serious risk among those who are depressed (Beck, 1967).

There are too many women today struggling to rear young children with inadequate incomes, many also struggling with the pain and hopelessness, the loss of energy and of self-esteem, of depression. These women come from all racial and ethnic groups and from all social backgrounds. They live in public housing projects and in privately owned rental housing and even in suburban houses. They form one of the largest and fastest-growing client populations at mental health centers across the country, and those who reach out for help represent only the smallest fraction of those whose suffering is severe. While the susceptibility to depression of low-income mothers has been well-documented, many professionals in the mental health field remain unaware of the extent of the problem. Those who do realize the connection between poverty and depression often despair of treating poverty-related mental health problems, unaware of promising strategies which do exist for assisting low-income mothers.

The Stress and Families Project was funded by the National Institute of Mental Health to examine systematically the stresses which lead to high rates of depression among low-income mothers with young children and to develop knowledge on which to base future mental health services and public policy decisions. While not discounting the importance of other factors in the etiology of depression, the Stress and Families Project emphasized the investigation of environmental factors, both those which place women at high risk for depression and those which protect women from stress and depression. A major goal of the study was to understand the *causes* of depression in low-income mothers, and a second major goal was to understand some of the *consequences* of depression, particularly for the mother-child relationship. The project was designed to test several hypothesized relationships between women's life situations and their mental health and maternal behavior; to develop new hypotheses about such relationships; and to locate points at which intervention might be successful in protecting mental health and family functioning. Evidence from this study is relevant to the four million families and ten million children living in poverty in this country today, as well as to other families living above the poverty line but suffering from financial strain.

PLANNING THE STUDY

To study these issues a staff of women was assembled, representing many academic disciplines and a wide range of personal histories. The staff included white, black and Asian women, single women, married women, women with children and those without, women who had grown up in middle-class households and women who had been on welfare. Many of us had studied child development; others, social psychology, anthropology, or nutrition. We differed among ourselves in our ways of approaching research problems, in the research methods with which we were comfortable, and in our personal values and stance toward the research project. For some of us the project was an exciting intellectual challenge; for others, a chance to learn more about the lives of women; for others, an opportunity to help women by documenting their needs. Bringing together a group of researchers with such diverse backgrounds and interests led to a planning period of considerable conflict and excitement.

The planning period was particularly tumultuous because we tried to operate collaboratively, continuing our discussions until we reached a consensus.[1] Although the staff included a tenured professor, a woman who had recently earned a doctorate, and graduate students at various stages in their professional training, we sought to function in an egalitarian manner, ignoring the hierarchy implicit in our different statuses. We tried to judge each question on the merits of the arguments presented, rather than on the credentials of the advocates. As a consequence of this staff organization, every staff member was aware of and involved in the major decisions of the project. We believe this resulted not only in better decisions, because each woman's suggestions were heard and weighed by other staff members, but also in higher staff morale, as each staff member felt she had a personal stake in the outcome of the project.

The original design of the Stress and Families Project called for a survey study of several hundred families in two sites to test hypotheses about stress and depression in the lives of low-income mothers. As we began to plan the study we discovered that we had many different ideas about the kind of data we should be collecting. Were we simply looking for quantitative stress ratings to compare with depressive symptom levels? Did we need descriptive information about each respondent's living environment? Were we interested in the processes by which stress brings about depression? Did we need to learn about women's strengths, so that public policies and mental health services could build on these?

Within the staff there were disagreements about the best methods of achieving our goals. Some of us favored open-ended interviewing to learn how women construed their own life circumstances. Others believed that quantifiable data should be the first priority. Our staff meetings in this period were both exciting and frustrating, as we realized that several topics were indeed crucial to the study and that the different methodologies we favored would be highly complementary. Yet if we were to interview hundreds of women, we could spend only a limited amount of time with each woman and could never carry out the multimethod, multiinstrument study we began to envision.

For these reasons we decided first to carry out a pilot venture—an intensive, exploratory study of a small number of women. This would allow us time to talk with women and with their children, to make repeated observations in the home, and to gather both open-ended interview data and standardized, quantitative data. This "pilot" study grew in the planning until it became a major undertaking in its own right; it is the results of this exploratory work which we describe in this book. Later we designed a streamlined interview schedule to assess stress factors in women's lives and surveyed a large number of families. We believe that when these data are fully analyzed, they will complement and extend our earlier work. Yet the intensive study we report on here has illuminated many important issues in women's lives as well as prepared the way for a productive survey study. Concentrating on a relatively small number of families has allowed us to investigate lives in depth and to generate many new ideas about stress and depression in low-income families.

CONDUCTING THE FIELDWORK

Before meeting with families we held many staff meetings to discuss our hopes and fears about the fieldwork. We envisioned a relationship between researcher and respondent in which each respondent knew that we regarded her as the expert on her own life. We hoped that we could achieve rapport with women who might have had very different experiences from our own. We worried that as educated professionals we would be seen as social workers or clinicians. We did not want to find ourselves doing therapy instead of research. We did not want women to be defensive about their lifestyles or approaches to child rearing. While we later developed close relationships with many respondents, the first meetings between respondents and researchers were generally tentative. Respondents raised questions and reservations about the study before offering their formal consent.

For the researchers, the first visits to research families signaled that the planning, the pilot-testing, the rehearsals were over, and that we had really begun our research. As our work with families began, we discovered that many of our fears had been groundless. The respondents understood that we were not "helping professionals" like social workers. Instead, it was they—the respondents—who were helping us to learn about stress and depression in the lives of low-income women. We were not there to evaluate, assist, or change the respondents. We found that our relationship allowed us to give a kind of unconditional attention and respect, to listen and to learn. In turn, being on the other end of a helping relationship and receiving pay for their work was gratifying to many of the women we interviewed.

Early on we recognized the value of the time we spent with each research family before and after completing the research tasks for that visit. We were gaining rapport with the women and their children, and we were learning many things about the daily lives of the families. By visiting different respondents we saw firsthand how diverse the living environments of low-income mothers can be. Some of the women we interviewed lived in dilapidated public housing projects. Others lived in solidly built apartment buildings with the sort of architectural details much sought after by the young professional people moving into the neighborhood. Some respondents had attractive and comfortable apartments; other apartments lacked all but the most essential furnishings.

We wondered how we could capitalize on the "informal knowledge" we were gaining day by day. We tried using a debriefing questionnaire after each family visit, but this proved to be an imposition on the already hard-working researchers. More seriously, we realized that we did not have a sufficiently clear idea of what informal knowledge we wanted to gain. We decided to concentrate on the formal research procedures and to let the informal knowledge base build itself.

In the end, we found that we did not have to use questionnaires to make use of the insights we were gaining in the field. Certain images, experiences, and conversations impressed themselves on our memories and later informed our understanding of the formal data we had collected. Our own interests kept each of us attuned to different issues in the field. During my own work with families, for instance, I was especially interested in the importance of social relationships for well-being. I had read studies showing that long-standing relationships were important for mental health and that residential moves often had a disruptive effect on such relationships. I was curious to learn how residential stability or instability affected the women we were interviewing. One day, while a respondent was showing me the community garden and the grounds of the public housing project where she lived, I asked her to tell me how long she had known each of the people we met. After a while I turned to her and remarked with satisfaction, "You've known most of these people five or six years." To my way of thinking at that time, such stability promised many benefits. "Yeah," she said. "That's about how long it takes to get out of here." Her response opened my eyes to other implications of residential stability. When I discovered later that among the women we interviewed, longer residence in a neighborhood was not associated with a more positive assessment of the neighborhood or with mental health advantages, I had some possible explanations ready for this "unexpected" finding.

I worked with one respondent who lived in a public housing project only two blocks away from a large city park. My bus stopped close to the park, and I always enjoyed the walk across the park, admiring the trees, the grass and the open space. I was puzzled that my respondent and her son never seemed to go to the park, although it was so close, playing instead in the project's own asphalt playground. There was so much broken glass underneath the jungle gym and swings there that I feared a serious cut if he should fall. Eventually I asked the respondent why so few of the neighborhood children, including her own, were to be seen in the park, and why so many parents chose what seemed to me an inferior place to play. She told me that she would never take her son to the park. "People get *killed* there! That's where the dope dealers hang out." Such discussions gave the research staff a better understanding of the respondents' lives.

Over the months of fieldwork strong relationships developed between the researchers and the respondents. In some cases a common factor in women's personal histories contributed to the bond. A black respondent who had grown up in the South found how much she shared with a black interviewer who had also grown up in the South. A researcher who had been on welfare and gone on to complete a college education compared her own past experiences with those of a respondent who was struggling to go back to school. Women who did not share such experiences discovered common ground in personal philosophies or simply in mutual respect. We learned firsthand from many women who had been economically secure at an earlier time in their lives that their security did not survive a divorce or a disastrous illness. The realization brought home to us the precarious economic situation of women today. It also diminished our sense of separateness from the women we interviewed, to know that at some future time one of us might find herself rearing children in poverty.

In the midst of our fieldwork we experienced a stunning loss—the sudden death of our director, Marcia Guttentag. She had created the Stress and Families Project, built its staff, directed it through the critical period of planning and then through the first several months of fieldwork. The study reflected her passion for social justice and her concerns with poverty and with women in distress. She continually reminded us that our work was designed to lead to action and not simply to interest other researchers, that we were studying families and their pain, and that we should never mistake that pain for weakness.

Following her death we grieved for our loss and attempted to carry out the work Marcia Guttentag had begun in the way she would have wished. Because of the collaborative staff structure she had encouraged we were all aware of plans for the remainder of fieldwork and for data analysis, and we had a clear direction for our work. We also had the inspiration of her memory and the desire to accomplish our work in a way to justify her trust in us. We missed and still miss Marcia Guttentag—her insights, her intensity, her enthusiasm, and her laughter. We hope that our completion of one of the many tasks which she began will honor her memory.

IMPACT OF THE RESEARCH PROCESS

We are often asked about the effect of our research on the families who participated in the study, and we have monitored these effects. At the end of the research process we asked each respondent about the advantages and disadvantages of participation. We also left behind brief questionnaires that could be returned anonymously if there were concerns the respondent did not want to share with her interviewer. Overwhelmingly, the women who participated in the study found it a positive experience. When asked to state what was the best thing about participation, the most frequent response was the opportunity to reflect on one's own life. One woman said: "By being in your study, the questions you've been asking me about myself, I've really found myself out."

Next to the opportunity for reflection, women named the hope of helping others. One woman said that it had been "an honor to be in the study, because my experiences have not gone unsaid and will perhaps help others." Another said: "Maybe it will shake up a few people." Women liked getting to know the researchers too. One said that the researchers she worked with were "two of the most humane people I've met in a long time. Both have feelings and depth for others." Another said the best thing was meeting her interviewer and observer and that "there are still some decent people in the world." Other women stated that the study was interesting, that they liked talking things over, and that they enjoyed the money they earned through participation. Most women said there was nothing we could have done to make the research process more comfortable for them or their children.

Discontents were also voiced by some women, and some of these were related to the very advantages already discussed. The woman who said that meeting the researchers was the best thing about being in the study also recommended that in future work with families we "don't be too friendly or get too close. Parting is such sweet sorrow." One woman said she didn't like such questions as, "Would you do anything differently if you had to go through it again?" She said: "Those made me worry more and cause regrets. It helps me not to think that way."

Not a single family dropped out of the study once work had begun. The absence of attrition is particularly striking because many of the respondents continued to meet with us during stressful times, such as when separating from husbands, starting new jobs, or while relatives were living temporarily with the research families. Return visits after the end of the fieldwork indicate that the good feelings which were described as the research ended still exist, and that women would choose to repeat their experience with the project if they were making the decision over again. In some cases, it appears that women initiated positive changes in their lives as a result of their involvement with the project.

We did not question children systematically about their experiences with the research project, so we must rely on their mothers' statements, children's spontaneous comments to us, and our own impressions. In conducting observations in the home we found that the first, practice observation session was a strange experience for most children and an uncomfortable one for many. Even though we had explained to children that we would be working and writing for a half hour and would not be able to talk with them, children found it strange to have us present and yet unresponsive. It was not easy for us, either.

At the end of the practice observation session we showed the child and the mother what we had written and offered the child our attention again. Seeing our notes and being able to talk with us again seemed to reassure children. By the next observation, which was the first from which we took data for analysis, almost all of the children appeared comfortable with the observation procedure, even if somewhat impatient for us to finish our work and become available for conversation and play. A few children remained noticeably uncomfortable during succeeding observations, although none was so unhappy that we or their mothers suggested an end to observing.

After we had done a number of observations, we could almost believe that the mothers and especially the children were oblivious to our presence. They no longer attempted to talk with us during the observation period and seemed to pay little attention to us. However, our hope of being completely forgotten for those half-hour periods was not satisfied. In one family, for instance, when the observer believed she had become an accustomed part of the family routine, a squabble broke out between two of the siblings she was observing when their mother was in another room. When the mother was called in to mediate and asked who had started the fight, one of the children told his mother she should "ask the lady there. She's writing it all down." Clearly, the presence and purpose of the observer had not been forgotten.

We also interviewed children, and they generally seemed interested in these sessions. They enjoyed the tape recorder and liked talking about the topics we raised. During one interview session a six-year-old girl responded to a question about mothers and children and then remarked to her interviewer: "And I think that was a very good decision, so thank you very much." The interviewer asked, "What was a good decision?" The child answered: "That you got me into this, and my mother got me into this, and you're doing me an interview, and I never had an interview in my life." Her pleasure in being interviewed was delightful to see.

While pleasure and interest were expressed by many children, some of the very young children had trouble understanding some of our questions. More disturbingly, a few children became unhappy when asked to talk about their relationships with their parents. In these cases the interviews were ended, and the interviewer turned the conversation to happier topics.

The respondents were not the only ones affected by the research process. Researchers, too, experienced moments of self-discovery, strong attachments to the women and their children, and a sense of loss as the fieldwork came to an end. During the months we spent with families, hardly a staff member escaped a moral crisis in which she wondered how her own role as researcher was justified when she saw so much pain and injustice. We accused ourselves of parasitism or voyeurism or simple uselessness in the face of great need. While we shared our worries with each other, we experienced these crises as strangely solitary. We found that no words from colleagues were helpful. We all knew intellectually the answers to our dilemma: we were studying the problem in order to help find ways to remedy it; we were not hurting individuals or families, but even helping in small ways; many of the problems we saw were beyond our own powers to solve; we had carefully refrained from offering more to families than we could provide. Yet the questions and the guilt remained until we worked them through and came to accept the answers emotionally as well as intellectually. A legacy of these crises is the urgency we feel to find solutions to the problems we documented and to alert others to the needs of low-income mothers and their children.

FORMAT OF THE BOOK

While staff members shared fieldwork and planning responsibilities, each of us also took responsibility for a specific topic within the study: searching the relevant research literature, adapting or designing an interview schedule, overseeing data collection with this instrument, and then analyzing data and writing reports. At each stage these efforts were discussed with other staff members, who also pilot-tested the interview schedules, suggested data analysis approaches, and commented on successive drafts of written reports. In some cases a new staff member took over at the data analysis phase or assisted the staff member who had originally directed research on a given topic. The chapters, therefore, represent the work of individuals or small groups, informed by the advice of other staff members.

The chapter titled "Research Methods and Sample Characteristics" explains how the study of 43 women and their families was conducted. Methods of sampling and recruiting families, characteristics of the respondents, methods of working with families, the measures which were used to assess mental health, and the limitations and strengths of the book's data base are discussed. The mental health of the respondents is compared to that of other research populations.

Part II of the book, "The Ecology of Poverty" considers the current and past life situations of the respondents. "Sources of Stress: Events or Conditions?" considers the impact of important recent events and current life circumstances on the mental health of the respondents. This chapter explains and defines stress as it was measured in this study. "Daily Lives" explores how the respondents spent their days and the mental health impact of daily routines. "Growing Up: The Impact of Loss and Change" investigates factors in the respondents' early lives which have implications for their present-day circumstances and their emotional well-being.

Part III, "Women and Society," turns to the social institutions and forces which shape the lives of the respondents. "Work: Its Meaning for Women's

Lives" examines the work experiences and work ambitions of the respondents in relation to their family responsibilities and considers the mental health implications of employment for women. "The Public Welfare System: Regulation and Dehumanization" explores the circumstances which drove women to apply for welfare benefits, their experiences as welfare recipients, and the implications of the welfare system for all women, including those who never receive welfare benefits. "The Human Cost of Discrimination" looks at both the injuries and the insults suffered by women who experience discrimination because of their race, sex, level of education, or other attributes. The chapter considers both the emotional toll taken by discriminatory incidents and the barriers discrimination places in the way of women attempting to improve their lives. "The Politics of the Poor" investigates the respondents' political views, particularly in regard to issues that directly concern low-income women, as well as their political behavior.

The next section of the book is titled "Relationships," and it focuses on the personal relationships of the respondents and the importance of such relationships for emotional well-being. "Social Ties and Social Support" considers the friends and relatives respondents describe as important to them and the respondents' involvements in neighborhood sociability and exchange. "Fathers' Support to Mothers and Children" discusses the men with whom the respondents live and the assistance these men provided to the respondents and their children.

"Mothers and Their Children" is devoted to the mother-child relationship and to the impact of stress and depression on that relationship. "Parenting Philosophies and Practices" reports on open-ended interviews with the respondents concerning their child-rearing beliefs and practices. "The Quality of Mother-Child Relationships" turns to observational data and interviews with children to explore the effect of stress and depression on maternal behavior and on mothers' relationships with their children.

"Well-Being" is the section of the book which considers women's coping efforts and their mental and physical health. "The Challenge of Coping" examines coping as a process by which stressful experiences are digested by respondents, and presents a theoretical model for understanding how stressful conditions erode mental health. "Mental Health Problems and Their Treatment" turns to the respondents' conceptions of mental health problems and their experiences in seeking professional help with such problems. "Physical Health Issues" looks at the physical health status of the respondents, the relationship of stress and depression to physical health, and some of the difficulties the respondents face in maintaining good physical health.

A year after all of the initial fieldwork with families had been completed we made return visits to families to discuss the study's findings with them, to hear how they viewed participation in the study after the intervening time period, and to catch up on their lives. "Families Revisited" reports on these visits. "Summary and Conclusions" reviews the major findings of the study and discusses the implications of these findings for mental health services and public policy.

To protect the identity of the respondents and their families, code names are used throughout the book to designate the women who were interviewed. These names were chosen by the research staff and bear no resemblance to those of the women themselves. Characteristics of families which might be used to identify them have also been changed. Each woman is referred to as "Ms." The decision to use this form of address was made by the research staff; it does not necessarily represent the usage each woman would have chosen for herself. In this book a woman living with a husband or boyfriend is referred to as "coupled" and the man with whom she lives is referred to as her "partner." Women living without partners are designated "single."

ACKNOWLEDGMENTS

The efforts of many individuals have contributed to the Stress and Families Project and to this book. The project would not have been begun without the efforts of Marcia Guttentag, would not have been sustained without the commitment of Susan Salasin, and would not have been possible without the generosity of the 43 respondents and their children. We are grateful to the many researchers who worked with us in designing interview schedules, conducting interviews and observations, and analyzing data. We wish to thank the members of our advisory committee, and especially its chairperson, Jeanette Williams, who provided expert counsel and encouragement through every phase of our work. The Stress and Families Project was supported by grant number MH28830 of the Mental Health Services Development Branch of the National Institute of Mental Health, and we are grateful for this support. Many individuals read earlier drafts of all or part of this book and offered constructive criticism. We thank each of them, and especially Jessie Bernard, Nancy Colletta, Lois-ellin Datta, and Jean Baker Miller, who offered substantial assistance.

NOTE

1. We were later intrigued to read a study contrasting successful to unsuccessful applied research projects which found that the less successful projects were characterized by calm during the early planning stages, while the successful projects were dynamic and laden with conflict (see Glaser & Taylor, 1973). We believe that the variety of viewpoints represented by our staff and the insistence on discussing issues until reaching consensus, rather than relying on top-down decision making, resulted in better decisions than would have been reached otherwise.

REFERENCES

Beck, A. T. *Depression: Clinical, experimental, and theoretical aspects.* New York: Harper & Row, 1967.

Barrett, N. Women in the job market: Occupations, earnings, and career opportunities. In R. Smith (Ed.) *The subtle revolution: Women at work.* Washington, DC: Urban Institute, 1979.

Brown, G., Bhrolchain, M., & Harris, T. Social class and psychiatric disturbance among women in an urban population. *Sociology,* 1975, *9* (2), 225-254.

Glaser, E. M., & Taylor, S. H. Factors influencing the success of applied research. *American Psychologist,* 1973, *28,* 140-146.

Goldman, N., & Ravid, R. Community surveys: Sex differences in mental illness. In M. Guttentag, S. Salasin, and D. Belle (Eds.) *The mental health of women.* New York: Academic Press, 1980.

Guttentag, M., Salasin, S., & Belle, D. (Eds.). *The mental health of women.* New York: Academic Press, 1980.

National Advisory Council on Economic Opportunity. *Critical choices for the 80's.* Washington, DC: Government Printing Office, 1980.

Pearce, D. Women, work, and welfare: The feminization of poverty. In K. W. Feinstein (Ed.) *Working women and families.* Beverly Hills, CA: Sage, 1979.

Pearlin, L., & Johnson, J. Marital status, life-strains and depression. *American Sociological Review,* 1977, *42,* 704-715.

Radloff, L. Sex differences in depression: The effects of occupation and marital status. *Sex Roles: A Journal of Research,* 1975, *1,* 249-266.

Ross, H., & Sawhill, I. *Time of transition: The growth of families headed by women.* Washington, DC: Urban Institute, 1975.

Sawhill, I. Women with low incomes. In M. Blaxall and B. Reagan (Eds.) *Women and the workplace: The implications of occupational segregation.* Chicago: University of Chicago Press, 1976.

U.S. Bureau of the Census. *Money income and poverty status of families and persons in the United States: 1979 (Advance Report).* Current Population Reports, Series P-60, No. 125. Washington, DC: Government Printing Office, 1980.

Weissman, M., & Klerman, G. Sex differences and the epidemiology of depression. *Archives of General Psychiatry,* 1977, *34,* 98-111.

2

RESEARCH METHODS AND
SAMPLE CHARACTERISTICS

DEBORAH BELLE AND DIANA DILL

This account of the mental health and life circumstances of low-income mothers is based on a study of 43 Boston-area low-income families and is a product of several research methodologies. Beginning in the summer of 1978 and continuing for approximately one year, respondents and their children were interviewed with both open-ended interviews and structured, standardized psychological instruments. In addition, mothers and children were observed in their homes. In this chapter we tell about the process of finding research families, the characteristics of the sample, our methods of working with families, and the measures of mental health we used in the study. We also discuss the limitations and strengths of the study's data base.

SAMPLING AND RECRUITNG FAMILIES

Rather than being randomly selected, our research families were recruited to represent the range of circumstances faced by low-income mothers. White women living with husbands or boyfriends, single white women, black women living with husbands or boyfriends, and black single women were recruited in approximately equal numbers. Women with a wide range of educational backgrounds, employment histories, and early life experiences were recruited as well. We included women with many children and women with only one child, women living in nuclear families and women living with their sisters or mothers, women who had always been poor and women who had only recently become poor. We also attempted to keep income and educational differences between single and coupled women and those between black and white women as small as possible, so that these variables were not confounded with other differences.

The 43 research families were drawn from three Boston area neighborhoods where many low-income families live. One of these neighborhoods is ethnically heterogeneous and in recent decades has been home for a predominantly poor and working-class population. It is now the scene of rapid change as wealthy and professional people purchase and rehabilitate houses in the area. The second neighborhood is politically a separate city, populated largely by white working-class families. The third area in which the study was conducted is a predominantly black community with some fine old houses as well as much deteriorated housing.

Before beginning to recruit families we met with community leaders to learn about each community, to discuss our research objectives, and to seek help in recruiting. The meetings with community leaders proved to be invaluable, both in orienting us to each community and in providing personal contacts which led to the recruitment of families. We used recruiting strategies designed to locate representatives of populations traditionally unavailable to research, such as the illiterate and those without telephones, and to include families which were in contact with social agencies as well as families which were not. We offered $150 to families for participation in the study and secured from the Massachusetts Department of Public Welfare a written assurance that accepting this money would not jeopardize respondents' welfare payments.

To find research families we contacted personnel at housing projects, day care centers, settlement houses, political action groups, community groups, and schools. We also posted notices on local bulletin boards and ran advertisements in local papers. Some women who had been in the study referred other women to us. Our suspicion that random selection of research families would be difficult was confirmed by the failure of door-to-door recruitment to obtain any interested respondents. We recruited 43 research families, seeking data from at least 40 families and anticipating attrition. However, none of the research families dropped out of the study, and we collected data on all 43 of the original families.

CHARACTERISTICS OF THE SAMPLE

The 43 women who participated in the research ranged in age from twenty-one to forty-four with an average age of thirty, and represented every legal marital status. Each woman had at least one child between the ages of

TABLE 2.1   Characteristics of the Respondents

Race	
Black	21
White	22
Marital Status	
Married	12
Divorced	10
Widowed	2
Informally separated	10
Legally separated	2
Never married	7
Age	
20-24	5
25-29	18
30-34	11
35-39	4
40-44	5
Education	
No high school	4
Some high school	11
High school diploma or equivalent	20
Some college	6
College degree	1
Graduate school	1
Number of children under 16 years of age	
1-2	26
3-4	11
5 or more	6

five and seven. Twenty of the women were single-parent heads of household, 12 lived with their husbands, and 11 lived with boyfriends. Per capita household income for the families ranged from $500 to $4500, which meant that some families lived far below federal poverty lines, and some lived just above poverty lines. Of the 43 respondents, 33 received government welfare payments, and most of the remaining 10 had received these benefits in the past or participated in other public assistance programs, such as food stamps. The sample was almost evenly divided by race: 21 women were black and 22 were white. Educational attainments of the respondents ranged from fourth grade to graduate school, with a mean educational level of 11.8 grades.

Our selection procedures resulted in a sample of respondents more highly educated than the population of low-income women from which the sample is drawn (U.S. Dept. of Health, Education and Welfare, 1978). Black respondents did not differ from white respondents in age, income, or education, but did tend to have more children living at home. Respondents living with husbands or boyfriends had a significantly higher mean per capita household income than did single respondents, but did not differ significantly from single respondents in age, educational level, or number of children at home. We found that respondents with smaller families, younger respondents, and more highly educated respondents were likely to have higher incomes. Younger respondents were also likely to have higher levels of education and fewer children than older respondents.

WORKING WITH FAMILIES

We chose to study 43 families intensively so that adequate attention could be given to each family and to each of a number of interrelated issues in the lives of low-income families. Each of the 43 women who participated in the study worked with one interviewer and one observer for several months of weekly or twice-weekly meetings. Interviewers gathered information from the mothers on recent life events, enduring life conditions, daily routines, childhood histories, work experiences, experiences with social service and political institutions, experiences of discrimination, social relationships, parenting philosophies and practices, coping efforts, and nutrition. At least one meeting was devoted to each topic. Brief measures of mental health were administered at the beginning and end of the series of interviews.

While some interview questions were asked using a forced-choice or brief answer format, many interviews were of the semistructured variety and created opportunities for the resondents to describe their experiences and personal philosophies in their own words. The interview schedules are described in the relevant chapters which follow. Most of the interviewers were graduate students at the Harvard Graduate School of Education, and many were themselves mothers of young children. Each respondent was interviewed by a woman of her own race.

Children in each family were also interviewed to discover their perceptions of the parent-child relationship. We interviewed children from five to eighteen years of age in the research families. Family interaction was observed in each home by the researcher who interviewed the children. Six half-hour periods of nonparticipant observation were conducted with each family, focusing on a five- to seven-year-old child. The children we observed included an equal number of boys and girls and did not include children with severe physical disabilities. We attempted to match the race of the observer to that of the research family, but logistical considerations made this impossible in approximately one-fourth of the research families.

Before and after the formal research tasks of interviewing and observing, the researchers spent many hours in the homes and in the neighborhoods of the research families. We met relatives, neighbors, friends, and social workers. We visited families when there was no money in the house, when a child had to be rushed to the hospital, and the day after a burglary. We accompanied mothers on shopping trips and on tours of the community garden. We talked with children about their school work and watched them perform acrobatic feats on the housing project jungle gym. Such experiences also form part of the data on which this book is based.

MEASURING MENTAL HEALTH

To assess each woman's mental health we administered five brief self-report scales which measure depression, anxiety, self-esteem, stability of self-esteem, and mastery. The scoring conventions of these scales dictate that a high score reflects *poor* mental health. This can be confusing, since some of the scale names reflect *good* mental health. We have, however, retained the scoring conventions and the scale names developed by the authors of each measure. Thus, the higher the scores on these scales, the greater the depressive symptoms, anxiety, poor self-esteem, instability of self-esteem, and lack of mastery. It may help the reader to keep in mind that high scores on any of these measures reflect poor mental health.

Each scale was administered at the beginning and at the end of the period in which we worked with the respondent, and scale scores were relatively stable from one administration to the next. Paired t-tests showed that only the anxiety scores changed over the course of the study. The respondents reported significantly fewer symptoms of anxiety at the end of the study than at the beginning. The mean of each respondent's two scores is used in most of the analyses we report, although in cases where scores from one administration are missing, the remaining score is used.

Depressive symptomatology was measured by the Center for Epidemiologic Studies Depression (CES-D) Scale, which was developed for population surveys at the National Institute of Mental Health. The scale includes 20 items which represent the major components of the depressive syndrome: depressed mood, feelings of guilt and worthlessness, helplessness, despair, retarded activity and change in eating or sleeping patterns (Radloff, 1977). The respondent is asked to rate how frequently she experienced these depressive symptoms over the past week. Scores on this measure do not necessarily indicate whether or not a person is suffering from the clinical syndrome of depression, but scores have been found to discriminate well between psychiatric inpatient and general populations and to discriminate moderately well within patient groups by severity of illness (Radloff, 1977).

Stress and Families Project (SFP) respondents reported significantly more depressive symptoms than have been reported for the general population. The distribution of depressive symptom scores of the respondents fell midway between the distribution of scores in the general population and those among psychiatric patients (Radloff, 1977). The average CES-Depression score among the respondents is high, similar to that which has been reported for individuals who have recently separated from their spouses or experienced the death of a spouse.

As a measure of *anxiety* we used the Anxiety Section of the Multiple Affect Adjective Checklist developed by Zuckerman and Lubin (1965). We used the "In General" form of the scale, which measures anxiety as a trait rather than as a current affective level. The respondent was read a list of 21 adjectives, including "anxiety-plus" words, like "afraid" and "nervous," and "anxiety-minus" words like "calm" and "secure." She was asked to choose all words which best described her usual frame of mind. Mean anxiety scores for Stress and Families respondents were at normal levels for women according to standardization studies (Zuckerman and Lubin, 1965).

The Pearlin Mastery Scale was used to measure the degree to which respondents felt they were in control of their lives. Seven statements are included in the scale, and the respondents were asked to indicate their degree of agreement or disagreement with each statement. *Mastery,* the feeling of being in control of one's life, is indicated by agreement with statements such as, "What happens to me in the future depends mostly on me." Lack of mastery, the feeling that one's life is determined primarily by factors beyond one's control, is indicated by agreement with statements such as, "Sometimes I feel that I'm being pushed around in life." SFP respondents' scores are distributed more heavily on the high-external end of the scale than are those of a general population sample (B. Brown, University of Chicago, personal communication, 1978). The difference is significant at the .005 level when both sexes in the sample are grouped together, and at the .01 level when SFP respondents are compared with the female respondents in Pearlin's sample. Thus, the Stress and Families respondents as a group appear to experience less mastery over their lives than does the general population.

The measure of *self-esteem* we used is one developed by Rosenberg (1965) to measure level of self-acceptance in late adolescence. Ten statements were read to the respondent, and she was asked to rank her degree of agreement or disagreement with the statement. Positive statements such as, "I take a positive attitude toward myself," and negative statements such as, "I certainly feel useless at times," were read alternately. The respondent was asked to respond to these statements with general feelings about the self, rather than at-the-moment feelings. According to Rosenberg's scoring convention, the scores of 20 (47 percent) of the Stress and Families respondents reflect high self-esteem, the scores of 15 (35 percent) of the respondents reflect medium self-esteem, and the scores of 8 (19 percent) of the respon-

dents reflect low self-esteem. There was no significant difference in distribution between scores of SFP respondents and scores of female high school
students collapsed across social classes as reported by Rosenberg (1965).
The comparison is not precise, however, since Stress and Families respondents are women in their twenties, thirties, and forties, while Rosenberg's
respondents were ages fifteen to eighteen, when female self-esteem is nota-
bly precarious.

The Stability of Self-Esteem Measure was designed by Rosenberg (1965)
to assess stability of self-image in relation to self-esteem. The Stability of
Self-Esteem Scale presents five items, each of which concentrates on the
relative stability of the respondent's *valuation* of herself, rather than on other
aspects of the self-image; therefore, the scale is intrinsically related to
self-esteem. Stability of self-esteem is related to self-esteem empirically, as
well. In his sample of high school students of both sexes, Rosenberg found
that students with high self-esteem scores were three and a half times more
likely to have very stable self-valuations than were students with low self-
esteem scores. Conversely, students with low self-esteem scores were four
times more likely to have very unstable self-valuations than were students
with high self-esteem scores. Instability of self-valuation was also associated with higher anxiety, as indicated by psychosomatic symptomatology.
The scores of Stress and Families respondents generally indicated more
stability of self-valuation than Rosenberg found in his sample, although the
SFP sample included more respondents with very unstable self-valuations
than did Rosenberg's.

Within the sample of 43 women we interviewed, there was enormous
variation in mental health. Some respondents reported virtually no symptoms of poor mental health, while others reported almost as many symptoms
as the scales allowed. We used this naturally occurring variation in symptom
scores within the sample of respondents to explore factors which distinguished the women with excellent mental health from those with poor mental health. The respondents' interviews were analyzed to determine what life
situations were typical of the respondents with good mental health and what
circumstances were typical of those with poor mental health. Similarly, our
observations of maternal behavior and children's reports of the mother-child
relationship were analyzed to discover what characteristics of mother-child
relationships were associated with high levels of maternal depressive symptomatology and other indicators of poor mental health.

LIMITATIONS AND STRENGTHS OF
THE DATA BASE

This book is based on a small-scale, exploratory study, and caution
should be exercised in generalizing findings reported here to the population

of low-income women and their children. The small size of the sample means that trends which might attain statistical significance in larger samples may not reach statistical significance in this sample of 43 families. Thus, only the strongest trends in the data are reported. With a small sample one also runs a high risk that the sample fails in some ways to represent the population from which it was drawn. For instance, this sample includes more women with high school diplomas than is typical of the low-income population.

We also intentionally overrepresented certain rare types of low-income mothers in our sample, such as the college educated, and attempted to orthogonalize other variables. Thus, the black and white women, the single women and coupled women, have more characteristics in common (such as income level and educational background) than these groups actually do in the real world. If few important differences are found between the mental health of black women and that of white women, this result can only be interpreted to mean that when income, education, and marital status are held constant, black and white women will show similar levels of psychological well-being. However, in the general population these factors are not held constant. Black women tend to have lower incomes, less education, and to rear children without husbands more frequently than white women. Our approach thus cannot provide evidence on racial differences in mental health in the general population, but it could provide suggestive evidence on whether race itself is the important determinant of psychological well-being or whether the factors which vary with race are more important for mental health.

Each of the various research methods used in the study—open-ended interviews, standardized questionnaires, and home observations—has its strengths and its weaknesses. Open-ended interviews allow us to hear a woman's own words and help us to understand how she construed the questions we asked. However, open-ended interviews cannot capture what a woman might have said if asked a similar question in a forced-choice mode. Thus, a woman who is asked what she most wants her children to have when they grow up may speak of education or a good family life. When asked specifically if she wants her children to have these and other things, she might well name several more goals than she offered spontaneously. One must therefore be cautious in attributing too much significance to what women did *not* say in response to open-ended questions. Standardized questionnaries are sometimes interpreted by respondents in idiosyncratic ways, but they do yield data that are eminently comparable to data collected in other studies. Such questionnaries allow us to make comparisons among the respondents and between the respondents as a group and other research populations. Home observations permit mothers and children the comfort of familiar territory and enable us to observe how they behave *in situ*. Home observations do not, however, make possible the standardization of setting and actors that can be achieved in a laboratory.

The strengths of the data base lie in its profusion of qualitative and quantitative data, gathered from multiple informants in each family over a period of several months with high rapport between researchers and respondents. Few conclusions are reported in this book which are not corroborated by many informants and many analyses. The multiple methods we used, and the intensive and intimate fieldwork we conducted, enable this book to be both a descriptive report on the nature of contemporary poverty as it is experienced by women and their children, and an analysis of the stress factors and protective factors which affect the mental health of low-income mothers.

REFERENCES

Pearlin, L., & Schooler, C. The structure of coping. *Journal of Health and Social Behavior,* 1978, *19*, 2-21.

Radloff, L. The CES-D Scale: A self-report depression scale for research in the general population. *Journal of Applied Psychological Measurement,* 1977, *1* (3), 385-401.

Rosenberg, M. *Society and the adolescent self image.* Princeton: Princeton University Press, 1965.

U.S. Department of Health, Education and Welfare, Social Security Administration. *Aid to families with dependent children: 1975 recipient characteristics study.* HEW Pub. No. (SSA) 78-11777. Washington DC: Government Printing Office, 1978.

Weissman, M., & Locke, B. Comparison of a self-report symptom rating scale (CES-D) with standardized depression rating scales in a psychiatric population: A preliminary report. Paper presented at the Society for Epidemiologic Research, Albany, 1975.

Zuckerman, M., & Lubin, B. *Manual for the MAACL.* San Diego: Educational and Industrial Testing Service, 1965.

PART II
THE ECOLOGY OF POVERTY

3

SOURCES OF STRESS:
EVENTS OR CONDITIONS?

VIVIAN PARKER MAKOSKY

A variety of physiological changes and subjective feelings of stress are likely to be experienced when environmental demands (stressors) threaten well-being. Although it is argued that some stress for some people has positive effects (Kraus, 1979; Pfeiffer, Siegel, Taylor, & Shuler, 1979), most of the life stress research has focused on unpleasant or disease-producing stress (Selye, 1978). Such stress has been implicated in the etiology of numerous physical and mental health problems, ranging from football injuries to schizophrenia, from ulcers to depression. (For example, see the books by Dohrenwend & Dohrenwend, 1974; Gunderson & Rahe, 1974; Sarason & Spielberger, 1975, 1976; Selye, 1978; Spielberger & Sarason, 1975, 1977; or the *Journal of Human Stress*.)

Much of the research on stress has focused on stress resulting from change per se, hypothesizing that *any* change which requires readjustment in one's life causes stress (Holmes & Masuda, 1974). Even apparently benign changes, such as getting married or starting a desired job, can lead to stress and to the negative consequences of stress. Volume of change is important, and it has been found that people experience elevated risks for many physical and emotional problems when they experience numerous life changes in a short period of time. A clustering of life events or a high level of life change has been found to precede suicide and hospitalization for depression or schizophrenia and to be related to depressed mood and to psychophysiologic symptoms in the general population (see Paykel, 1974a, 1974b;

Brown, 1974; Coleman, 1973; Markush & Favero, 1974; Myers, Linden-thal, & Pepper, 1974; Dohrenwend, 1973a). In addition, there is evidence that the stress of events accumulates over time. The number of life events occurring over a period of years has been found to be related to physical illness (Holmes & Masuda, 1974; Bageley, 1979). Life changes over periods ranging from three weeks to one year have been related to depression, schizophrenia, and depressed mood (see Brown, 1974; Paykel & Tanner, 1976; Markush & Favero, 1974).

While the life events stress research has produced many provocative findings, this research tradition has not succeeded in answering adequately many important questions about the specific effects of stress in women's lives. As has been pointed out elsewhere, the majority of stress studies have focused on research populations which are exclusively or predominantly male, such as prisoners of war, football players, industrial emloyees, medical interns, and Naval personnel at sea, (Makosky, 1980). Sex comparisons were rarely reported, and the most frequently used lists of events included a disproportionate number of events which apply more often to men than to women, while excluding events which women are likely to experience. Thus, being drafted, being promoted at work, or having one's wife start work often appeared on inventories of stressful events, while experiencing an abortion, a rape, or a change in child care arrangements generally did not.

For the purposes of the Stress and Families Project, traditional inventories of stressful life events had another flaw: they tended to include events likely to happen to middle-class people and excluded events which were likely to happen to poor people. Taking out a mortgage would be reflected in higher stress scores on these inventories, while going on welfare would not. (Discussion of closely related issues is presented in Dohrenwend, 1974.) Therefore, in the current study, the standard lists were expanded to include many events likely to happen to low-income women rearing young children. This Life Events Scale contained 91 discrete events,[1] such as change of residence; starting work; deaths of relatives or friends; and going off welfare, AFDC, unemployment, or similar assistance.

Although life events must be considered, they are not the only source of life stress. Much of the stress in life comes not from the necessity of adjusting to sporadic change, but from steady, unchanging (or slowly changing) oppressive conditions which must be endured daily. Research suggests that stressful life conditions as well as discrete events contribute to mental health problems. For example, studies have reported group differences in depression or other psychiatric symptoms which are not accounted for by differences in life events scores: women, people of low socioeconomic status, and nonwhites all exhibit an elevation in symptom scores that is not explained by differences in events scores (see Radloff, 1974, 1975; Dohrenwend, 1973a).

Other researchers have related "life strains," "difficulties," and "vulnerability factors" to depression or depressed mood (for example, Pearlin & Johnson, 1977; Brown, NiBhrolchain, & Harris, 1975). To investigate systematically life conditions which might prove stressful to low-income mothers, a Conditions Scale was developed.[2]

The Conditions Scale includes questions about 11 areas of the respondents' lives: employment, extended family, friends, physical health, mental health, intimate (love/marital) relationships, the law and legal involvements, living environment, money, education, and parenting. The capacity to make comparisons between the various areas is necessary because researchers who have looked only at money, social isolation, and parenting have found that all three areas of strain are related to depression but that money seems to be the most important (Pearlin & Johnson, 1977). A major aspect of the present study was the attempt to isolate the conditions of the respondents' lives most closely associated with mental health.

The remainder of this chapter will present findings concerning the events and conditions experienced by the respondents. The contributions each source of stress makes to mental health will be examined and discussed. Analysis indicates that a measure of the ongoing conditions of women's lives is more powerfully associated with mental health than is a measure of life change. Financial problems, such as low income, unpredictable income, and lack of control over income, appear to be central to the respondents' experience of stressful life conditions.

THE LIFE EVENTS OF LOW-INCOME MOTHERS

The women we interviewed experienced more life events than have been reported in other life stress research. For the two years preceding the interview, respondents reported from 5 to 33 events, with a median of 13.5. In most community surveys respondents report an average of only 1 to 2 events per *year* (Coates, Moyer, Kendall, & Howat, 1976; Dohrenwend, 1973b). Although some of the events reported were those added to the life events list for this study, examining only those events contained in the classic Holmes and Rahe (1967) list still yields a high frequency of events (ranging from 5 to 27, with a median of 13.5).[3] Thus, it would appear that the respondents in this study were much above the average for a nonhospitalized group in exposure to life events. Although the in-depth nature of the interviews or other contextual factors may have led the respondents to recall or report more of their life events than they would have done in a community survey, some "real" elevation in exposure to life changes is consistent with the higher average levels of depressive symptoms discussed in Chapter 2.

Of the 91 events on our list, 80 were reported as having happened to at least one of the respondents during the last two years.[4] Understandably, since some of the events were benign, the 80 events constituted a complex mixture of good and bad experiences. Thus, whereas 12 women moved to a better place, housing changes for 11 were for the worse. Thirteen started to work after a long time without a job and 15 were fired, laid off, or quit working. Seventeen started a sexually intimate relationship and 11 reported broken love relationships, including being divorced or widowed. On the positive side, 24 women reported that they had taken a vacation (though some of these vacations were no more than a day at a local beach) and 15 reported an outstanding personal achievement in the past two years. Twenty started school or a training program and 14 completed such a program. But 12 borrowed a large amount of money and 14 had a big drop in income. Twenty-one women reported that friends or family members had died in the preceding two years, and the health and safety of the women themselves were cause for concern: 15 women reported hospitalization or surgery; 6 were unwilling participants in sexual acts; 18 were victims of crime; and 6 were hit or beaten by someone in the household. (This is a conservative estimate of the violence in the respondents' lives because several women reported more than one instance of a particular event and because beatings were reported as happening "off and on" or "whenever he's out of jail" were counted only once.) Seventeen of the women had changed child care arrangements, and 16 women made appearances in court.

Perhaps the mixture of positive and negative events reported accounts for the fact that the mere *number* of events which happened to the respondents in the preceding two years was not a strong correlate of mental health problems: the frequency of such events was correlated .27 ($p < .05$) with unstable self-esteem, but was not significantly correlated with any other mental health indicator. However, for each event reported, the respondent indicated on a scale from 1 to 8 the amount of stress (problems, upset, worry, or concern) which the event had caused for her, and these subjective ratings of stress correlated significantly with anxiety and unstable self-esteem, and marginally with depression. These correlations are the same order of magnitude as those typically published for life events research (Rabkin & Struening, 1976). See Table 3.1.

THE EFFECTS OF STRESSFUL LIFE CONDITIONS

In order to assess factors in women's lives which might be causing stress (stressors) a number of questions were asked in each of the 11 Life Conditions areas. These questions were designed to tap ongoing aspects of the respondents' lives, not discrete events. The questions were multiple-choice questions, and each possible answer was assigned a stressor score by the

TABLE 3.1 Correlates of Mental Health

	Anxiety	Mastery	Stability of Self-Esteem	Self-Esteem	Depression
Stress of life events happening to the respondent	.34*	.12	.36*	.20	.25†
Life conditions money stressors	.41**	.29*	.32*	.46***	.59***
Income	−.30*	−.25†	−.11	−.21	−.30*
Life conditions money stressors when income is controlled	.27†	.16	.28†	.40**	.50**
Life conditions stressors when income is controlled	.38*	.31*	.41**	.30*	.60***
Life events stress when life conditions stressors are controlled	.16	−.07	.19	.04	−.06
Life conditions stressors when life events stress is controlled	.35*	.36*	.32*	.30*	.61***
Life conditions total stressor scores	.45***	.37**	.43**	.35*	.64***
Life conditions total stress scores	.59***	.59***	.52***	.60***	.70***

† $p < .10$
* $p < .05$
** $p < .01$
*** $p < .001$
NOTE: High scores on mental health measures indicate *poor* mental health.

author of the measure. These scores were assigned on the basis of common sense, and answers reflecting conditions thought to be more stressful received a high number of stressor points on this scale.

In addition to this stressor score, a score was devised to indicate the intensity of the respondents' own feelings about the several areas of stress in their lives. Following the other questions in each area, the respondents were asked to indicate on a scale from 1 (no problems, upset, worries, or concern)

TABLE 3.2   Correlations among Stressors and Feelings of Stress

Area	Area Stressors & Feelings of Stress	Money Stressors & Stressors in Other Areas	Money Stressors & Feelings of Stress in Other Areas
1 Education	.11	.26*	.07
2 Employment	.02	−.15	.06
3 Living Environment	.27*	−.10	.27*
4 Law	.34*	.01	.01
5 Parenting	.32*	.33*	.36**
6 Friends	.20†	.18*	.33*
7 Family	.61***	.33*	.43**
8 Intimate Relations	.40**	.34*	.25†
9 Health	.47***	.25†	.34*
10 Mental Health	.59***	.36**	.37**
11 Money	.49***		
12 Total	.59***	.51***	.50***

† p < .10
* p < .05
** p < .01
*** p < .001

to 100 (severe problems, upset, worries, or concern all or most of the time) their ratings of the stress they felt within that area of their lives. This 1-100 score is the Conditions Stress Score.

The goal in this research was to investigate relationships between stressful conditions in women's lives and their mental health. In many ways this research is exploratory and represents an attempt to quantify the difficult ongoing aspects of women's lives which might predispose them to mental health problems. Because the measure of stressful life conditions was constructed for this study, it was necessary to establish whether the areas of potential problems included in the interview related to the stress the respondents were experiencing. This was determined by correlating the *stress* respondents reported in a given area with the obtained *stressor* score. With the exceptions of education and employment, each stressor score was correlated with its area stress score, and the total stressor scores correlated with the total stress scores (see Table 3.2). These results indicate that the inteview actually does tap aspects of the lives of low-income mothers which are associated with their feelings of stress.

Furthermore, the results indicate that if one knows about the conditions of women's lives, one also knows something about their mental health: the total stressor scores correlated significantly with all five mental health indicators (see Table 3.1). In examining responses to the Conditions questions, a number of patterns emerged which give a clearer picture of the quality of life for low-income mothers of young children. The discussion of the nine areas for which the stressor questions were correlated with feelings of stress will move, in general, from the weaker to the stronger correlates of the mental health indicators.

LIVING ENVIRONMENT

Compared to national averages, *all* of the respondents lived in high-density, high-crime, and low-income neighborhoods. All the respondents lived in neighborhoods that are partly commercial or industrial, and only 14 percent of the respondents lived in single-family dwellings. Income is related to living environment in many ways, and in this low-income group the fact that all of the respondents shared such stressful living conditions may have caused a "floor effect," resulting in nonsignificant correlations between living conditions and the mental health measures. This interpretation is supported by the finding that feelings of stress in this area are correlated with three of the mental health indicators (see Table 3.3).

LAW

Although women who had problems with the law also reported feelings of stress in this area, this did not seem to be a factor in the sample as a whole: only six of the respondents had an arrest record and only three had a criminal record. With a larger sample, the law might be an important factor in the lives of a significant subgroup. For this sample, problems with the law did not correlate significantly with any measure of mental health (see Table 3.3).

PARENTING

Life Conditions questions in the parenting area revealed that primary responsibility for children lay with the mothers, and they seemed to get little "time off": two-thirds of the respondents said they had primary child care responsibility; 24 percent said they had no regular periods of time away from their children; and another 49 percent had only work time away from their children on a regular basis; nearly one-fourth said they had no one to count on for nonemergency child care (just to do something they wanted). Among the respondents, over half had at least one child before the age of twenty, and nearly two-thirds said that none of their pregnancies was planned. Forty-eight percent reported at least one child with problems in school, and over one-fourth reported that their situations as parents had gotten worse over the last five years.

TABLE 3.3 Life Conditions Stressors (and Feelings of Stress) Correlated with the Mental Health Indicators

Area	Anxiety	Mastery	Stability of Self-Esteem	Self-Esteem	Depression
1 Education	.08 (.13)	.24† (.18)	−.01 (.12)	.10 (.17)	.24† (.31*)
2 Employment	−.22† (.39**)	.14 (.64***)	−.09 (.16)	−.22 (.38**)	−.10 (.43**)
3 Living environment	.10 (.34*)	.23† (.33*)	.10 (.12)	−.09 (.25†)	.12 (.31*)
4 Law	−.09 (.02)	−.21† (−.21†)	.09 (.10)	.09 (.05)	−.20 (−.19)
5 Parenting	.17 (.47***)	.26† (.41**)	.07 (.64***)	.06 (.58***)	.29* (.57***)
6 Friends	.34* (.26*)	.02 (.17)	.32* (.06)	.33* (.10)	.38** (.18)
7 Family	.28* (.44**)	.27* (.53***)	.23† (.33*)	.25† (.39**)	.40** (.62***)
8 Intimate relations	.34* (.21†)	.04 (.20)	.35* (.34*)	.24† (.28*)	.46*** (.35*)
9 Health	.43** (.42**)	.26† (.38**)	.39** (.45**)	.41** (.49***)	.43** (.47***)
10 Mental health	.65*** (.43**)	.38** (.38**)	.51*** (.63***)	.55*** (.56***)	.66*** (.52***)
11 Money	.41** (.53***)	.29* (.59***)	.32* (.26*)	.46*** (.43**)	.59*** (.60***)
12 Total	.45*** (.59***)	.37** (.59***)	.43** (.52***)	.35* (.60***)	.64*** (.70***)

† p < .10
* p < .05
** p < .01
*** p < .001
NOTE: High scores on mental health measures indicate *poor* mental health.

Women who lacked regular child care assistance were more depressed than those who had such assistance, and this is the parenting area in which higher incomes would be likely to have the greatest buffering effect on mental health problems. Conditions in the parenting area are significantly correlated with depression and are marginally correlated with a poor sense of mastery (see Table 3.3). There is no clear explanation for the finding that parenting problems are not more generally related to mental health indicators. One possibility, however, is that the women in this study had a restricted range of parenting problems (perhaps all at the high end), and thus there was not enough variability for a stronger relationship to emerge in this sample.

FAMILY AND FRIENDS

Although problems with extended family and friends are important, there was no clear consensus on the nature of the most frequent problems, except poor health of relatives. Women named a diverse array of problems with relatives and friends, and it is clear that those women naming more problems for relatives and friends were also likely to have more mental health problems (see Table 3.3). The life conditions family stressors correlated significantly with depression, anxiety, a poor sense of mastery, and marginally with unstable self-esteem and poor self-esteem. In the area of friends, the stressor scores correlated significantly with anxiety, unstable self-esteem, poor self-esteem, and depression.

INTIMATE RELATIONS

Many distressing findings emerged in the intimate relations section of the Conditions measure. In reporting about their intimate relationships, over one-third of the respondents said that during the preceding two years they had been separated from their current partners for more than a few days because of problems in the relationship. Two-thirds of the respondents living with partners said that the partner acted as if he were the only important person around, that their partners kept them from being the sort of people they would like to be, and that they could not completely be themselves around their partners. Over a third indicated that their partners did not spend money wisely. These factors, in addition to household violence, may account for the fact that even though coupled women had significantly higher incomes than single women, there was no difference in four out of five of their mental health scores. Among those women who did not currently have a partner, the most frequently reported problems concerning intimate relationships were not having a chance to have fun, not having the kind of sex life they would like, and wondering whether they were interesting people. The Conditions score in the intimate relationships area correlated significantly with anxiety, unstable self-esteem, and depression, and marginally with poor self-esteem (see Table 3.3). Thus, problems with intimate relationships were frequently related to mental health problems.

PHYSICAL HEALTH

The physical health of the respondents seemed to be strongly associated with mental health status. Twenty-three percent of the respondents rated their health over the preceding two years as poor or very poor. Over half reported that they had been kept from their usual activities two or more days in a row three or more times, and 72 percent said they had to stay in bed all day at least once because of a physical health problem. Many of the health problems the respondents reported are those typically associated with stress, including several cases of asthma, ulcers, colitis, tuberculosis, migraines, chronic colds, arthritis, recurring pneumonia, high blood pressure, alcoholism, and obesity. It should be remembered that these problems were reported by a group of women whose average age was thirty! Life conditions stressors in the health area correlate significantly with anxiety, unstable self-esteem, poor self-esteem, and depression, and marginally with a poor sense of mastery (see Table 3.3).

MENTAL HEALTH

When looking at the respondents' reports concerning their mental health, there are several causes for concern. Only 40 percent of the respondents rated their mental health as good or very good. As expected, the respondents' mental health stressor scores correlated significantly with all five mental health indicators (see Table 3.3). In addition, there were correlations ranging from .38 to .63 between the respondents' upset, worries, or concerns about their mental health and their mental health scores. Not only were these women showing signs of poor mental health, they were worried about their mental health as well. Forty-two percent said that they had problems they should or would like to talk over with someone, such as a counselor.

MONEY

In looking at the money problems reported by the respondents, it was found that nearly half (42 percent) knew less than a month ahead of time how much money they would have for their households. Forty-two percent reported that no one in the household had a savings account, and one-third either did not know whether they could get $100 on short notice or knew they could not. Forty percent said their money situation had gotten worse over the last five years. Life conditions stressors in the money area are correlated significantly with all five mental health indicators (see Table 3.3). Considering that the income range in this group was severely restricted, the fact that money is so strongly related to depression and anxiety indicates again the importance of this factor. Even increases of as little as $500 per year in per capita income were associated with decreases in depression and anxiety scores (see Figures 3.1 and 3.2).

Although income level is assumed to be an important factor in the conditions of life, especially relating to money problems, it was excluded from the money section scores of the Conditions measure for two reasons: first, because all the respondents had low incomes when compared to national averages and there were no clear a priori scoring units; and second, because income level was thought to be a powerful variable for study in and of itself. The Total Conditions Stressor Score was significantly correlated with in-

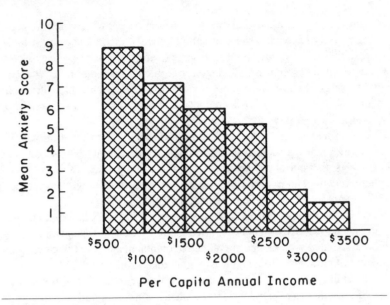

FIGURE 3.1   Income and Anxiety

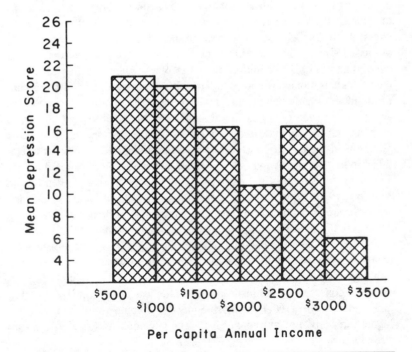

FIGURE 3.2   Income and Depression

come level ($-.29$), indicating that as income goes up, life conditions stressors generally decrease. The correlation between income and the stressor score in the area of money is even stronger ($-.52$), confirming the expected relationship between income and money problems. In addition, income and total feelings of stress were significantly correlated ($-.40$), indicating that as income goes up, the total amount of upset, worry, and concern in a woman's life goes down.

It is clear that money is a particularly important factor. Not only is the money area stressor score strongly correlated with mental health scores, but *income* is also correlated with some of these scores (see Table 3.1). Although income and money conditions stressors correlated with each other, they are not interchangeable variables.

When income is controlled, other money conditions continue to be important (see Table 3.1). That is, unpredictability, insecurity, and other problems associated with money are related to mental health apart from the total amount of money available (at least within this income range).

In addition to these conclusions about the stressfulness of the various conditions in the respondents' lives, their own comparative rankings of stressfulness were informative. At the end of all interviewing, the respondents were presented with a list of all 11 life conditions areas and were asked to indicate the most stressful, the second most stressful, the third most stressful, and the least stressful areas of their lives. In light of the findings discussed already, it is not surprising to find that according to the respondents' rankings of life conditions for stressfulness, the most stressful area in their lives was money, followed (not too closely) by parenting, living conditions, and intimate relationships, in that order. (These rankings support the argument that parenting and living conditions are not strongly correlated with mental health indicators because all of the respondents had many problems in those areas, and there was not sufficient variability for a relationship to emerge.) A total of 73 percent of the respondents rated money among the top stressors in their lives. This finding supports the Pearlin and Johnson (1977) case for the importance of money problems in people's lives. The area most frequently cited as least stressful was the law, chosen by 31 percent of the respondents.

In addition to the comparative rankings discussed above, we looked at the mean ratings of stressfulness assigned to each area by the respondents when they were asked to indicate on a scale from 1 to 100 the amount of upset, worry, or concern they felt in that area. The highest mean rating for stressfulness was for money (60.1), which was nearly 10 points higher than the next highest area (living conditions, 51.7). The law again emerged as the least stressful area.

THE CONTAGION OF STRESSORS AND STRESS

Money stressors are significantly correlated with problems in other areas of life more often than any other stressor: money stressors correlated with other stressors in the areas of family, mental health, intimate relationships, education, and parenting, and they marginally correlated with health (see Table 3.2). It seems that money problems indicated the likelihood of *generally* difficult life conditions. In addition, money stressors are correlated with the respondents' *feelings* of upset, worry, and concern in the areas of family, friends, health, mental health, living environments, and parenting, and they are marginally correlated with feelings of stress in the area of intimate relationships (see Table 3.2). One can conclude from the foregoing that there was a clear relationship between money stressors and the way women felt about many of the other areas of their lives.

Although individual problem areas can be identified, and the overlap in influence on mental health can be statistically controlled, such compartmentalization did not occur in the lives of the women themselves. Of the 55 intercorrelations possible among the life conditions areas, there are significant correlations among 33 of the stress pairs. This indicates that women who felt stressed in one area of their lives tended to feel upset, worried, or concerned about several other areas of their lives as well. Overall, there is strong evidence for the contagion of both stressors and stress.

THE RELATIONSHIP BETWEEN
EVENTS AND CONDITIONS

Looking at the total scores as they correlate with the five mental health indicators, we found that psychological well-being is more strongly related to life conditions than to life events. This general finding is quite clear in Table 3.1. Life events stress is significantly correlated with anxiety and unstable self-esteem and marginally correlated with depression, while the conditions stressor score is significantly correlated with all five mental health indicators. Again, it should be pointed out that the events stress correlations are of the same order of magnitude as those typically published for life events research using much larger samples than ours. It would seem that the events measure is at least as good as those used in previous research, so one can conclude that these results reflect a strong conditions effect, not a poor events measure.

Although the relatively greater power of conditions compared to events in predicting mental health was not expected when data gathering began, it was not surprising in light of work published by Pearlin and Lieberman in 1977.

Those researchers worked within the context of a project begun in 1972 to study problems of everyday life. At that time, the survey emphasized persistent problems; in a follow-up survey in 1976-77, this was enlarged to include a study of events in the intervening four years. Although their methods were different from the current project, and they reported only on the areas of occupation, marriage, and parenting, their conclusions support our own: they concluded that events affect a person's psychological well-being only when they alter enduring circumstances of the person's life. This is consistent with earlier work by Brown (1974), which emphasized the power of "threatening" events, which are those with long-term implications for the respondent. Based on this reasoning, a series of partial correlations were computed to determine whether the mental health indicators would be significantly correlated with events and/or conditions if the other source of variation were statistically controlled. All of the mental health indicators continued to be significantly correlated with conditions stressors when events stress was statistically partialed out. None of the correlations of events stress with the mental health indicators was significant when conditions stressors were controlled. Indeed, as can be seen in Table 3.1, in some cases the direction of the correlation was even reversed. Thus, it would seem that there is relatively little relationship between events in general and psychological symptoms which cannot be subsumed under the effects of stressful life conditions. A series of multiple regressions demonstrated that life events add nothing to the predictability of mental health measures beyond the contribution of life conditions. It may well be that events affect mental health only when they change the enduring conditions of one's life.

SUMMARY AND CONCLUSIONS

The women who participated in this study represent a population at high risk for mental health problems: low-income mothers of young children. In attempting to delineate some of the factors which put them "at risk" it was found that they were constantly confronted with the necessity of adjusting to stressful life events—they reported more than three times the number of events typical for the population at large! Nevertheless, the women in this study who experienced the most changes in life were not necessarily those who experienced the greatest risk for depressive symptoms, anxiety, and poor self-esteem. It was the women who had endured the most difficult stable conditions of life for the two years prior to the study who were at greatest risk. There was no evidence that life events are related to psychological well-being except as they might have affected the ongoing conditions of the respondents' lives.

Although researchers continue to report relationships between life events and various illnesses, injuries, and/or psychological states (for example, Coddington & Troxell, 1980), one must seriously consider the possibility that life stress research in the past has overemphasized events and change. Rabkin and Struening (1976) commented on the low-level correlations commonly reported in the literature, and more recently a number of studies have found "no effects" for life events. For example, Knapp (1979) did not find a correlation between life events and emotional disturbance in a college student sample. Gersten, Langner, Eisenberg, and Simcha-Fagan (1977 studied both the amount of change and the undesirability of events, defined both objectively and subjectively, and found that events made no contribution to the prediction of any disturbed behavior for a large sample of mothers. Bieliauskas (1980) concluded that for adult males any relationship between stress and illness is questionable in low-stress, low-maladjustment populations.

Broad individual differences in response to stress have long been recognized, and now Baum, Singer, and Baum (1981) have presented the appraisal of stressors as a transmission variable, affected by such factors as attitudes toward the stressor, perception of risk and danger, and perceived control. Several recent studies have integrated life events and such variables as need for power, inhibition, sensation seeking, and other psychosocial modifiers of responses to stress (McClelland & Jemmott, 1980; Jenkins, 1979; Johnson, Sarason, & Siegel, 1979). Thus, one new trend in the study of life stress would seem to be the integration of event characteristics with the individual's intrapsychic characteristics. A second new direction, discussed by Eckenrode and Gore (1981) recognizes the importance of context in the study of life stress. These authors have commented that, historically, the significance or meaning of life events was assumed to be determined by the characteristics of the events themselves, rather than by a "dynamic interaction" between the individual and the particular event(s) in question; they endorse the use of contextual analysis in order to determine more accurately the stressfulness of events to the individuals experiencing those events. My own position is more nearly that of Gersten et al. (1977). These authors investigated the role of events in the etiology of psychological disorders in children and concluded that such long-standing difficulties as poverty or a chronically ill mother are more important. Further analysis of discrete events may be less fruitful than attempts to quantify further the stressfulness of ongoing life conditions, or an investigation of the relationship between specific events and the conditions of people's lives.

Finally, we must address the issue of money in the lives of women at risk. The women who participated in this study were chosen to represent a population at high risk for depression: women are much more likely than men to be diagnosed depressed, and the women most likely to become depressed are low-income women with young children. There is strong evidence in the present study that the critical attribute may be "low income." Money stressors are correlated with all five mental health indicators and with problems and feelings of stress in more areas of life than any other single variable studied. The economic status of women in the United States has been documented again and again (see, for example, Bernard, 1981). At the same time, more households than ever before are headed by women, and the consequences may be devastating. Corcoran (1979) reported that women who were married in 1968 but divorced or widowed in 1975 had suffered a 40 percent decrease in real money and a decrease of more than 10 percent in the ratio of income to family needs. They were able to make up only 40-60 percent of this loss through additional earnings, transfer income, or contributions of other household members. Fifty-five percent of the divorced women received no welfare, alimony, or child support, and 38 percent of the widows received no retirement benefits. For those who did receive support, welfare averaged $2150; alimony and child support averaged $1930; and retirement benefits averaged $2860. The rising divorce rate, particularly in families with young children, and the low probability of regular child support payments from the absent father (Ross & Sawhill, 1975) mean that increasing numbers of mothers with young children live in poverty. Even families receiving AFDC benefits would have incomes below the poverty line if they did not have additional income from other sources (Pearce, 1979). At the same time, women's earnings, relative to those of men, have actually declined in recent years, and over half of the occupations women typically enter will not support a family of four above the poverty level (Barrett, 1979; Sawhill, 1976).

In his book, *What Money Buys: Inequality and the Social Meaning of Income,* Rainwater (1974) stops short of saying money will buy happiness, but he certainly documents the importance of money for psychological well-being. Our findings support that documentation. During an interview on mental health problems and the use of mental health services, respondents were asked what they would see as emotional problems. At the core of many responses was a concern with lack of money and with the related problems of paying bills, finding a decent place to live, putting food on the table, and getting adequate medical and child care. One woman said: "Welfare, you know, is an emotional strain." Another woman succinctly stated: "No money or food would cause emotional problems." As long as women are disproportionately represented in low-income groups, they will also be disproportionately represented among the depressed.

NOTES

1. This measure (the Life Events Measure) was constructed by Vivian Parker Makosky. Many of the items included in this list also appear on lists of events used in other research, but the overlap in content of such lists makes specific acknowledgments impossible. The procedures used for this interview were patterned after those reported by Dohrenwend et al. (1977). Many valuable suggestions concerning content and phrasing were made by the members of the Stress and Families Project staff. See also note 3.

2. This measure (the Life Conditions Measure) was constructed by Vivian Parker Makosky. In constructing this measure, a number of items were taken either directly or with modification from questionnaires or surveys done by others. In addition, a number of items were suggested by the research literature. I wish to acknowledge particularly the work of Leonard Perlin, George Brown, Urie Bronfenbrenner, and Leo Srole and their colleagues, as well as the *Current Estimates from the Health Interview Survey: United States–1974*. The members of the Stress and Families Project staff made many valuable contributions to the content and phrasing of the questions, as well as to the thinking behind the measure as a whole.

3. Other items were included in our interview so that we would be able to make direct comparisons between our measure and the measures used by others as they relate to the five Mental Health Indicators. The two lists of most interest to us are those of Holmes and Rahe (1967) and of Dohrenwend, Krasnoff, Askenasy, and Dohrenwend (1977). A chart of which events appeared on the Holmes and Rahe and/or Dohrenwend et al. lists is included in a Stress Supplement to this report, which is available upon request.

4. No respondent reported the following events for the two years preceding the interview: birth of first child, child died, went on probation, went on parole, failed to get out of jail when expected, decrease in workload, promotion, demotion, business failure or loss, being on strike, or starting work for the first time.

REFERENCES

Bageley, C. Control of the emotions, remote stress, and the emergence of breast cancer. *Indian Journal of Clinical Psychology,* 1979, *6* (2), 213-220.

Barrett, N. S. Women in the job market: Occupations, earnings, and career opportunities. In R. E. Smith (Ed.) *The subtle revolution: Women at work.* Washington, DC: Urban Institute, 1979.

Baum, A., Singer, J., & Baum, C. Stress and the environment. *Journal of Social Issues,* 1981, *37* (1), 4-35.

Bernard, J. *The female world.* New York: Free Press, 1981.

Bieliauskas, L. Life events, 17-OHCS measures, and psychological defensiveness in relation to aid-seeking. *Journal of Human Stress,* 1980, *6* (1), 28-36.

Brown, G. W. Life-events and the onset of depressive and schizophrenic conditions. In E. K. E. Gunderson and R. H. Rahe (Eds.) *Life stress and illness.* Springfield, IL: Charles C Thomas, 1974.

Brown, G. W., NiBhrolchain, M., & Harris, T. Social class and psychiatric disturbance among women in an urban population. *Sociology,* 1975, *9,* 225-254.

Coates, D. B., Moyer, S., Kendall, L., & Howat, M. G. Life-event changes and mental health. In I. G. Sarason & C. D. Spielberger (Eds.) *Stress and anxiety* (Vol. 3). Washington, DC: Hemisphere, 1976.

Coddington, R. D., & Troxell, J. The effect of emotional factors on football injury rates: A pilot study. *Journal of Human Stress,* 1980, *6* (4), 3-5.

Coleman, J. C. Life stress and maladaptive behavior. *American Journal of Occupational Therapy,* 1973, *27* (4), 169-180.

Corcoran, M. The economic consequences of marital dissolution for women in the middle years. *Sex Roles,* 1979, *5* (3), 343-353.

Dohrenwend, B. P. Problems in defining and sampling the relevant population of stressful life events. In B. S. Dohrenwend & B. P. Dohrenwend (Eds.) *Stressful life events: Their nature and effects.* New York: John Wiley, 1974. Pp. 275-312.

Dohrenwend, B. S. Social status and stressful life events. *Journal of Personality and Social Psychology,* 1973, *28,* 225-235. (a)

Dohrenwend, B. S. Life events as stressors: A methodological inquiry. *Journal of Health and Social Behavior,* 1973, *14,* 167-175. (b)

Dohrenwend, B. S. & Dohrenwend, B. P. Social class and the relation of remote to recent stressors. In M. Roff, L. N. Robins, & M. Pollack (Eds.) *Life history research in psychopathology* (Vol. 2). Minneapolis: University of Minnesota Press, 1972. Pp. 170-185.

Dohrenwend, B. S., & Dohrenwend, B. P. *Stressful life events: Their nature and effects.* New York: John Wiley, 1974.

Dohrenwend, B. S., Krasnoff, L., Askenasy, A. R., & Dohrenwend, B. P. Exemplification of a means for scaling life events: The PERI life events scale. Unpublished manuscript received 5/27/77.

Eckenrode, J., & Gore, S. Stressful events and social supports: The significance of context. In B. H. Gottlieb (Ed.), *Social networks and social support.* Beverly Hills, CA: Sage, 1981.

Gersten, J., Langner, T., Eisenberg, J., & Simcha-Fagan, O. An evaluation of the etiologic role of stressful life-change events in psychological disorders. *Journal of Health and Social Behavior,* 1977, *18* (3), 228-244.

Gunderson, E. K. E. Introduction. In E. K. E. Gunderson and R. H. Rahe (Eds.) *Life stress and illness.* Springfield, IL: Charles C Thomas, 1974.

Gunderson, E. K. E., & Rahe, R. H. (Eds.). *Life stress and illness.* Springfield, IL: Charles C Thomas, 1974.

Holmes, T. H., & Rahe, R. H. The social readjustment rating scale. *Journal of Psychosomatic Research,* 1967, *11,* 213-218.

Holmes, T. H., & Masuda, M. Life change and illness susceptibility. In B. S. Dohrenwend & B. P. Dohrenwend (Eds.) *Stressful life events: Their nature and effects.* New York: John Wiley, 1974.

Jenkins, C. D. Psychosocial modifiers of response to stress. *Journal of Human Stress,* 1979, *5* (4), 3-15.

Johnson, J., Sarason, I., & Siegel, J. Arousal seeking as a moderator of life stress. *Perceptual & Motor Skills,* 1979, *49* (2), 665-666.

Knapp, S. Life events, rationality and emotional disturbance. *Psychological Reports,* 1979, *45* (2), 510.

Kraus, S. The crisis of divorce: Growth promoting or pathogenic? *Journal of Divorce,* 1979, *3* (2), 107-119.

McClelland, D., & Jemmott, J. Power motivation, stress and physical illness. *Journal of Human Stress,* 1980, *6* (4), 6-15.

Makosky, V. P. Life stress and the mental health of women: A discussion of research and issues. In M. Guttentag, S. Salasin, & D. Belle (Eds.) *Mental Health of Women.* New York: Academic Press, 1980.

Markush, R. E., & Favero, R. V. Epidemiologic assessment of stressful life events, depressed mood, and psychophysiological symptoms—A preliminary report. In B. S. Dohrenwend &

B. P. Dohrenwend (Eds.) *Stressful life events: Their nature and effects.* New York: John Wiley, 1974.

Myers, J. K., Lindenthal, J. J., & Pepper, M. P. Social class, life events, and psychiatric symptoms: A longitudinal study. In B. S. Dohrenwend & B. P. Dohrenwend (Eds.) *Stressful life events: Their nature and effects.* New York: John Wiley, 1974. Pp. 191-206.

Paykel, E. S. Recent life events and clinical depression. In E. K. E. Gunderson and R. H. Rahe (Eds.) *Life stress and illness.* Springfield, IL: Charles C Thomas, 1974. Pp. 134-163. (a)

Paykel, E. S. Life stress and psychiatric disorders: Applications of the clinical approach. In B. S. Dohrenwend & B. P. Dohrenwend (Eds.) *Stressful life events: Their nature and effects.* New York: John Wiley, 1974. Pp. 135-150. (b)

Paykel, E. S., & Tanner, J. Life events, depressive relapse and maintenance treatment. *Psychological Medicine,* 1976, *6,* 481-485.

Pearce, D. Women, work and welfare: The feminization of poverty. In K. W. Feinstein (Ed.) *Working women and families.* Beverly Hills, CA: Sage, 1979.

Pearlin, L. I. & Johnson, J. Marital status, life-strains, and depression. *American Sociological Review,* 1977, *42,* 704-714.

Pearlin, L. I., & Lieberman, M. A. Social sources of emotional distress. In R. Simmons (Ed.) *Research in community and mental health.* Greenwich, CT: Jai Press, 1977.

Pfeiffer, M., Siegel, A., Taylor, S., & Shuler, L. Background data for the Human Performance in Continuous Operations Guidelines. U.S. Army Research Institute for the Behavioral & Social Sciences, 1979, TR 386, 110 p. Cited from *Psychological Abstracts, 65:* 11354.

Rabkin, J. G., & Struening, E. L. Life events, stress, and illness. *Science,* 1976 *194,* 1013-1020.

Radloff, L. Sex differences in mental health: The effects of marital and occupational status. Draft of text for presentation at APHA, New Orleans, 1974.

Radloff, L. Sex differences in depression: The effects of occupation and marital status. *Sex Roles: A Journal of Research,* 1975, *1* (3), 249-266.

Rainwater, L. *What money buys: Inequality and the social meanings of income.* New York: Basic Books, 1974.

Ross, H. L., and Sawhill, I. *Time of transition: The growth of families headed by women.* Washington, DC: Urban Institute, 1975.

Sarason, I., & Spielberger, C. *Stress and anxiety* (Vol. 2). New York: John Wiley, 1975.

Sarason, I., & Spielberger, C. *Stress and anxiety* (Vol. 3). New York: John Wiley, 1976.

Sawhill, I. Women with low incomes. In M. Blaxall & B. Reagan (Eds.) *Women and the workplace: The implications of occupational segregation.* Chicago: University of Chicago Press, 1976.

Selye, H. *The stress of life* (revised paperback ed.). New York: McGraw-Hill, 1978.

Spielberger, C., & Sarason, I. *Stress and anxiety* (Vol. 1) New York: John Wiley, 1975.

Spielberger, C., & Sarason, I. *Stress and anxiety* (Vol. 4). New York: John Wiley, 1977.

4

DAILY LIVES

DIANA DILL AND ELIZABETH GREYWOLF

What characterizes the daily lives of urban low-income women? How is their time utilized, and is there such a thing as a "typical lifestyle" for these women? To answer these questions we looked at sample days in the lives of the 43 women we interviewed. By having the respondents describe a "normal day" (from the time they woke until going to bed), we hoped to build a window through which to view their daily activities. What we found was a great variety in lifestyles, daily occupations, and social contexts in which days were spent. But we also found a common denominator for most of the women in the way they spent their days—too little satisfaction with the quality of their daily lives.

An influential behavioral theory of depression (Lewinsohn, Biglan, & Zeiss, 1976; Lewinsohn, Sullivan, & Grosscup, 1979) points to a low rate of pleasant daily events and/or a high rate of aversive daily events as etiological factors in depressive symptomatology. In this view, mood swings closely parallel the degree to which daily events are welcomed. Dysphoric mood, therefore, is a predictable result of a person's having few experiences which are reinforcing, frequent experiences which are punishing, or unpleasant, or a combination of both types of experience. Lewinsohn and his colleagues (1976, 1979) note that, while for some individuals such a schedule of events may result from their lack of skill in eliciting pleasant events or in coping with aversive events, for others the environments in which they live simply provide too few opportunities for pleasant experience and too high a frequency of aversive experiences. The frequency with which low-income mothers have been shown to experience aversive events in the contexts of their daily lives (see Makosky on Life Conditions Stressors) gives weight to the argument that environmental conditions for low-income mothers are punishing.

When we look at the daily routines of low-income mothers, we find that it is difficult to identify *specific* routines with which increased stress and depression are associated. For instance, women who spend their entire days at home caring for children, without the company of other adults, are no more likely to exhibit higher levels of depressive symptomatology than are women who spend their days outside the home engaged in work or educational pursuits which bring them into contact with other adults.

What the daily routine data do illustrate, however, is that it is the relative availability of *free* time and the relative opportunity to schedule portions of one's day *to suit oneself* rather than to meet external demands which differentiate women without depressive symptoms from depressed women.

This chapter presents an overview of the range of activities and time schedules of the profiles of women who illustrate the daily routines of "a worker," "a student," and "a homemaker," and hypothesizes about the relation of daily routines to mental health and stress and depression.

OVERVIEW

Within the sample we found that there is little consistency about the time span constituting "a day." Many of the women begin activity as early as 6:00 a.m., like Ms. Walker and Ms. Ramsey. They wake their families, help to dress their children, and then prepare breakfast for everyone so that the entire family begins its day together. Other women play the role of "starter." Ms. Sanders is one of these. She wakes her nineteen-year-old son at 6:00, goes back to sleep, and then wakes again at 7:00 to feed her two younger daughters.

Some women, however, are really "night people." Ms. Webb, for example, normally sleeps until 10:00 a.m. or noon because she is up and working (either doing housework or building maintenance) until 2:00 or 4:00 in the morning. Several women also indicated they suffer to varying degrees from insomnia—although they may go to bed at an early hour, they are actually awake for hours longer.

In many of the families, such as the Newmans, Trents, and Everetts, the school-age children either get their own breakfasts or eat at school. Some children even seem to have traded roles, to some extent, with their mothers, and play the role of "starter." Ms. Newman's youngest daughter, for instance, wakes herself and then her siblings before going off to school alone.

Within some families—the Webbs, for example—individual members maintain radically different schedules. Ms. Webb's two-year-old daughter has adapted to her mother's schedule and sleeps quite late in the morning, while her older sister spends each night in her grandmother's house next door and gets up at 8:00 a.m. with her. But while the children in these families usually adapt to the patterns set by adults, they sometimes develop patterns of wake and sleep which are unique to themselves. Ms. Rand's independent five-year-old son, for instance, goes to bed at 7:30 but wakes typically between 10:00 p.m. and midnight when he spends time by himself, sometimes until 2:00 a.m. The child never sleeps straight through an evening; apparently he always "cat naps."

On the average, however, a day in the life of most respondents and their families begins sometime between 6:00 and 8:00 a.m. and ends between 10:00 p.m. and 1:00 a.m. Within that time-span the respondents complete the normal activities of eating, housework, child care, and some form of interaction with the outside world—whether formally through employment or studies, or informally through encounters with shopkeepers and sales personnel, relatives, friends, doctors, and others. Specific activities and the times the activities occur vary widely from family to family.

The extent of daily contact with others outside the household is virtually nonexistent for some of the women and almost continuous for others. Ms. Taylor, in one day which she considered normal, took her younger child to his day care center, returned home and discussed work with her husband, entertained old friends for lunch, commuted to a suburban city where she works in human services, returned home after dinner and talked with her children, joined with friends until midnight, and then conversed for several hours with her husband before going to sleep.

While many respondents, for different reasons, spend most of the day away from home, in contrast, ten respondents rarely leave the house during the day. Ms. Marshall, for example, who has four children of her own, is employed at home as a babysitter and telephone salesperson.

Many other women are also at home all day, spending most of their waking hours inside alone while their children are at school. Ms. Walker is alone for almost seven hours each weekday, from the time her husband and children leave until midafternoon, when the children return. She may leave the house to do errands but is always home by the time her children return from school.

The viewing of television is one activity common to each family, although the amount of time spent in front of the set or simply having a set on for companionship varies among families a greal deal. As might be expected, preschool children who are at home all day seem to have the greatest exposure. Ms. Everett's five-year-old son, for example, watches television intermittently from the time he gets up until bedtime. Many older children watch television from the time they come home from school in midafternoon until dinnertime, and after dinner until they go to bed. Some respondents are more selective than others about TV. While Ms. Wade prepares dinner in the afternoon, her children watch programs mainly on the public television station for entertainment. Others are too busy for television viewing during the day and confine this activity to a few hours here and there. And some adults, like Ms. Ross and her partner, watch very little television, although their children generally watch the set each afternoon and evening before going to bed.

The following family profiles are based on interviews with three women. While they were chosen because their daily routines illustrate the range from virtual isolation to days filled with numerous complex interactions, they are also indicative of the limitations to personal freedom which many low-income women find prevent fuller satisfaction with their lives.

THE RAND FAMILY

Ms. Rand divides her personal time among three residences. She begins her day at 5:00 a.m. in the home of either her twin sister or an older sister who lives in the same housing project. Although she has an apartment of her own, she spends most of her free time at her twin's because her own apartment is not completely furnished. When Ms. Rand rises at 5:00 it is not to wake her own two children (David, five, and Mary, four), but her niece and nephew (seven and five). She bathes them, makes lunches for them to take to school, and then prepares breakfast. As they are eating she combs their hair and wakes her own children. She then walks her niece to the bus stop (the nephew leaves by himself) after putting food on the table for her own children.

At 7:35 Ms. Rand returns and dresses her son and daughter, who watch television and have their hair combed. The family catches a bus at 8:30 to their apartment and from there Ms. Rand walks her children to school. After returning home she may sleep a bit or watch television. This very brief period is the only "free time" she has during the day. At 10:30 she catches another bus for work. After an hour-and-a-half commute, she begins her current job—temporary work as a housekeeper at a Boston-area hotel.

While their mother is on her way to work, the two Rand children are picked up at school by their aunt at 11:30 and taken to one home or the other, where they are given lunch. David is put into pajamas and either plays in his room or cleans it if it is messy, until it is time for the cartoons on TV. His cousin arrives and the children may play alone or together and watch TV until 5:30 or 6:30, when they have supper.

Finishing her job at 5:00, Ms. Rand catches a bus and arrives at her sister's house at about 6:30, greets the children, and eats the supper her sister has prepared. Ms. Rand will then either go to bed or watch TV with David, who often falls asleep while watching. But (as previously mentioned) David usually wakens while everyone is sleeping (from 10:00 p.m. to midnight) and spends time alone until 2:00 a.m. or so. On weekends David stays with the family of the respondent's separated husband, and a sister may keep Ms. Rand's daughter for part of the weekend. During the summer the children usually stay with their grandmother. The living patterns of the family are closely interrelated with those of extended family members.

Ms. Rand's daily life is obviously full of activity, especially those related to child care responsibilities within her extended family. She is unhappy with her job and finds it difficult to make time to take her children places.

THE ROSS FAMILY

Ms. Ross is a student and divides her time among classes, housework, studies, and the care of her two sons (ages eight and five). She is pregnant with another child, and is expecting a teenage foster child to enter the household soon. Her partner works from noon until 10:00 p.m. and is able to help her with some child care responsibilities, but the two children need to be picked up in the afternoon by Ms. Ross, one from a day care center and one from a day care mother's home.

A typical weekday for the Rosses begins at 7:00 a.m., when both adults wake and dress. The children wake between 7:00 and 7:30, and Ms. Ross helps dress the younger child and makes breakfast for the entire family. The children leave for school about 8:00 and for approximately 15 minutes Ms. Ross and her partner have time for coffee and talk. Then Ms. Ross does household chores and leaves at 9:30 to take her younger child to his day care mother. She then goes straight to her classes until 1:00 p.m. Her partner remains at home and does some chores until noon, when he leaves for work nearby. At 11:00 a.m. the younger child is picked up at school by his day care mother and is taken to her home.

By 1:00 p.m. Ms. Ross has finished her classes and has one hour to herself. She either goes home or to the library, and at 2:45 she picks up her younger child at his day care mother's house and returns home to relax a bit, do chores, and talk or play with her children. Her older son returns from school at about 3:00.

The children vary their predinner time with snacking, television, play, or talk. At 5:00 the family eats dinner. Ms. Ross's partner returns from work just in time to eat and help her feed the children. After helping to clean up, he leaves again for work at 6:30. From 7:00 to 8:00 Ms. Ross can either relax briefly, spend time with her children, read or do school work, or do additional household chores. At 8:30 the younger child goes to bed, then, her older son at 9:00, when Ms. Ross can continue her school work. Her partner returns from work at 10:00 and the two adults spend the rest of the evening together until 12:00 or 12:30.

On weekends the family can sleep a little later, spend more time with each other or with friends, and get any shopping done which they did not have time for during the week. Ms. Ross says it is hardest for her to find time for homework and time for herself, to relax or to deal with feelings, "expressing them constructively with thinking behind them."

THE BARNETT FAMILY

Ms. Barnett is a forty-year-old mother of three children, ages six, eight, and fifteen. In contrast to Ms. Rand and Ms. Ross, Ms. Barnett spends most of her time at home and experiences few time constraints. Her husband died a year before she was interviewed and she was still deeply upset and attempting to cope with the problems of providing total emotional support to her children during this difficult time. Ms. Barnett has several serious health problems, including failing eyesight, and has had financial problems for as long as she can remember, even when her husband was alive and working. Ms. Barnett used to work to add to the family's income, but now she cannot see well enough even to crochet (a pastime she said used to give her considerable pleasure and relieved her stress). She is at home most of the time, taking care of her own children and others (for whom she does child care). A typical weekday for Ms. Barnett begins at 6:00 a.m., when she wakes her oldest child, Diane. Ms. Barnett can then sleep a little longer, until about 7:00, when Diane leaves for school. Ms. Barnett wakes her two youngest children at that time and prepares breakfast, which they all eat at about 7:30 before the children leave for school.

Ms. Barnett has just enough time to do the dishes before the children for whom she babysits arrive. She does her wash, plays with the children and cleans until lunch time. After the noon meal the children nap until 1:30, when they require continued care. Diane arrives home from school around 2:30 and plays with the children while Ms. Barnett begins preparing for dinner, which is usually made ahead of time. Her day care charges are picked up around 4:15 and then Ms. Barnett can rest before the family eats dinner together at 6:00. After the evening meal Diane usually goes out with friends, and the two youngest draw or watch television until their bedtime at 9:00. Ms. Barnett finishes any leftover housework, bathes, and goes to bed when Diane returns home around 10:00 or 10:30.

In addition to severe emotional and financial difficulties, Ms. Barnett's life is further complicated by her housing situation and an ongoing battle with the owner of her building. Ms. Barnett's apartment building is periodically flooded (when it rains or when snow melts) and drains back up into her rooms. This situation has caused her considerable stress and has been going on for over a year and a half. Much of her contact with people outside her household has to do with attempts to rectify this situation, but when she was last seen, nothing had been done to alleviate the problem.

Ms. Barnett's life is relatively isolated, child-centered, and involves fewer formal time constraints than the lives of Ms. Rand and Ms. Ross. She says she usually finds time to do everything she needs to do. Ms. Barnett is, in this regard, typical of many women living in low-income housing projects. Rainwater (1970) found that, because of child care responsibilities and safety concerns, women in a St. Louis housing project spent no more than 10 hours per week outside their apartments, on average. This included shopping and visiting time.

CHILD CARE AND HOMEMAKING

The average respondent regularly spends five hours a day alone with her children, and some women spend virtually all of their time in this manner. We reasoned that many hours spent alone with children daily would be a possible indicator of both isolation and overload of responsibility. Nearly half of the respondents reported spending more time with their children than they wanted to spend, and these women also tended (although the relationship was not statistically significant) to report more symptoms of depression than did women who are satisfied with the amount of time they spend this way and women who want to be with their children more often. A simple count of hours alone with children is not significantly correlated with any mental health or stress measures, indicating that the subjective appraisal of time allotment is more relevant to this issue than a more objective measure.

The average respondent daily spends nine hours actively caring for children, running household errands, and doing housework. Several respondents report feeling they do not have enough time for homemaking due to the time demands of work or school. More hours spent homemaking—which necessarily implies less time interacting with the world outside the home— is associated with less frequent life events and related stress, and with fewer life conditions stressors in the area of friends. More hours spent homemaking was also found to be associated with increased stress in the area of parenting. It was not, however, associated with any of our measures of mental health.

FAMILY INTERACTION

The average family in the study spends three hours together daily (when respondents' partners and/or other adult family members and all the children are home). For four families, there is no time during the day when all resident family members are together. If family time together is considered a pleasant event, we wondered if lack of time together might be associated with stress and depression. Alternatively, if family time together is tension-producing, we might expect women who spent more time with their families to be more stressed and depressed. We found, however, no across-the-board relation of family time together and either stress or depression.

SOCIAL CONTACT

Hours spent with other adults without children is an index of sociability, and several respondents report feeling they do not have enough time to pursue a social life with other adults. Ms. Lewis, for instance, says that the hardest thing to find time for is "socializing with adults the way I'd want to." Hours spent this way is also an indicator of the respondent's major daily activity. If she is primarily a homemaker, she is less likely to spend as much time with other adults as is the respondent who is employed or goes to school. The average respondent spends four hours daily with other adults away from her children. Four respondents have regular contact only with adults who are household members. Three respondents have daily contact with other adults only through work or school. The remaining respondents see other adults daily in a variety of context, for instance, while running errands, visiting, or participating in group leisure or volunteer activities.

More hours spent with adults, without children, is associated with more frequent life events and higher stress associated with life events. Women who spend more time daily with other adults, away from their children, are also more likely to have more stressors in the areas of friends and intimate relations but fewer stressors in the parenting area. This count of hours was not associated with any of our measures of mental health.

These relationships and the associations we found between stressors and time spent homemaking seem to suggest that a woman is likely to experience stress in those areas of life which occupy the major portion of her daily routine. The woman who spends much of her day in the company of other adults tends to find relationships with other adults stressful; in contrast, the woman who spends much of her day homemaking and caring for children is likely to find parenting, but not relationships with adults, stressful. Neither type of routine was, in itself, related to increased incidence of depressive symptomatology.

DISCRETIONARY TIME AND
SATISFACTION WITH TIME ALLOTMENT

As a means of discerning what impact control over events would have on mood—given the hypothesis that lack of control over events, whether they are pleasant or aversive, lends itself to depression—we wanted to find out whether or not a woman who had little opportunity to take time out of a routine to spend as she liked would be more susceptible to stress and depression than a woman who had such opportunity. Respondents often mentioned time strain as an important source of stress. For instance, Ms. Wade has claimed Sundays as her day for herself after a serious argument with her partner over "the working issue." She felt she had "too much to do all the time cooped up in the house cleaning and the rest of the time cooking, washing, and looking after the children." Another respondent said she would like at least nighttime to herself: "I can only get time when I steal it, pretend I am going to the store and stay for two hours." Still another respondent said: "I don't get enough time for myself. If both kids were in school . . . to go somewhere and scream would make me feel better. Showing my feelings is the hardest thing to do. When I was a kid, I'd go off alone but now there is *no* being alone."

We attempted several ways to assess the relation of discretionary time to stress and depression. We made a count of hours of both time alone and time free of responsibility. Time alone was not necessarily time to spend as one liked, as much of the time respondents spent alone was allotted to housework, homework, working at other jobs at home, or doing errands outside the house. We found, using these counts of hours, that the average respondent spent three hours of her average day alone. Time free of responsibility, in contrast, was defined as hours during the day in which the respondent could devote her full attention to whatever she chose to do; when, for instance, there was someone else at home available to be responsible for a sleeping child or a child who was playing outside, and when household tasks were completed and work or study was finished for the day. Using this index of time allotment, we found that the average respondent had one hour of her average day to spend as she liked, and nearly half the respondents had no time during the day in which they were considered, by the above definition, free of responsibility. This index was problematic, however, because the "average" days reported by respondents usually did not include weekends, when there was more time available, and because what we considered to be time free of responsibility was not necessarily congruent with respondents' perceptions of time to themselves. Therefore, when we found that neither of the above indices was associated with any of our measures of mental health, we did not take this as hard evidence against our hypothesis, but instead looked at respondents' reported perceptions of the availability of free time. It should be noted in passing, however, that hours free of responsibility, using the above definition, was associated with total self-reported stress across all areas of life. That is, women with more free time felt less stress.

When we asked respondents how much time they could get for themselves during the average week, we found that 14 percent reported getting no time for themselves, 11 percent reported having fewer than 7 hours a week to themselves, 37 percent reported 7 to 16 hours a week, or one or two hours a day, and 37 percent reported having more than 16 hours a week to spend as they liked. Most of the respondents were dissatisfied with the amount of time they could get for themselves. Sixty-seven percent wanted more time to themselves than they found was available to them. Only one respondent reported having too much free time. We found that the women who were dissatisfied with the amount of free time available to them were more likely to exhibit symptoms of depression. That the respondents as a group tended to have so little free time belies one stereotypic image of the welfare mother—a woman who is bored and discontent due to inactivity.

Finally, we asked respondents to describe to us their experiences with time constraints. When asked "What are the hardest things for you to find time to do?" respondents listed taking care of themselves, being alone, socializing, spending time with their children, and taking care of the house. Only four respondents felt they had enough time to take care of all their needs and responsibilities. Women who experienced these stressful time constraints were more likely as a group to exhibit depressive symptoms than were women who felt they had all the time they needed.

In summary, we found that specific patterns of time-use were stressful but did not differentiate depressed from nondepressed women. What was relevant in daily time use for understanding vulnerability to depression were women's subjective appraisals of how they spent their time. Too little discretionary time and too little time to meet pressing needs and responsibilities were typically reported by depressed women. This suggests to us that it is the woman's satisfaction with and control over her time use, rather than particular patterns of time use, which should be of most interest in understanding the patterns of stressful conditions which lead to stress and depression.

This finding supports the behavioral theory of depression previously cited. In the view of Lewinsohn and his colleagues (1976, 1979), the occurrence of pleasant events has less impact if they are not perceived by the person as being a result of her own efforts. Likewise, unpleasant events have increased potency to affect mood negatively when they are perceived as uncontrollable. For a low-income mother, according to this theory, pleasant but serendipitous events would not contribute as strongly as they might in countering dysphoria. Pleasant occurrences which are perceived to result from one's own efforts do contribute to feelings of well-being. If, however, one's daily routine is so circumscribed by obligations that little opportunity exists to provide oneself with pleasant events, dysphoric mood is a predictable result.

An alternative interpretation of these findings is also possible, however.

It may be that dissatisfaction with time use, rather than contributing to vulnerability to depression, proceeds from the generalized dissatisfaction with one's life which is characteristic of women in a depressive state. The helplessness which depressed women often feel may prevent them from using their time in ways which they would find more satisfying.

NOTE

1. Events, in this sense, are not the dramatic life events, such as deaths of intimates, discussed by Makosky in the preceding chapter on stress. Events, as used by Lewinsohn et al., refer rather to the smaller events which make up the context of daily life. A pleasurable event, for instance, might be a compliment from a respected acquaintance. An aversive event might be an argument with one's partner or receiving a bill for which funds are not availaable.

REFERENCES

Lewinsohn, P., Biglan, A., & Zeiss, A. Behavioral treatment of depression. In P. O. Davidson (Ed.) *The behavioral management of anxiety, depression, and pain*. New York: Brunner/ Mazel, 1976.

Lewinsohn, P., Sullivan, J., & Grosscup, S. Changing reinforcing events: An approach to the treatment of depression. Unpublished paper available from the Department of Psychology, University of Oregon, 1979.

Rainwater, L. *Behind ghetto walls: Black family life in a federal slum*. Chicago: AVC, 1970.

5

GROWING UP:
THE IMPACT OF LOSS AND CHANGE

MAUREEN FOLEY REESE

Childhood has been romanticized as a time in life when one is protected from the stresses and strains of the adult world. However, such an idyllic situation is not a reality in the lives of those who experience parental deaths, divorces, or other disruptive events during childhood, as was the case for many of the Stress and Families Project respondents.

Childhood experiences of parental loss have often been implicated in the etiology of depression, schizophrenia, psychoneurosis, and suicide. However, research on this topic has yielded many contradictions and few widely generalized findings. Thus, Brown (1961) and Beck, Sethi, and Tuthill (1963) find the death of a parent predisposes an individual to depression in later life, while Crook and Raskin (1975) find the intentional separation of parents but not the death of parents more common in the history of suicide attemptors. In opposition to these results, Gregory (1958, 1966) and Munro (1965) report that neither death nor prolonged separation from parents is associated with a vulnerability to mental illness of any type. These contradictory findings have been attributed to methodological flaws, such as the use of inconsistent definitions of parental deprivation, nonrepresentative samples, and the difficulty of establishing the frequency of parental loss of all types in the general population (Gregory, 1958; Munro, 1965, 1969; Beck et al., 1963; Kulka & Weingarten, 1979).

A glaring omission in most retrospective studies is failure to control for socioeconomic status in childhood and adulthood. Low socioeconomic

status is related to shorter life span (Brenner, 1979) and an increased frequency of marital dissolution and mental illness (Langner & Michael,
1963). Therefore, failure to control for socioeconomic status may result in
spurious associations between parental loss in childhood and mental illness
in adulthood. Since parental loss is confounded with poverty, one may
question whether it is the loss of a parent per se, or the preceding or subsequent events and conditions surrounding the loss, that have a deleterious
effect on the child's life course and mental health.

This chapter focuses on the childhoods of the SFP respondents, identifies
childhood stress factors, investigates how these stress factors are intertwined, and considers the implications of early hardship on the women's
adult lives and psychological well-being. The data on which this chapter is
based come from an interview which contained both forced-choice and
open-ended questions which explored the women's experiences in childhood. Rich qualitative data were used to augment the quantifiable data we
collected on loss and change.

The findings indicate that women who experienced deprived and disrupted childhoods were more likely to experience both difficult life conditions and depression in adulthood. Women who experienced economically
advantaged childhoods and women who experienced poor but stable childhoods accrued a buffer against depression under difficult life circumstances
in adulthood.

RANGE OF CHILDHOOD EXPERIENCES

The sample is comprised of women who grew up in middle-class homes
but became poor in adulthood, as well as women who experienced economic
deprivation throughout their lives. This reflects the precarious financial
situation of mothers with young children, regardless of their socioeconomic
background (Pearce, 1978; Ross & Sawhill, 1975; Brandwein, Brown, &
Fox, 1974).

Since data were not systematically collected on the occupations and
incomes of the women's fathers, all women cannot be categorized into
specific class backgrounds. However, responses to open-ended questions
indicate a wide variety of fathers' occupations, ranging from professional to
blue-collar worker, and including corporate executive, broker, clergyman,
military officer, carpenter, factory worker, serviceman, and porter. Further
evidence of economic disparity among the women in childhood is indicated
by the fact that some women's mothers worked as paid domestics, while
those of other women actually *hired* domestic helpers. Some women
dropped out of school at an early age—one as early as the fourth grade—and
others attended college. Many women lost one or both parents in childhood

through death, divorce, or desertion, and others lived continuously within the relative stability of their nuclear or extended families. Some women moved frequently—one as many of thirty times; others never moved at all.

Ms. P is a thirty-year-old divorced mother of four. Although born in the South, she moved to Boston at the age of four. Her father left before she remembers, and her mother married and divorced her stepfather twice. By the time she was fourteen, she had lived in 30 places around Boston. During that time, Ms. P's mother worked full-time, and her only sibling was watched by a neighbor while she "hung around" a teen center. Ms. P does not remember a time when she was not responsible for the housework, but realistically she knows that her mother must have done it when she was too small to do it herself. "When I was a kid growing up there was very little in the house. I mean we always ate . . . but it just left the fear in me that if my food supplies go down I find myself very nervous." Ms. P told the interviewer that her mother always let her know that "she could have done something with her life if it wasn't for me." During the years she was growing up, Ms. P's mother tried to commit suicide several times. Since she was sixteen, Ms. P also made several attempts to end her own life. When asked what she thought her children's chances were of not being poor, she replied: "Very good, if, you know, they got the education and all this type of thing. I hope they're stronger than I was."

Ms. Rand is a twenty-five-year-old mother of two. She was one of five siblings. Her father was a sailor and was away at sea most of the time. Her mother worked as a truck driver. When Ms. Rand was seven years old, her twin sister drowned. Two weeks later her mother died of a stroke. After her mother's death, Ms. Rand's grandmother took care of the children, but she died when Ms. Rand was thirteen. Eventually, Ms. Rand's father remarried a woman who neglected his children when he was away. Later they were divorced. By the time she was seventeen, Ms. Rand had lived in 20 different places. When asked what the people who brought her up taught her about being poor, she answered:

> That we couldn't eat all the time. That we could have no Christmas, no holidays, no carnivals, no playful things that children should have. I mean we didn't have no underclothes. We had to wear shorts in place of underclothes. Sometimes we couldn't take baths. . . . After my mother died I never remember sitting in people's front rooms watching TV with them or sitting at a dinner table with them. We had to make our lives more outdoors than in.

Now Ms. Rand vows her children will have a better life. "I plan to see them through their first couple of years and making the right decisions. . . . My mother died when I was seven, and a child needs at least one parent's support that sees them through some of the trials and tribulations."

While childhoods such as Ms. Rand's were not unusual among the women we interviewed, several women had extremely different childhood experiences. In marked contrast to Ms. Rand and Ms. P, Ms. J spent her entire childhood in a comfortable house in a suburban community where her father was an executive and her mother was a full-time homemaker. At eighteen, Ms. J ventured off to college, but, unlike her two older sisters, she was not ready for school. Instead, she decided to travel abroad, where she married and had a child. Several years later the marriage ended, and Ms. J found herself and her child in dire financial circumstances. While her current economic resources are limited, her still wealthy parents do provide expensive gifts to her son.

When asked what she had to learn to adjust to her present financial situation, Ms. J answered: "I had to learn that I couldn't have what I wanted even by waiting and saving. I was not used to working hard, saving money, and being responsible. I also learned to do housework. . . . The only way I know how to deal with it is to get rich." Pride and a sense of independence make it impossible for her to ask her parents for financial assistance. However, she admits that her son is "being raised at a standard above my own. I tend to indulge him, and, of course, my parents make sure he is dressed as well as his rich cousins." Ms. J thinks her child's chances of not being poor are "pretty good—I'll try pretty hard to prepare him for the realities of life—one of which is that money is power, prestige, and freedom. I would not say that money is happiness or dignity, and being poor is fine if that's your chosen way of life. Otherwise, it's better in this society to be rich . . . it just makes things so much easier."

The women like Ms. J who grew up in middle-class families had important advantages over other women in the sample. They were more likely to have grown up in stable two-parent families, to have traveled abroad, and to have gone to college. In addition to cultural advantages, money ensured them important social connections and a personal sense of power and control. This was reflected in their language, demeanor, attitudes, and expectations. Although these women were poor, in most ways, they resembled the service providers with whom they came into contact, which made it easier for them to get the services to which they were entitled. When times were especially trying, they could also rely on their parents for financial support. As a result of coming from a middle-class background, current poverty was a very different experience for this subsample of women. A middle-class childhood left these respondents with many resources that were denied to women who grew up in poverty. Elder (1974) found similar protective factors among middle-class families who dropped into poverty during the Great Depression.

Despite the considerable variation in respondents' childhood experiences, it was possible to identify two dimensions along which all respondents could be compared. One was the type of family structure the woman grew up in, including the amount of time the woman lived with both natural parents, and whether the woman came from a stable or disrupted home. The other dimension was the type of loss and change that occurred within the family, including parental death, divorce, remarriage, and household moves. We hypothesized that a "rough" childhood, one characterized by loss and change, would be related to current adverse life circumstances and to poor mental health. We calculated Pearson product moment correlation coefficients between the childhood variables and indicators of current life situation and mental health.

TYPES OF FAMILY STRUCTURES

Only 37 percent of the respondents lived continuously with both parents during the years they were growing up, while the same percentage lived with both parents for only part of their childhoods. Another 16 percent lived with only their mothers, and 9 percent lived with neither parent. According to the literature on attachment (Bowlby, 1969), one would expect to find that women who always lived with both biological parents during childhood would fare better as adults than women who did not. As Table 5.1 indicates, being raised by both biological parents does not appear to be a protective factor for the women in our sample.

Over half came from homes in which the marital status of their parents (or custodial parents, who in all cases were the grandparents) remained the same, while 44 percent had parents who married, died, divorced, or remarried one or more times. Seven women had mothers who changed marital status two or more times. Since continuity and predictability are important during a child's formative years, we were not surprised to learn that women who grew up in families that were disrupted in these ways currently experienced more difficult life situations, as reflected in the Life Condition Stressor Score, and more depression and anxiety than women who experienced stable living arrangements. This was true regardless of whether these stable living arrangements were with both, one, or neither parent. In fact, Table 5.1 shows that as the number of changes in parents' marital status increases, so does the risk of experiencing difficult life conditions and poor psychological well being. These findings indicate that stability in childhood was a protective factor for the women in adulthood.

TYPES OF LOSSES AND CHANGES

After testing for associations between family structure variables and current life situations and emotional well-being, we turned our attention to

TABLE 5.1   Correlations of Family Structure Variables with Life Conditions Stressors, Life Conditions Stress, and the Mental Health Indicators

	Life Conditions Stressor	Life Conditions Stress	Depression	Anxiety	Mastery	Self-Esteem	Stability of Self-Esteem
Lived with both natural parents until leaving home							
1 = yes							
2 = no	.10	.16	.27*	.17	.13	.08	.08
Disrupted versus stable family structure	.42**	.38**	.38***	.32*	.29*	.32*	.28*
Number of changes in parents' marital status: none, one, two or more	.50**	.34**	.42**	.31*	.26*	.33*	.35**

* p < .05
** p < .01

the issue of loss and change. Sixteen percent of the women experienced a parental death, 30 percent experienced a parental marital dissolution (included in these percentages are three women who experienced both a parental death and a divorce), and 27 percent lived with a stepfather for some part of their childhoods. The average number of household moves for the sample was five.

Losses and changes during childhood, including parental marital dissolution, parental remarriage, and moving, are associated with current reports of difficult life conditions and poor psychological health, as can be seen in Table 5.2. Other researchers have also found parental marital dissolution (McDermott, 1970; Crook & Raskin, 1975; Schooler, 1972; Langner & Michael, 1963), parental remarriage (Kellam, Ensiminger, & Brown, 1979; Langner & Michael, 1963; Pope & Mueller, 1976), and childhood moves (Moore, 1969) to be associated with negative outcomes. Surprisingly, parental death is not significantly associated with any deleterious outcomes in this study.

The number of childhood events of loss and change was staggering. For this reason, we decided to create an index of loss and change. Every time a woman mentioned having someone leave or join her family structure, or when the woman mentioned being sent to live with relatives, foster parents, or to an institution, she was coded as having an event of loss and change. Table 5.2 shows that as the index of childhood loss and change increases, so do current reports of troublesome life circumstances and poor emotional well-being. Similar findings were reported by Jacobson, Fasman, and Di Mascio (1975) in an assessment of early childhood experiences in the etiology of depression. These researchers studied three groups of women: depressed psychiatric inpatients, depressed psychiatric outpatients, and a group of normal controls. While the three groups did not differ with respect to parental death during childhood, depressed women reported more negative childhood experiences, including more parental separations, than did nondepressed women. Among the depressed women, psychiatric inpatients reported the greatest number of negative childhood experiences.

INTERRELATIONSHIPS AMONG
CHILDHOOD LOSSES AND CHANGES

The strength of these childhood stress factors may well lie in their interrelatedness. As Table 5.3 shows, parental divorce is related to parental remarriage and to frequent moves during childhood. Interestingly, parental death in our sample is not related to any of the other events of loss and change. This may account for its lack of power in predicting mental health outcomes. Conversely, it appears that parental divorce is not one stressor on its own,

TABLE 5.2 Correlations of Childhood Loss and Change Variables with Life Conditions Stressors, Life Conditions Stress, and the Mental Health Indicators

	Life Conditions Stressor	Life Conditions Stress	Depression	Anxiety	Mastery	Self-Esteem	Stability of Self-Esteem
Parental death	.29	.15	.15	-.08	.08	-.07	-.07
Parental marital dissolution	.43**	.27*	.42**	.36**	.11	.29*	.37**
Lived with stepfather	-.31*	-.26*	-.24	-.21	-.28*	-.26*	-.21
Number of household moves	.15	.06	.38**	.29*	.26	.40**	.41**
Index of childhood loss and change	.43**	.19	.42**	.26*	.22	.29*	.32**

* $p < .05$
** $p < .01$

TABLE 5.3   Intercorrelations Among Childhood Stress Factors

	Lived with Both Natural Parents until Leaving Home. 1 = yes, 2 = no	Disrupted Family vs. Stable Family	Parental Death	Parental Marital Dissolution	Lived with Stepfather	Number of Household Moves	Index of Loss and Change in Childhood
Lived with Both Natural Parents until Leaving Home. 1 = yes, 2 = no							
Disrupted Family vs. Stable Family	x^2 = 10.6**						
Parental Death	x^2 = 2.6	x^2 = 2.0					
Parental Marital Dissolution	x^2 = 8.2**	x^2 = 22.2**	x^2 = .4				
Lived with Stepfather	x^2 = 4.2*	x^2 = .5	x^2 = .1	x^2 = 5.1 *			
Number of Household Moves	r = .21	r = .35**	r = .07	r = .41**	r = −.29*		
Index of Loss and Change in Childhood	r = .44**	r = .52**	r = .53**	r = .67**	r = .38**	r = .64**	

NOTE: Pearson product moment correlation coefficients were calculated for continuous variables. Chi-square tests were done for discontinuous variables.

* $p < .05$
** $p < .01$

but rather often leads to other stress-provoking events to which a child must adjust. An investigation of families in chronic stress (Rutter, 1979) shows that children were not at risk when they experienced a solitary stress factor; yet, when any two stressors occurred simultaneously, the risk to the children increased at least fourfold.

RELATIONSHIP BETWEEN PAST
AND CURRENT STRESS FACTORS

Women who talked about experiencing rough childhoods, in terms of loss and change, also reported more difficult current life circumstances. Among the 19 respondents who experienced disrupted childhood family arrangements (including deaths, divorces, remarriages), only 7 were living with a man at the time of the field study. Only two of these men were fathers of the target child who was observed during mother-child interactions. Since poverty and family instability are intertwined, we consider this evidence of a cycle of disadvantage in our sample.

When we investigated factors that intervened between childhood and adulthood, we noted that women from disrupted homes were more likely to have left home at an earlier age, to have had less education upon leaving home, and to have given birth at a younger age than women who were raised in stable living arrangements. Among the 19 women with disrupted child-hood histories, 42 percent left home by the age of seventeen, 71 percent (N = 17) had less than high school diploma upon leaving home, and 58 percent had given birth by the age of nineteen.

RELATIONSHIPS AMONG PAST STRESS,
CURRENT LIFE CONDITIONS, AND MENTAL HEALTH

Women who reported several events of loss and change in childhood also reported more symptoms of depression, anxiety, low self-esteem, and low stability of self-esteem. We consider this evidence that stress in childhood is related to poor psychological health in adulthood. However, as Chapter 3 demonstrates, current life conditions are also related to poor emotional well-being. The index of childhood loss and change accounts for 18 percent of the variance in current Life Conditions Stressor scores, while it bears little association to current Life Conditions Stress (feelings about current life conditions). This indicates that stressful events from childhood and current stressful life circumstances are confounded in their relation to mental health in adulthood. On the other hand, past stress is not associated with feelings about current life circumstances. One route by which adult mental health becomes impaired is that of family disruption in childhood leading to stressful life circumstances and a psychological risk factor. A continuation of these stressful life circumstances in adulthood, combined with responsibility for young children and further family disruption, may activate the psychological vulnerability that was sustained in childhood. A study of social class and psychiatric disturbance (Brown, Bhrolchain, & Harris, 1975) found that loss of a mother before the age of eleven was a risk factor for working-class women *only* in the presence of a major event or severe life difficulty.

We asked ourselves the following question: "If we know a woman has experienced a lot of loss and change in childhood, how much do her current life circumstances contribute to negative psychological outcomes?" To answer this, a multiple regression analysis was performed with the index of childhood loss and change and current Life Conditions Stressors. We also did a multiple regression with the index of childhood loss and change and Life Conditions Stress. Table 5.4, column 2, indicates that adding current Life Condition Stressors to the index of childhood loss and change explains a larger proportion of the variance in all the mental health indicators. Table 5.4, column 3, indicates that the additional amount of variance explained by current Life Conditions Stressors is significant for depression, anxiety, and stability of self-esteem. On the other hand, current Life Conditions Stress (feelings associated with current life conditions) adds significantly to the predictability of all the mental health indicators. We infer from these findings that current life circumstances and feelings about such circumstances are more powerfully related to psychological well-being in adulthood than are childhood life circumstances. Langner and Michael (1963) drew a similar conclusion in the Midtown Manhattan study of 1660 adults. While childhood stress factors were associated with an increased mental health risk, they were also associated with an increased probability of experiencing stress factors in adulthood. These adult factors were much more strongly associated with mental health impairment among Midtown respondents than were the childhood stress factors.

DISCUSSION

Peter Marris states, in his book *Loss and Change* (1974), that predictability is a fundamental need of human beings; without predictability life can be a threatening, even debilitating, experience. An investigation of the childhoods of the Stress and Families respondents suggests that more than needing both parents, children need a stable, loving environment in which to grow and discover the world around them. For respondents in our sample one event of loss and change was related to several other events of loss and change. Respondents who reported more difficult childhoods in terms of

TABLE 5.4 Amount of Variance in Mental Health Indicators

	Amount of Variance (R^2) Explained by Index of Childhood Loss and Change Alone	Amount of Variance (R^2) Explained by Index of Childhood Loss and Change Plus Current Life Conditions Stressors and Stress		Test for Significance (f) of Additional Variance Explained by Current Life Conditions Stressor Score and Current Life Conditions Stress Score	
Depression	17%**	Stressor	44%**	Stressor	15.61** d.f = 1,37
		Stress	58%**	Stress	34.11**
Anxiety	7%*	Stressor	21%**	Stressor	6.82* d.f = 1,38
		Stress	37%**	Stress	18.14**
Mastery	5% (N.S.)	Stressor	14% (N.S.)	Stressor	3.97 (N.S.)
		Stress	36%**	Stress	17.47** d.f = 1,36
Self-Esteem	10%*	Stressor	15%*	Stressor	2.26 (N.S.)
		Stress	39%**	Stress	18.69** d.f = 1,38
Stability of Self-Esteem	12%*	Stressor	21%*	Stressor	4.37* d.f = 1,38
		Stress	32%**	Stress	11.28**

* p < .05
** p < .01

disruption also reported more adverse current life conditions and poor psychological health. While difficult childhoods were related to difficult adulthoods, *current life conditions* were a more powerful predictor of poor psychological functioning than were childhood experiences of loss and disruption.

These findings suggest two recommendations for research in the area of parental loss in childhood. First, as was mentioned earlier, it is necessary to control for socioeconomic status in childhood and adulthood, since socioeconomic status is confounded with parental loss and mental illness. When Langner and Michael (1963), Brown et al. (1975), and Kulka and Weingarten (1979) considered these background variables, they found a greater risk of unpleasant sequelae from parental death, divorce, or separation among those people from a low socioeconomic background than among those from higher social classes. Langner and Michael (1963) noted that when the number of childhood stress factors was controlled, there was still a residual effect on mental health related to socioeconomic status. Thus, Kulka and Weingarten (1979) caution that any attempt to disentangle the factors which constitute the social context within which the parental divorce was experienced may be theoretically misleading.

Second, parental divorce is not an independent event. Instead, "it may well be a 'shorthand' or a 'metaphor' for a complex web of interacting social influences" (Kulka & Weingarten, 1979, p. 72). At the outset of this Chapter I suggested that the deleterious outcomes of parental loss in childhood may not be related to the loss of the parent per se, but to the impact the loss has on other areas of the child's life. Therefore, parental death and parental divorce may have dissimilar concomitants, which explain their differential effects on adult adjustment. For one thing, widowed parents and their children are not socially stigmatized in the same manner as divorced mothers and children from so-called "broken" homes. In our sample, parental death was not related to remarriage or to frequent moves during childhood, while parental divorce was.

A parental divorce is often surrounded by conflict—an experience that is known to be extremely upsetting to children (Rutter, 1971). A parental divorce is often preceded, and even more often followed, by hardship (Brandwein et al., 1974). The loss of income following divorce generally forces a mother to get a job or go on welfare. The family's standard of living is reduced, which may involve a houshold move. Ross and Sawhill (1975) argue that female-headed families are only transitional units that are later transformed into parent/stepparent families. As researchers have found, "remarriage cannot be accurately described as the 'repair of a broken home'" (Langner & Michael, 1963, p. 187). Instead, remarriage has been associated with additional negative outcomes for children. There is also evidence that children from voluntarily disrupted homes are more likely to become divorced or separated as adults than are children from intact homes (Mueller & Pope, 1977; Pope & Mueller, 1976; Kulka & Weingarten, 1979; Langner & Michael, 1963). However, when Kulka and Weingarten (1979) controlled for social class, religion, and region of upbringing, the intergenerational trend of marital instability in their data disappeared.

Consequently, retrospective research which only considers whether a person has lost a parent through death or divorce may tell us very little about why parental loss does or does not affect one's future life circumstances and subsequent psychological adjustment in adulthood. Developmental psychologists (Rutter, 1977; Longfellow, 1979; Moore, 1969; Benswanger, n. d.) have advocated an ecological or contextual approach to studying stressful life events in childhood, in order to determine how the event is experienced, coped with, resolved, or not resolved. Researchers interested in the long-term impact of childhood parental loss must also consider adopting such a methodological approach in order to discover the pathways through which affective disorders and marital instability occur in adulthood.

The question still remains: "How do stressful life conditions get transmitted from one generation to another?" In an attempt to isolate mediating factors between parent-child marital instability, Mueller and Pope (1977) identified what they call high-risk mate selection associated with early and limited education marriages. Expanding on the notion of intergenerational transmission in a review of the literature, Rutter and Madge (1976) consider the route by which cycles of disadvantages are perpetuated through marital instability. For children who grow up in disrupted homes characterized by poverty and disadvantage, opportunities are limited. Such children often drop out of school at an early age and soon afterward get married and become parents. Their spouses are often young adults from similar disadvantaged circumstances. Youth and a lack of education, combined with family responsibilities, make it difficult to achieve financial security. This often leads to a recapitulation of the hardship and disruption the parents experienced a generation before (Rutter & Madge, 1976). Rubin (1976) and Liebow (1967) vividly capture this process by portraying the individual hopes and failures of working-class men and women caught in the cycle of poverty.

It seems likely that children from poor and disrupted families would find consolation in the hope of growing up and sharing in the American Dream: a spouse, children, and a home around which to build a loving, stable environment. Instead, many of the women we interviewed have endured the loss of their children's father, loss in the belief that you can have a decent comfortable place in which to live your life, and, finally, loss of the hope that you can give your children all the things you have never had. Feelings of loss in adulthood which recapture childhood experiences of loss have been found to precipitate the onset of depression (Brown, 1961; Beck et al., 1963; Brown et al., 1975). It is disheartening to know that the depressed mothers had children who were more likely to report feelings of unhappiness compared to other children in the sample.

CONCLUSION

The intent of this chapter is not to present a deterministic view of the Stress and Families respondents' lives. Rather, it is intended to elucidate the ways in which past experiences affect current life circumstances and emotional well-being. For the women in the sample who had advantaged childhoods, the current stress they experience is a detour in their life courses; but for those who had rough childhoods, poverty and stress *are* their life courses, all they have ever known.

We found, as did Langner and Michael (1963), that childhood stress may leave some scars but that present life circumstances are a more powerful predictor of poor mental health. Moreover, Brown et al. (1975) and Rutter (1979) have demonstrated that even in extremely disadvantaged circumstances, positive environmental supports can have an ameliorating effect on mental health. Therefore, we believe that efforts aimed at mitigating stressful life conditions through adequate day care, improved job opportunities, and better housing will lead to improved mental health for mothers and happier homes for children. Nevertheless, if these environmental supports are not forthcoming, research suggests that these family histories will be a legacy to the respondents' children.

REFERENCES

Beck, A., Sethi, B., & Tuthill, R. Childhood bereavement and adult depression. *Archives of General Psychiatry,* 1963, *9,* 295-302.

Benswanger, E. Stressful events in early childhood: An ecological approach. Unpublished paper, University of Pittsburgh, Pennsylvania, n.d.

Bowlby, J. *Attachment and loss Volume 1: Attachment.* New York: Basic Books, 1969.

Brandwein, R., Brown, C., & Fox, E. Women and children last: The social situation of divorced mothers and their families. *Journal of Marriage and the Family,* 1974, *9,* 498-514.

Brenner, M. Mortality and the national economy: A review, and the experience of England and Wales, 1936-76. *The Lancet,* 1979, 568-573.

Brown, F. Depression and childhood bereavement. *Journal of Mental Sciences,* 1961, *107,* 754-777.

Brown, G., Bhrolchain, M., & Harris, T. Social class and psychiatric disturbance among women in an urban population. *Sociology,* 1975, *9* (2), 225-254.

Butler, E., McAllister, R., & Kaiser, E. The effects of voluntary and involuntary mobility on males and females. *Journal of Marriage and the Family,* 1973, *5,* 219-227.

Crook, T., & Raskin, A. Association of childhood parental loss with attempted suicide and depression. *Journal of Consulting and Clinical Psychology,* 1975, *43* (2), 277.

Elder, G. *Children of the great depression.* Chicago: University of Chicago Press, 1974.

Gregory, I. Studies of parental deprivation in psychiatric patients. *American Journal of Psychiatry,* 1958, *115* (1-6), 432-442.

Gregory, I. Retrospective data concerning childhood loss of a parent. *Archives of General Psychiatry,* 1966, *15,* 362-367.

Jacobson, S., Fasman, J., & Di Mascio, A. Deprivation in the childhood of depressed women. *Journal of Nervous and Mental Disease,* 1975, *160,* 5-14.

Kellam, S., Ensiminger, M., & Brown, H. Epidemiological research into the antecedents in early childhood of psychiatric symptoms and drug use in mid-adolescence. *Society for Research in Child Development, Inc. Newsletter,* 1979, Winter, 6-7.

Kulka, R., & Weingarten, H. The long-term effects of parental divorce in childhood on adult adjustment. *Journal of Social Issues,* 1979, *35* (4), 50-78.

Langner, T., & Michael, S. *Life stress and mental health.* New York: Free Press, 1963.

Longfellow, C. Divorce in context: Its impact on children. In G. Levinger and O. Moles (Eds.) *Divorce and separation in context: Causes and consequences.* New York: Basic Books, 1979.

Liebow, E. *Tally's corner: A study of Negro streetcorner men.* Boston: Little, Brown, 1967.

McDermott, J. Divorce and its psychiatric sequelae in children. *Archieves of General Psychiatry,* 1970, *23,* 421-427.

Marris, P. *Loss and change.* New York: Pantheon Books, 1974.

Moore, T. Stress in normal childhood. *Human Relations,* 1969, *22* (3), 235-250.

Mueller, C., & Pope, H. Marital instability: A study of its transmission between generations. *Journal of Marriage and the Family,* 1977, *2,* 83-92.

Munro, A. Childhood parental loss in a psychiatrically normal population. *British Journal of Preventive Social Medicine,* 1965, *19,* 69-79.

Munro, A. Parent-child separation: Is it really a cause of psychiatric illness in adult life? *Archives of General Psychiatry,* 1969, *20,* 598-604.

Munro, A., & Griffiths, B. Some psychiatric non-sequelae of childhood bereavement. *British Journal of Psychiatry,* 1969, *115,* 305-311.

Pearce, D. The feminization of poverty: Women, work and welfare. *The Urban and Social Change Review,* 1978, *11* (1, 2).

Pope, H., & Mueller, C. The intergenerational transmission of marital instability: Comparisons by race and sex. *Journal of Social Issues,* 1976, *32* (1), 49-66.

Ross, H., & Sawhill, I. *Time of transition: The growth of families headed by women.* Washington, DC: Urban Institute, 1975.

Rubin, L. *Worlds of pain: Life in the working class.* New York: Basic Books, 1976.

Rutter, M. Parent-child separation: Psychological effects on children. *Journal of Child Psychology and Psychiatry,* 1971, *12,* 233-260.

Rutter, M. Protective factors in children's response to stress and disadvantage. In M. W. Kent and J. E. Rolf (Eds.) *Primary prevention of psychopathology. Vol. III. Social Competence in children.* Hanover, NH: University Press of New England, 1979.

Rutter, M., & Madge, N. *Cycles of disadvantage: A review of research.* London: Heineman, 1976.

Schooler, C. Childhood family and adult characteristics. *Sociometry,* 1972, *35* (2), 255-269.

PART III
WOMEN AND SOCIETY

6

WORK: ITS MEANING FOR WOMEN'S LIVES

RUTH TEBBETS

The belief that poor women do not work and do not want to work is not new: in 1751 the "Society for Encouraging Industry and Employing the Poor" was organized in Boston with a stated purpose of employing "women and children who are now in great measure idle" (Abbott, 1910, p. 21); the Boston Centennial reported in 1788 that a factory would soon be completed to "give employment to a great number of persons, especially females, who now eat the bread of idleness" (p. 39). Contemporary concern with the large number of women on welfare rolls has intensified the belief that poverty and the foundering of the work ethic go hand in hand. It is assumed that poor women are too lazy, too overwhelmed with their chaotic home lives, or too alienated from the mainstream of working America even to want to participate in the work world.

Beliefs about the orientation of poor women toward work have been formed with little information from the women themselves. The Stress and Families study provides an opportunity to look at the importance of work force participation to poor women from the vantage point of poor women. This chapter first examines women's work histories and patterns, then turns to respondents' perceptions of the benefits and drawbacks of

AUTHOR'S NOTE: Portions of this chapter were presented at the NATO-sponsored symposium on women and work which was held in Portugal in 1980 and will be published in the book, *Women and the World of Work* (New York: Plenum).

workforce participation, and finally, to statistical correlations among women's life cycle stage, work experience, and psychological depression. These sources of information all lead to the conclusion that, contrary to popular images, participation in the workforce is an integral part of women's life histories, central to their thoughts about themselves and their futures, and important to their well-being. Some of the socio-economic trends related to women's labor force participation and the implications they hold for the lives of the women in this study are then discussed in light of these findings.

WORK HISTORIES AND PATTERNS

Whether ringing cash registers, operating lathes, or caring for patients in hospitals, most women in the Stress and Families Project sample have extensive work histories. Only two women report no work experience for which they were paid, and many had held jobs even before their tenth birthdays. One woman had a history of 15 jobs (the maximum number of jobs the interview recorded), and the respondents had an average of 4 jobs prior to the interview.[1] The majority of these jobs were held for six months or longer. This work force participation in respondents' histories corresponds to nationwide statistics showing that over 90 percent of welfare mothers have worked at some time, and three-fourths have worked full-time (Pearce, 1979).

The type of work respondents engaged in also parallels nationwide patterns. Waitressing and kitchen work alone accounted for over one-sixth of all jobs named, and factory work rivaled these jobs in frequency. Nursing, child care, and housekeeping also accounted for large numbers of jobs. Almost all of the jobs listed by respondents could be categorized as service jobs, manual labor, sales positions, and clerical positions, job categories that have been found nationally to account for 80 percent of all female jobs (National Commission on Working Women, 1979). These jobs are generally low in required education, pay, and prestige, demanding hard work for minimal returns. Sawhill (1976), for instance, reports that one-half of the predominantly female occupations typically held by high school graduates aged twenty-five to thirty-four pay less than $3000 a year for full-time work. In contrast, only 20 percent of predominantly male jobs have a similarly low earning potential.

Respondents' working histories and patterns are tied closely to events in their own and their families' life cycles. To illustrate the contingencies women experienced between these major social roles, a composite work history was created for a typical respondent. This typical respondent began work as a youngster, picking fruit during school vacations and contributing the proceeds to the family budget. On her own at seventeen, she held a succession of jobs at franchise restaurants that never paid more than $2.00 an hour and often required working late shifts. She married at nineteen, and stopped working at twenty when she was five months pregnant with her first child. When the baby could walk, she started working in part-time cleaning jobs to supplement her husband's salary, leaving the baby with her sister when possible and taking him with her when necessary. She had two more children in the next four years. No longer able to get away during the day, she sometimes worked evenings at the fast food restaurant where she had worked before marriage. Now she is separated from her husband and works part-time in a nursing home to supplement her government welfare checks.

As this typical work history exemplifies, work and family events are closely intertwined for the SFP respondents. In a society such as our own that is organized around the assumption that women are primarily home-makers and men breadwinners, combining work with family responsibilities is not easy for anyone. The work roles of low-income mothers, however, are less pervious to demands from the home than those of women with higher incomes (Mott, 1972; Hoffman & Nye, 1978, p. 18). Women with little education (which is strongly associated with low income) participate in the work force at rates approximately equal to those of women with more education in the early stages of family formation. After having two or more children, however, relatively educated women are more likely to stop work-ing. One can assume that financial necessity plays a strong role in keeping low-income mothers in the labor force even when family conditions are so demanding that similar circumstances cause women who can better afford it to drop out of the labor force temporarily.

Limited funds also make it more difficult for low-income mothers to purchase substitutes for their own labor that would ease the strain of dual roleholding. Studies of contemporary spending patterns show that above a minimum economic threshold, families with working mothers spend more money on goods and services that ease the strain of combining work and family roles (Reynolds, 1980). Eating meals in restaurants, purchasing time-saving appliances, and contracting for reliable and convenient child care are all ways in which money can buy time and comfort. Few women in the Stress and Families sample had any such conveniences, and most did not even own appliances or durables that are considered by many women to be necessities for homemaking, such as a car with which to do grocery shop-ping or a washer and dryer to do the laundry. In such ways, poverty com-pounds the already significant problems of combining work and family that mothers of all economic levels face.

At the time of the study, half of the respondents were engaged in full-time employment. While circumstances did cause some respondents to stop work, other respondents did not drop out of the labor force altogether, but compromised by taking work that was more compatible with their commitments at home. For this they turned to part-time work, work during evening or nighttime hours, and work which could be done at home or on a flexible schedule. In the three years prior to the study, when all respondents had child care responsibilities, only about 20 percent of all jobs were full-time, nine-to-five jobs. Telephone sales, knitting and crocheting, child care, and janitorial work were home-based jobs commonly taken by women to minimize conflicts between work and home. The drawbacks of jobs that offered such flexibility were unfortunately high. These jobs were generally very poorly paid and did not provide benefits such as unemployment insurance, health insurance, or opportunities for advancement that would provide long-term security or mobility within the labor force.

In summary, an examination of the work histories and patterns of respondents indicates that work is an important theme in the lives of members of the SFP sample. Many women have worked for pay since childhood and stop working temporarily only when home responsibilities are impossible to coordinate with work force participation. Some women minimize the conflict between work and home by taking part-time or home-based work, which in turn exact their own costs. To understand how these aspects of women's work lives are experienced and interpreted by the respondents, we next explore their responses to questions that elicited women's own views of the role of work in their lives.

VIEWS ON WORKING

In one question, respondents listed the good and bad points of the different jobs they had held. On the positive side of many respondents' perceptions of work were its intrinsic interest, the pleasant relations with co-workers and supervisors that sometimes accompanied jobs, and, occasionally, good pay and good hours that jobs provided. Other responses were more idiosyncratic to a particular job or respondent: pleasant customers (in a doughnut shop), the freedom of setting one's own hours (as a housekeeper), the belief that one was needed (in a nursing home), and the acquisition of skills (in a bookkeeping job). When asked about the meaning of work to them, respondents tended to associate work with confidence, self-esteem, accomplishment, dignity, and independence. As one woman said, "I want to feel I can say I took care of myself." Mothers also identified work force participation as resulting in benefits for their children. The belief that having a working mother fosters independence and self-reliance was frequently mentioned in this respect.

The benefits of work force participation were discussed most poignantly by the unemployed. Two-thirds of the women not working reported feeling lonely every day, or at least a few times a week. Few unemployed women reported more than occasionally feeling happy that they were not working. A woman who had worked at renovating old houses recalled with much pleasure the "great skills" she had learned before an injury had forced her to quit. For some of the women, the frustrated desire to work was very troubling. One respondent described herself as having been in a tense and irritable state until she had finally found a job.

Although many wanted to work, the unemployed respondents also identified important barriers preventing them from taking work. The unavailability of jobs, particularly those compatible with motherhood, was a problem frequently mentioned by respondents. Three-fourths of the mothers agreed with the statement: "Some women find it very hard to get the kinds of jobs they can do while being a mother." The most common reasons given for stopping work were family events, such as pregnancy, birth of a child, or problems with child care.

Several respondents pointed out that the high cost of child care can destroy the economic rationale to work. One respondent told the interviewer, "More than half of my paycheck would be gone before I saw it. It's hopeless. Why bother?" While many respondents had at least occasional child care help from paid sitters, day care centers, and the public schools, relatives were the most common source of child care assistance. Such help is often characterized as a simple gift, but as Chapter 10 explains in more detail, it is not without cost, for many relatives often expect assistance in return. For example, in return for the care of her two children in the evenings, one respondent felt obligated to provide babysitting help every morning for her sister's two children. Her child care responsibilities, therefore, were not substantially reduced by this help, but merely shifted to different children at different times of the day.

Another major barrier to employment for many women is the fear of losing medical insurance should their incomes rise above limits set by the welfare department. While many families experienced serious health problems requiring expensive treatment, few of the respondents' jobs provided medical coverage for themselves or their children. One woman in the study was paying installments on a large medical bill accrued when she was hospitalized at a time when neither she nor her husband had medical insurance. Her weekly payments of $2.00 toward this bill placed an additional strain on an already tight budget, and at this rate of repayment, it would take at least 100 years to cancel the debt.

When asked whether they would give up AFDC benefits to start work if they could keep their Medicaid and food stamp benefits, most respondents who were not employed said they would do so. Those who said they would not most often cited continuing child care responsibilities and their inability to earn enough to support their families as reasons for not wanting to relinquish welfare benefits. One respondent succinctly captured the plight perceived by this group of women: "The problem with most jobs is that you just can't afford to take them."

Some respondents saw their lack of education as the most important barrier to decent employment. Like many other women in the study, one respondent expressed the hope that things would be different for her own children.

> For all my kids, my daughter included, I would push for education. . . . The more education you have the more freedom you have, because you have more money. You don't owe anybody anything. The more money you have, the more power you have. . . . I would push for the education, a good job, and somewhat of a career for all my kids. . . . And I would hold myself up as an example. I married young; I didn't complete my education; we ended up in the projects. If I'd had an education, I'd be able to get a job and everything else and wouldn't end up in the projects. I have no skills in anything.

Even though child care responsibilities and poverty made the enterprise a particularly difficult one, several of the women in the study had returned to school to complete their high school education and to go to college. Others had participated in training programs, and half of these programs had resulted in jobs.

Positively though work was viewed, it was not seen as an unmitigated blessing. Low pay, bad hours, boring work, high pressure, and environmental hazards were commonly listed as negative features of jobs. One woman who worked behind a counter in a record store was constantly fearful of robbery (the store had been robbed several times before). Another woman would walk up and down six flights of stairs to a card factory rather than trust a faulty elevator. Transportation to and from work frequently posed problems of both safety and convenience and in at least two cases caused women to give up their employment. Many respondents mentioned the kinds of jobs they had already held so often—waitressing, kitchen work, and housekeeping—as the work they would take only as a last resort. Sometimes a job could be so draining and unrewarding that ending it was a marked change for the better.

Even though many women were dissatisfied with the quality of the jobs they had held and that were most frequently available to them, they had aspirations for better work. Not a single woman reported that she did not ever want to work. Most women's ideal jobs were quite practical to attain because they built upon some aspect of earlier work or training. For example, one woman selected nursing as her ideal job; she had trained and worked as a health attendant and nursing aid. Another who had extensive training in hairstyling wanted to operate her own barber shop.

Pay level was frequently mentioned as an important attribute of an ideal job, in part because a high rate of pay was perceived as a way of gaining some power over the conflicting demands of work and family. Many women mentioned that their jobs would provide a salary high enough to allow them time with their children. One respondent, for example, felt that an ideal job would be one in which she could work 20 hours a week and earn enough money to support herself and her daughter.

As discussed elsewhere in this book, the quest for a decent salary takes on additional meaning against the backdrop of poverty, for economic problems were at the root of many of the respondents' difficulties. One-third said they did not have enough money to buy adequate food for their families. Low income often meant poor housing, discrimination, and exposure to violent crime, and money difficulties were related to worries over parenting as well as the mothers' own mental health. Jobs that paid well were thus important to respondents as a possible route out of poverty and its stresses that so deeply penetrated many aspects of their lives.

In summary, respondents reported that work was important in their lives. Even those working under objectively difficult conditions, and especially those who were temporarily unemployed, reported important benefits to working—that it gave them a sense of competence and independence as well as a more secure economic base. Barriers to employment mentioned by women include the unavailability of inexpensive but reliable child care, the loss of health insurance that would accompany taking a job, and education. Despite the fact that some jobs were so dangerous, fatiguing, or low paying that the end of the job had been viewed as a positive event, all women had a realistic vision of what an ideal job would be. At best, it was a route out of poverty and a source of fulfillment.

WORK STATUS AND DEPRESSION

A considerable amount of research has addressed the question of whether working enhances women's well-being or detracts from it (for one review, see Hoffman & Nye, 1978). The findings from such studies have been characterized by inconsistencies; some find that working women are better off than homemakers, some report the opposite, and still others find no association. One review (Tebbets, 1981) suggests that inconsistencies and nonresults are due to the fact that women's work status (working or not working) is not in itself a "master variable" around which other dependent variables fall in line; rather, work status is a variable whose impact on well-being is sensitive to other social characteristics, such as education and stage in the family life cycle, that determine the quality of women's work experiences. Although some evidence points to work as enhancing the well-being of older women with exceptional IQs (Sears & Barbee, 1977) and well-educated women (Birnbaum, 1975), there is little evidence to suggest what its impact is on women living under poverty conditions. One review confidently states that there is evidence for an overall positive relationship between working and well-being (Kanter, 1977, p. 62). Given the bias toward studying middle-class women in much of the literature reviewed, however, the generality of this finding for the poverty-level women in the Stress and Families Project is questionable.

To address the question of the relationship of work to well-being among low-income mothers, a series of correlations were computed between depression scores and aspects of women's working experience. Because both work experiences and depression scores are also related to women's stage in the family life cycle, some life cycle variables were included in the correlation matrices. Significant correlations resulting from these tests are presented in Figure 6.1.[2] This chart contains eight variables: four life cycle variables (age of women at the birth of their first child, number of children they have under eighteen, number of preschoolers for whom they are responsible, and their level of education); two work history variables (total number of jobs held in their lives and the duration of time they have been employed in the last three years); current work status; and depression scores.

As the typical work history described earlier in this chapter indicated, current work status is highly contingent upon women's other life commitments and experiences. Women were more likely to be currently working if they were older when they had their first child, if they have fewer children, fewer preschoolers, and higher levels of education. They were also more likely to be working if they held many jobs in the past and worked longer in the past three years.

Work histories are also associated with life cycle variables. Women who are responsible for more children held fewer jobs overall than those responsible for fewer children, and women who were older at the birth of their first child and who had more education worked longer in the past three years than did those who had children earlier and were less educated. There are significant associations between the work history variables and depression scores. Women who have held more jobs and who have worked longer in the past three years report lower depression scores than women with less extensive work histories.

There is no significant biserial association between women's current work status and their reports of depressive symptoms. Because of the high degree of association between work status and the other life indicators included in this diagram and reported above, the question arises as to

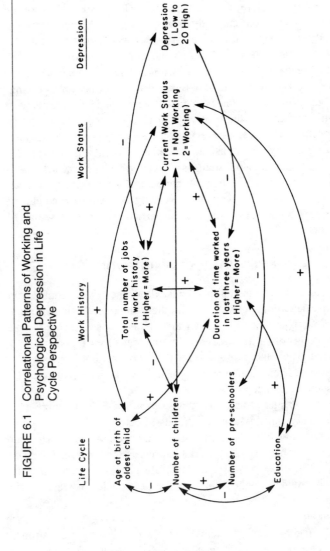

FIGURE 6.1   Correlational Patterns of Working and
Psychological Depression in Life
Cycle Perspective

The signs on each bidirectional arrow indicate the direction of the association.
Only correlations significant at the p ≤ .05 are reported.

91

whether there is an association between current work status and psychological depression if these other variables are held constant. To address this question, a regression equation was computed using the work history and life cycle variables, as well as current work status, to predict depression scores. With the work history and life cycle variables controlled, there is a very strong ($b = -11.1$; $F(1,27) = 10.425$, $p \leq .001$) association between work status and depression; currently working women are much less depressed than those who are not. The seven predictors together account for a significant 48 percent of the overall variance in depression scores.

In addition, mean depression scores of women who were not working but who wanted to work were compared to those of women who were working. The average scores of women who wanted to be employed but were not were fully 10 points higher than those of women who worked. The frustrated desire to work can thus be seen as a very strong associate of high depression.

In summary, having an extensive work history is associated with low depression scores. Current work status is associated with prior work experience and closely tied to family commitments, and when these factors are controlled, whether or not a woman is working is a strong predictor of depression. The frustrated desire to work is a particularly strong associate of high depression.

CONCLUSION AND DISCUSSION

In conclusion, far from being disinterested or otherwise alienated from work force participation, low-income mothers interviewed in this study report that work is a central theme in their lives. This is evident in the extensive work histories of these women, in their own reports of their experiences in the paid labor force, and in their work aspirations, as well as in the significant correlations between women's work experience and their reports of psychological depression.

The expectations and aspirations of women in the SFP study are highlighted when viewed against national trends affecting the social and economic environment within which women live and work. Most women interviewed in this study had extensive work histories and, even if they were not currently working, expected to work in the future. This expectation is reasonable, for the trend throughout this century has been for increasing numbers of women in all socioeconomic strata to work, and this increase has taken place at all points in the family life cycle (Taeuber & Sweet, 1976; Waite, 1976). Since women's participation in the paid labor force is strongly related to development in an advanced industrial economy (Oppenheimer, 1970), there is no reason to foresee that the trend toward increased participation would taper off or reverse itself.

The expectation of women that they will work in the future is also reasonable in light of the economic meaning of work. As more women work for longer periods in the paid labor force, family economic standing becomes increasingly tied to women's contribution to family income. High divorce rates also make it increasingly likely that women will be called upon to support their families for at least some segment of the family life cycle (Ross & Sawhill, 1975). In short, it is already the norm for women to work, and all signs indicate that women can look forward to a life in which work force participation is increasingly important for the standard of living they achieve for themselves and their families.

In this study, women with more extensive work histories had lower depression scores than those who had worked less, and the frustrated desire to work was associated with high depression. As work becomes more normative for women, it is reasonable to expect that mental health will be even more closely tied to work roles. One study examining the association of unemployment rates to psychiatric hospital admissions over time gives weight to this expectation. Men's admission rates have consistently evidenced a direct relationship with unemployment since the early years of this century. Women's rates did not show such a sensitivity, however, until World War II, a time at which there was an especially sharp increase in the number of women workers (Brenner, 1973). This trend for women's mental health to be tied to unemployment points to an alarming possibility, for unemployment has risen in recent years at a faster pace among women than among men (U.S. Department of Labor, 1975). If these trends continue, unemployment, which is concentrated among relatively uneducated women such as those in the Stress and Families sample (U.S. Department of Labor, 1975), will pose an increasing risk to the mental health of women in this demographic group.

The conditions of employment for women are also important, and, here again, contemporary trends are alarming, for women's increased participation in the labor force has been accompanied by a drop in women's earnings relative to those of men. In the mid-1950s, a full-time employed woman earned, on average, 63 cents for every dollar earned by a male counterpart. By the mid-1960s and 1970s, this figure had declined to below 60 cents (Barrett, 1979), and this gap is considerably wider in work roles that require few skills and are already poorly paid. This study suggests that this drop in earning power is accompanied by an increase in emotional distress among women like those in the SFP study. Psychological depression resulting from this lack of earning power could compound the problems women face in respect to employment by discouraging them to the point that they would not even look for work.

These trends clearly point to the need for recognition of the importance of work to the emotional as well as financial well-being of most women. More to the point than accusations of poor women who "eat the bread of idleness" are social programs that eliminate barriers to employment and remove discriminatory pay scales and working conditions that prevent work from being the route out of poverty that poor women dream it could be.

NOTES

1. Lest the reader think that this average number of jobs reflects an unusual lack of commitment to any one job, Wilensky (1961) reports that the average American male holds at least a dozen jobs in a 46-year working life, many in quite different industries and occupations.

2. It should be noted that this is not a path diagram, which was precluded due to the small sample size. It is a diagram in which correlation coefficients significant at the $p \leq .05$ level have been drawn as lines.

REFERENCES

Abbott, E. *Women in industry.* New York: Appleton, 1910.

Barrett, N. S. Women in the job market: Unemployment and work schedules. In R. E. Smith (Ed.) *The subtle revolution: Women at work.* Washington, DC: Urban Institute, 1979.

Birnbaum, J. Life patterns and self-esteem in gifted family-oriented and career-committed women. In M. Mednick, S. Tangri, & L. Hoffman (Eds.) *Women and achievement: Social and motivational analyses.* New York: John Wiley, 1975.

Brenner, M. H. *Mental illness and the economy.* Cambridge: Harvard University Press, 1973.

Hoffman, L. W., & Nye, F. I. *Working mothers.* San Francisco: Jossey-Bass, 1978.

Kanter, R. M. *Work and family in the United States: A critical review and agenda for research and policy.* New York: Russell Sage, 1977.

Mott, F. L. Fertility, life cycle stage, and female labor force participation in Rhode Island: A retrospective overview. *Demography,* 1972, *9* (1), 173-185.

National Commission on Working Women. *National survey of working women: Perceptions, problems, and prospects.* Washington, DC: Author, 1979.

Oppenheimer, V. K. *The female labor force in the United States.* Berkeley: University of California Press, 1970.

Pearce, D. Women, work, and welfare: The feminization of poverty. In K. W. Feinstein (Ed.) *Working women and families.* Beverly Hills, CA: Sage, 1979.

Reynolds, R. T. All about working women. *American Demographics,* 1980, *2* (1), 40-41.

Ross, H. L., & Sawhill, I. V. *Time of transition: The growth of families headed by women.* Washington, DC: Urban Institute, 1975.

Sawhill, I. Women with low incomes. In M. Blaxall & B. Reagan (Eds.) *Women and the workplace: The implications of occupational segregation.* Chicago: University of Chicago Press, 1976.

Sears, P. S., & Barbee, A. H. Career and life satisfactions among Terman's gifted women. In J. Stanley, W. George, & C. Solano (Eds.) *The gifted and the creative: Fifty year perspective.* Baltimore: Johns Hopkins University Press, 1977.

Sweet, J. A. *Women in the labor force.* New York: Seminar Press, 1974.

Taeuber, K. E., & Sweet, J. A. Family and work: The social life cycle of women. In J. M. Kreps (Ed.) *Women and the American economy: A look to the '80's.* New York: Prentice-Hall, 1976.

Tebbets, R. Thirty years of research on working women: A review of the empirical literature. Unpublished manuscript, University of California, Berkeley, 1981.

U.S. Department of Labor, Women's Bureau. *1975 handbook on women workers.* Bulletin 297. Washington, DC: Government Printing Office, 1975.

Waite, L. Working wives: 1940-1960. *American Sociological Review,* 1976, *41* (February), 65-80.

Wilensky, H. L. Orderly careers and social participation: The impact of work history on social integration in the middle mass. *American Sociological Review,* 1961, *26* (4), 521-539.

7

THE PUBLIC WELFARE SYSTEM: REGULATION AND DEHUMANIZATION

NANCY MARSHALL

Goffman (1963) has defined a stigma as an attribute that is deeply discrediting. A person who is stigmatized is "reduced in our minds from a whole and usual person to a tainted, discounted one" (p. 3). Stigmatization makes the individual seem less than human, allows others to explain her difficulties as a result of her inferiority, and to exercise discrimination in ways that effectively reduce her life chances. Goffman also suggests that, because the stigmatized individual tends to hold the same beliefs about her stigma as does the rest of society, self-derogation is likely. All of these aspects of stigma hold true of welfare recipients. The stigma of being a welfare recipient labels an individual as flawed and therefore responsible for her own poverty.

Women on welfare have been variously characterized as lazy, cheating, promiscuous, dependent free-loaders, and the daughters of mothers of equally poor character. Welfare recipients are also generally assumed to be Black. However:

(1) Fifty-two percent of all welfare recipient families are white. Outside the South and Mid-Atlantic states, 70 percent of all welfare recipient families are white (U.S. Department of Health, Education and Welfare, 1977).
(2) At least 90 percent of mothers in AFDC households have been employed (U.S. Department of Health, Education and Welfare, 1977). As the chapter on work noted, these women expect to work and to derive considerable satisfaction from working.

(3) In national surveys of welfare fraud, only 3 percent of all cases showed eligibility errors—and these cases were primarily a result of mistakes on the part of the agency (U.S. Commission on Civil Rights, 1974).

(4) Sixty-four percent of all AFDC families have only one or two children (U.S. Department of Health, Education and Welfare, 1977).

(5) Less than 10 percent of those who ever go on welfare are heavily dependent on it—that is, stay on for nine or ten years and derive 50 percent or more of their family income from welfare (Rein & Rainwater, 1978).

(6) There is no tendency for welfare to be perpetuated into the second generation, once the earnings of the parents are considered (Rein & Rainwater, 1978).

By denying these realities, the stigma associated with being a welfare recipient allows other assumptions and prejudices to operate. These assumptions are reflected in the public welfare system, one of the more salient institutions in the lives of low-income mothers. We found that women on welfare must bear not only the burdens of poverty but also the stigma of being a welfare recipient, and must face frustration, dehumanization, and lack of control in their dealings with the bureaucracy of the welfare system. In this chapter we will explore these aspects of the lives of women on welfare.

Each of the women who participated in the Stress and Families Project had some experience in applying for public assistance benefits. Thirty-three women had applied for and were receiving AFDC benefits at the time of the study. Three others applied for these benefits and were turned down. Two women participated in the AFDC program in the past but were not clients of the program at the time we interviewed them. The five remaining respondents' experiences with public assistance programs were limited to participation in the food stamp program, Medicaid, or child care.

This chapter discusses the experiences of the 35 SFP respondents who received AFDC benefits at some point in their lives and who discussed their experiences with this program during tape-recorded interviews. Throughout the chapter there are references to the number or proportion of respondents who reported a certain experience or point of view. It should be noted that these percentages represent respondents who mentioned this information in the course of a wide-ranging, open-ended discussion. Information from such interviews probably underestimates the number of women who actually experience each item, and the percentages are offered only as rough guidelines to the frequency of each experience and opinion.

LEVEL OF BENEFITS

One of the most popular beliefs about welfare is that it provides a family with unearned wealth. However, a Massachusetts family of three on AFDC receives benefits and food stamps worth $465.70 per month, or $5588.40

per year (Massachusetts Department of Public Welfare, 1980). Nationally, 94 percent of AFDC families headed by women who were receiving only public assistance were living below the national poverty line. Even when women receiving AFDC also work, as they legally may do, they are unable to bring their families out of poverty. In 1976, 60 percent of female-headed families receiving AFDC and wages were still below the poverty line (U.S. Department of Labor, 1978).

Poverty is clearly a major aspect of these women's lives. Sixty-six percent of the respondents spontaneously talked about how stressful it is to receive such inadequate benefits from welfare. While the effect of insufficient and unpredictable income on mental health has been statistically documented in other chapter, Ms. Paine's comments provide a personal account:

> They used to say you shouldn't pay more than a third of your income for rent; I'm paying half. Every time that school starts I end up having to go into hock for clothes. As the kids get older, you can't say, look, don't touch the milk. You are not alloting the cereal; next thing you know, you have no cereal. You really start worrying how to cut corners. You don't buy the extra tonic or whatever. . . . They don't allow for extras—carfare, or you want to take your kid to the show, or get your kid into Boy Scouts, Girl Scouts, or parochial school. They don't think that you might like to take a bus somewhere, or once in a while you might want to take the kids for an ice cream cone.

GOING ON WELFARE

For each of the women interviewed by the Stress and Families Project, going on welfare came at a time of considerable stress, when other options were closed. Ms. Stevens described her circumstances:

> At first, well, I was working after my husband and I separated. He was giving me support money . . . and then I got sick and I had to have an operation on my stomach. While I was in the hospital a social service lady came in and talked to me and told me that I would have to, you know, go to apply for welfare, you know, so they could pay for the hospital bill.

Ms. Sawyer talked about a somewhat different experience:

> I had a job, and at that time my husband decided that he'd stay at home even though he was quite capable of holding a job, and securing a job. He decided he'd stay home and let me do the work, bringing in the paychecks, while he stayed in bed all day. And I found myself expecting my first child, and during the later months, it was necessary for me to stop working. So when my paychecks stopped coming in, I was forced to cash in my life insurance policy which I had had since I was a young girl. He . . . just started acting to the point where I just couldn't manage at all. He was contributing nothing. If it hadn't been for friends I would have literally starved to death. He used to go on

disappearing binges, he would go out supposedly to bring in food as there was no food in the house, and not come back for about two or three weeks. . . . The last time he disappeared, I got the stamina and courage to move, because before I was afraid of physical assaults on my person by him. Verbal assaults I could take, but physical assault, you know, was devastating. So I got the courage to get up and move, and I went down and applied for help . . . until I could get myself back up on my feet. Meanwhile I was in stark terror that he'd find out where I was.

Ms. Ross preferred not to leave her child to work after her husband left, and felt she lacked the education and skills to find reasonable employment:

Rick was about fourteen months old, and his father and I had separated, and he was in California. He had been working, and had been making an adequate income. . . . But then he split to California. He was unhappy about the separation and he wasn't giving me any money. It was a matter of having to go out, and get a job, probably in a factory or as a waitress, because I didn't have enough education to probably do anything else. At that time, I didn't even want to leave my child. I didn't feel good about leaving him at that young an age. I also didn't want to work at a shit job, with wages basically just getting me by, and maybe not even adequately doing that.

These women's experiences are not unique but are linked to experiences and conditions common to women in this country.

These women might have been expected to work. Indeed, the women themselves expect to work. But the likelihood of their earning enough to keep their families out of poverty is slim. Nationally, in full-time, year-round civilian employment in 1974, women earned 57¢ for every dollar earned by men (Pearce, 1979). Eighty percent of women workers are concentrated in predominantly female occupations. While only 20 percent of predominantly male occupations pay poverty-level wages, 54 percent of predominantly female occupations pay poverty-level wages (Pearce, 1979). These earning gaps cannot be explained by differences in education or full-time versus part-time labor (U.S. Commission on Civil Rights, 1974).

Although the women in the SFP study had extensive work histories, they had worked primarily at low-paying jobs, as is true for most women in this country. Their chances of finding a well-paying job are further reduced by the low educational levels of many of them. Of the women in the study, almost half (44 percent) had less than a high school education when they applied for welfare. Several women had less than an eighth-grade education. Nationally, the picture is even bleaker. Of those households for which there is information, 63 percent of mothers in AFDC households had less than a high school education (U.S. Department of Health, Education and Welfare, 1977).

Even against these odds, some of the respondents might have found employment at a level to support themselves. However, all of them had to financially support children as well. Perhaps even more critical, they all had major child care responsibilities. At the time they applied for AFDC, 12 of the respondents were pregnant and another 11 had a child under the age of one year, a total of 70 percent of the respondents. Given the scarcity of affordable child care, especially for infants, these women had even fewer real choices. Faced with such barriers to economic autonomy, the economic security of women in this country often rests on the men in their lives, their fathers, partners, and sons.

However, none of the women interviewed by the Project could rely on a man's income to support herself and her children at the time she applied for welfare. Eighteen of the women had been recently widowed, divorced, separated, or deserted by their partners; another four were single. Of the seven women who were married or living with a man at this time, none was able to count on regular economic support. Their partners were either unemployed, were employed at jobs that were unstable or unpredictable, or were employed but gave the respondents no money.

At a time of considerable stress in each of their lives, with all other options closed to them, these women turned to welfare for assistance. As Ms. Sawyer put it, "Certainly no one has any business to allow themselves or their family to starve to death, or to go without." They found some financial assistance and individuals who actively cared and worked to get them back on their feet. But by and large, they were forced to cope with continued poverty and the regulation and dehumanization of the public welfare system.

REGULATION

Reading through the respondents' descriptions of what it is like to be on welfare, several themes stand out as they are repeated over and over. Many of the women had to contend with the extent to which the welfare system controlled their lives, with inadequate information about what was available to them, and with the amount of time involved in getting through the system.

LACK OF CONTROL

Bureaucracies, with their ambiguous regulations and their own goals which often conflict with the goals of their clients, promote behavior in lower-level bureaucrats, such as welfare caseworkers, that include routinization and control over their clients (Lipsky, 1980).

Twenty-five different women, or 71 percent, reported that welfare controlled their lives in one or more areas. Many women felt this control over their *personal* lives; they felt that their privacy was violated, but that to object would cost them their benefits. Ms. Moore described one such incident:

> This man talked to me for an hour and asked me everything . . . why my marriage broke up, why did I want to go to school, oh, I couldn't believe the things he said to me. I mean, he even brought sex into it. I couldn't believe it. He wanted to ask, and all I wanted to do was to find out about babysitting. Looking for statistics, and we were all the same. You know . . . he went back to when I was sixteen, was I happy when I first got married, why did I get married, and I said because I was pregnant and he said, well, other than that, why? And, oh, everything!

Fully 34 percent of the women reported some such control over their personal lives. As Ms. Sawyer says: "You own nothing when you become a welfare recipient of any sort, you have no privacy any more. Everything that you ever have had or done in your life belongs to the welfare department."

Some women (34 percent) also felt a lack of control as *consumers*. One woman wanted to buy lumber to make furniture at a time when furniture allowances were given, but was told that she must buy ready-made furniture instead. Welfare recipients are limited in their choice of housing to those landlords who will put up with the unpredictability of welfare income, and in the stores where they shop to those which will extend credit when necessary to a woman on welfare.

Finally, 63 percent of women felt a lack of control over their *economic security*. They reported that their cases are frequently reviewed and their benefits may be cut or terminated at any time. Because the women are not told how decisions are made about the size of their allotment, these changes are not predictable. And because an allotment depends on the particular caseworker's interpretation and knowledge of the regulations, these decisions can be as arbitrary as they seem. As Ms. Norton put it: "It is not a sure thing. I can never feel sure about it. Tomorrow they could write me a letter and say that they are cutting me off welfare."

INADEQUATE INFORMATION

Another aspect of bureaucracy is the system's control over, and selective release of, information. Fifty-four percent of the women spoke spontaneously about receiving inadequate information about the benefits and programs available to them. For example, Ms. Page commented:

> It was weird. It wasn't that they were kind or unkind, they just didn't tell you anything. . . . What made me angry was at the time they had what they called "special needs" that no one told me about. They didn't tell me that I could get what they consider a pregnancy diet which meant something like $37 extra every two weeks.

This lack of information means that women sometimes are denied services that are important to their health and well-being and that of their children. In addition, inadequate information can lead to chronic insecurity and limit a woman's ability to make informed decisions about her options to have some control over her life. While current laws require the provision of information to all welfare recipients, there is great variation in compliance with this law. "They have a welfare rights book, I do know there is one that is printed, and every time I asked them [the welfare office] they always tell me they don't have any left" [Ms. Stevens].

WAITING

A third aspect of bureaucracies is the amount of time involved. First there is the time spent waiting in the office—as one woman put it, "the good old hurry up and wait deal." Then there is the wait between the time of application and the first welfare check, a period that can range from two weeks to two months. Some women got through this time with emergency aid from welfare or another agency, or with the help of family and friends who could tide them over. But for some women there was no such help:

> I remember we didn't eat very much food and for a while I didn't have a refrigerator, so we were really confined to eating things like peanut butter and pasta—you know, I remember eating spaghetti a lot—something that didn't need to be refrigerated. Finally someone gave me a refrigerator . . . then I just had to worry about food and rent [Ms. Palmer].

But even more costly in terms of time were the inefficiencies of the welfare system that required repeated visits to the welfare office (54 percent of the women mentioned this). For example:

> The hours [for purchasing food stamps] are just ridiculous. They're 9 to 2:30 on Tuesday through Thursday—inconvenient because I have to make an extra trip. Also, if I run out of food stamps on Friday I can't buy them; I have to wait till Tuesday, so it's expensive.

DEHUMANIZATION

A central aspect of bureaucracies like welfare is the extent to which they are demeaning and dehumanizing (Silver, 1978; Weiss, 1973). Thirty-seven percent of the respondents felt demeaned by having to apply for welfare, and 29 percent felt demeaned by ongoing interaction with the welfare system. While 31 percent of the women mentioned a caseworker who was competent or dependable, and 57 percent felt their caseworker was a good person, 60 percent reported experiencing derogation from their caseworker. One woman said that they "never look at you and see your face." Another woman felt that the caseworkers "act like they were taking money right out of their pocket and giving it to you . . . they're supposed to be an agency for helping people, but they don't really act like it." Attitudes like these were experienced as demeaning and dehumanizing. As one respondent put it, "When you go in you feel like the lowest of the low. . . . You don't need any snide remarks. If anything, you need somebody to pat you on the back and say, look, better things are coming."

These dehumanizing attitudes were found both at the welfare office and outside. Ms. Taylor commented that "people [on welfare] sometimes feel depersonalized, [they] aren't treated with dignity or respect." Ms. Walker felt that what should change about the welfare system is "the outlook people have on people who are on welfare . . . the inferiority that people begin to feel, knowing they are dependent on that system." Twenty-six percent of the respondents reported derogation from people outside the welfare office. Several mentioned being derogated by sales people and others because they were using food stamps or receiving AFDC benefits. Ms. Palmer's estranged husband threatened to have her declared an unfit mother if she went on welfare and threatened to take her children away from her. Ms. James commented:

> You can't tell people that you're on welfare because you'll get shunned. People think you're a sleazy hooker and you couldn't keep a husband.

THE ROLE OF REGULATION AND DEHUMANIZATION

The preceding sections raise questions about the reasons the welfare system is like this. Because caseworkers are the most visible part of the system, we might first look to them for the answer. In fact, many of the respondents' criticisms of the welfare system were directed at the caseworkers. Forty-six percent reported experiencing stress as a result of an unfamiliar caseworker. They often were not notified of changes in their caseworkers, and each time a new caseworker was assigned to them, they had to go over the same information with them. The respondents found that they often could not reach their caseworkers, and that caseworkers made appointments and then did not keep them. While 31 percent reported their caseworkers as competent and dependable, 54 percent reported the workers as inefficient and failing to meet the expectations of the respondents.

> I don't mean to make the social worker out to look bad, but I don't have a lot of respect for a lot of them. . . . Maybe their hands are tied so that they can't do anything or they'll lose their jobs. Or they just see so many cases they become hardened to people's problems [Ms. Ross].

The respondents reported caseworkers who promised to fix errors in allotments but did not follow through, others who did not inform recipients of the benefits available to them, and others who, in general, did not get their jobs done as the respondents thought they should.

> It was clear that not everyone working there understood the procedures. . . .
> You know the procedures keep changing, too. There seem to be a lot of

incompetent people there . . . and [the competent caseworkers] knew very well that if they weren't there, no one else seemed able to do it [Ms. Taylor].

But to blame the caseworkers for the failings of the welfare system is too easy an answer. Several respondents' comments indicate their awareness of the context in which their caseworkers must function. Respondents pointed out that the workers themselves are frustrated by the system—they are given inadequate resources to solve the problems they see, the procedures they must follow keep changing, and they may risk their jobs if they "do anything" for the recipients.

The caseworkers' actions are constrained by the implicit purposes of the welfare system. Various authors (Piven & Cloward, 1971; Pearce, 1979; Withorn, 1981) have pointed out the uses of low welfare benefits and of the stigma of welfare to ensure a ready labor force of low-wage labor. Life is so difficult on welfare that many recipients will get off at the first chance—often to take a low-paying, deadend job. On the other end, employed women are reluctant to fall into "the welfare trap"; they accept low wages and poor working conditions to avoid going on welfare.

In addition to keeping wages down, the specter of welfare, combined with the reduced earning power of women and the limited social acceptability of single mothers, can reduce a woman's autonomy within the family and limit her ability to make choices about her own life. In these ways, the welfare system is integrally involved in restricting the lives of low-income mothers; it indirectly affects the lives of others who never come into direct contact with it.

SURVIVING THE SYSTEM

Seventy-seven percent of the respondents reported some way in which they "manage" the system, in an attempt to circumvent its most damaging aspects. These techniques include getting more information, empowering themselves, and learning to act according to the expectations of welfare workers.

GATHERING INFORMATION

A prerequisite for managing the system is to get enough information to be able to decide what to do. Since it is often difficult to get information from the welfare office itself, many women rely on learning from their own experience and that of others, and on access to the Welfare Manual. Twenty-five different women (71 percent of the respondents) reported getting more information in at least one of these ways. Sometimes the women learned from their own experiences which time of day was the best to guarantee little waiting at the welfare office or which place was best for buying food stamps.

One woman who had been on AFDC before felt that this experience helped her the second time: "I had to apply at a different office. I got a lot of things again, the second time, that I'm sure they never would have allowed me, that they didn't know about" (Ms. Ross).

At other times, women learned from others about benefits to which they were entitled, or got other information that made things easier. For example, Ms. Marshall learned from her neighbor about a nearby bank at which to buy food stamps. Ms. Palmer is part of a network of welfare mothers who share information with each other.

Finally, several women had access to a copy of the Welfare Manual and learned what they were entitled to and what procedures to follow to get it.

> They [a welfare rights organization] have a manual, same as they have at the welfare department. So I would go through the manual and then I would call my social worker and I'd tell her "well, I got my manual, so look in yours" [Ms. Hill].

LEARNING TO MEET THE EXPECTATIONS OF THE SYSTEM

When caught in a situation that deprives one of power or of one's ability to affect the outcome of the situation, one option any individual has is to attempt to meet the expectations of those with the power. This is particularly likely when the system seems beyond individual control (Glass & Singer, 1972). A few of the women (14 percent) mentioned doing exactly this at times:

> I shut my mouth, I didn't say anything anymore—and I found out later that as long as you went along with him [the caseworker] and you . . . play this sort of innocent naive who was taken in by this horrible person, he would be alright. But if I tried to pursue the argument further with him, he probably would have gotten mad at me. His sympathies lay with young innocent things who were coerced or victimized by men. But if you didn't fit that mold, he, uh, was not too friendly [Ms. Page].

> [I remember being] angry that I had to go on welfare, that I had to be subservient. . . . I remember always going in there with the feeling of not wanting them to think that I knew as much as I did know, because I was afraid that would disturb them or alarm them. When they would tell me what my budget was, although I knew exactly how much I was supposed to get to every penny, you know, I always acted somewhat surprised [Ms. Ross].

EMPOWERMENT

Another option, when placed in a situation that deprives one of power, is to seek to empower oneself—in some way to get more power on one's side. There seem to be three major ways in which the respondents did this: by acting as their own advocates with their caseworkers, fighting directly for what they were entitled to; by having someone else act as their advocate; and by using pressure tactics—such as hearings, lawyers, and calls to supervisors.

Thirty-four percent of the women mentioned taking some direct action on their own behalf, such as calling a caseworker and insisting on benefits to which they knew they were entitled. Ms. Hill comments, "I usually get what I want. I'm not the type of person to sit down and wait. I walk right in to my social worker and say what I want." Ms. Ross uses similar tactics:

> I have trucked in the back door—you are supposed to come in the front door—and demanded to see people, when I have had to wait for too long, or feel like people have been just passing the buck and pushing me around. I don't go in and holler and scream and make a big ruckus. But I have pretty well gone in there, demanded to get what I thought that I should get. And I feel that I have probably been treated differently because of it.

A few of the women have also used advocates or acted as advocates themselves for other women. Ms. Ramsey describes how this helps:

> As soon as I got an advocate to come with me to the welfare office, everything changed, and I found out that I was eligible for a lot of things that he [the caseworker] didn't tell me. . . . A good friend of mine used to work at the welfare office and she knew the laws and what people were entitled to. . . . She went to the office with me and told him that she was there to see that I got what was coming to me. If she hadn't come with me, I wouldn't have known that I had any rights. . . . Once I had her come with me, he changed his tune.

A third way mentioned by respondents to get some power over the situation is through the use of pressure tactics. Several women mentioned requesting hearings or getting a lawyer to appeal a welfare decision. When Ms. Wade was asked if she thought a hearing could do some good, she replied, "Sure. They don't want to be hassled." Other women talked about telephone calls and visits to supervisors to get things done. When asked what she would do if welfare was taking too long to make a decision, Ms. Wade said that she would talk to the worker and the supervisor at her office, "and then I'd call the people downtown and bug the people downtown." The next step after that, as Ms. Hill saw, are those who make the laws:

> When they said they couldn't find my ex-husband who owes support money, even after I'd given them his work number and all, I said "Bullshit, I'm going to go to the State House and I'm going to complain." I'd even demonstrate down there by myself.

CONCLUSION

Women on welfare are caught between myth and reality. The reality of their lives is that they are hard-working women attempting to raise their children in a society where they have limited access to well-paying jobs and insufficient child care support. They have turned to welfare in an attempt to cope with these conditions.

In the face of this reality, the myths live on. Women on welfare are stigmatized, seen as less than human and as responsible for their own poverty and misery. This stigma allows others to see them as lazy and promiscuous and not deserving of a decent income from welfare benefits. By labeling welfare recipients dishonest, society is able to justify the controlling regulations of public welfare. Since the stigmatized individual is "different," others can treat her as less than human, "the lowest of the low," without challenging their own humanity.

This interlocking web of personal prejudice and systematized practice has serious consequences for the lives and emotional well-being of women on welfare. Some accept the myths about their lives, blaming themselves and feeling dehumanized, unworthy of esteem. For others, the welfare system is a source of frustration, anger, and a sense of powerlessness. As Ms. Newman put it:

> I don't ever want to go on welfare because it is a trap. I call it the welfare trap. . . . [When I was on before] I was so grateful that they accepted me that I didn't want to complain. But it was mine to begin with. I want that changed.

While none of the women interviewed would abolish welfare, they would all change it, in ways they believe would give them back their human dignity and their ability to affect the course of their own lives. As Ms. Taylor put it:

> With all the trouble and mismanagement and unjust decisions and incompetence, . . . I think it still helps people to keep their families together and keep themselves going.

REFERENCES

Glass, D. C., & Singer, J. E. *Urban stress: Experiments on noise and social stressors.* New York: Academic Press, 1972.

Goffman, E. *Stigma: Notes on the management of spoiled identity.* Englewood Cliffs, NJ: Prentice-Hall, 1963.

Lipsky, M. *Street-level bureaucracy.* New York: Russell Sage, 1980.

Massachusetts Department of Public Welfare. *A Massachusetts chartbook: Aid to Families with Dependent Children,* 1980.

Pearce, D. Women, work and welfare: The feminization of poverty. In K. W. Feinstein (Ed.) *Working women and families.* Beverly Hills, CA: Sage, 1979.

Piven, F. F., & Cloward, R. A. *Regulating the poor: The functions of public welfare.* New York: Random House, 1971.

Rein, M., & Rainwater, L. Patterns of welfare use. *Social Service Review,* 1978, *52,* 511-534.

Silver, M., & Geller, D. On the irrelevance of evil: The organization and individual action. *Journal of Social Issues,* 1978, *34* (4), 125-136.

U.S. Commission on Civil Rights. *Women and poverty.* Washington, DC: Government Printing Office, 1974.

U.S. Department of Health, Education and Welfare. *Aid to Families with Dependent Children: 1975 recipient characteristics study.* HEW Publication No. (SSA) 77-11777. Washington, DC: Government Printing Office, 1977.

U.S. Department of Labor, Bureau of Labor Statistics. Women who head families: A socioeconomic analysis. *Monthly Labor Review,* 1978, *101,* 32-37.

Weiss, R. S. Helping relationships: Relationships of clients with physicians, social workers, priests and others. *Social Problems,* 1973, *20* (3), 319-328.

Withorn, A. Retreat from the social wage: Human services in the 1980's. *Radical America,* 1981, *15,* 23-31.

8

THE HUMAN COST OF DISCRIMINATION

EMILIE STEELE, JACQUELYN MITCHELL,
ELIZABETH GREYWOLF, DEBORAH BELLE,
WEINING CHANG, AND RONNA BARBARA SCHULLER

The experience of discrimination is not a new phenomenon for women; it has been a part of American life for centuries. Historically, women have suffered from oppression and discrimination simply because of their sex (Gornick & Moran, 1971; Rosaldo & Lamphere, 1974). In addition, women (and men) encounter discrimination because of their racial or ethnic backgrounds (Willie, Kramer, & Brown, 1973). They have also—and continue in increasing numbers—to experience oppression due to single-parent status as members of the most hard-pressed economic group in America (Brandwein, Brown, & Fox, 1974). Many black women suffer the most severe exposure as a result of sexual, marital, class, and race discrimination (Staples, 1976; Gordon, 1965).

Discrimination can affect women on two levels: the personal, when it is the result of an action of one person or of a small group; and the institutional, when it occurs as a result of actions taken and approved of as part of the normal operations of an institution (Feagin & Feagin, 1978). Both kinds of discrimination were present in the lives of the women interviewed by the Stress and Families Project; both had insidious and devastating effects on their lives.

While discrimination has often been studied, much of the literature focuses either on the nature of prejudice or the definition of minority status (Feagin & Feagin, 1978). However, controlled laboratory experiments on discrimination indicate that individuals subjected to discrimination perform less well on tasks and become less likely, after such an experience, to volunteer help to a peer (Glass & Singer, 1972). These results are particularly striking because they were found after only one episode of discrimination, and that one of a rather mild kind. Discrimination experienced as a continuing part of daily existence would most likely have an even more devastating impact on individuals.

Dion and Earn (1975) emphasize the pressing need for researchers to listen to people who suffer discrimination, to discover the oppressed's perceptions of prejudice and discrimination. They raise the question, "What are the affective consequences of confronting contempt from others by virtue of minority membership?" (p. 944). One could extend the question to other nonminority but stigmatized status attributes. The Stress and Families Project did address this question by means of a semistructured interview with respondents in which women were asked to describe the experience of discrimination and the role of discrimination as a barrier to the attainment of their life goals.

This chapter, therefore, considers the experience of discrimination of women who are often multiply stigmatized; as women, as poor people, as blacks or members of other ethnic groups, and often as single parents. The responses to this interview show that discrimination creates added barriers to life goal attainment in the lives of low-income women. The women told how discrimination occurs and who the discriminators were; they told what they did to handle the situations; they talked about how discrimination affected their own lives, their behavior as parents, and the lives of their children.

THE BARRIERS OF DISCRIMINATION

It's very hard. I think I'm not getting my full quota of life. Prone to live in the ghetto—this is what society says. . . . I can't find sufficient housing. You're put in a category. I'm not sure if society does this or if it's my own making, but society helps [black respondent].

To investigate the ways in which discrimination was perceived as preventing women from achieving certain societal goals, the women were asked about difficulties in obtaining decent housing, entry into a good training program, good jobs, promotions or raises, good education, credit or loans, and respect. They were asked whether their race or ethnicity, sex, single parenthood, income, or education made obtaining these goals easier or harder or made no difference. Next they were asked, "which of these [attributes] makes it hardest for you to get decent housing [and good jobs, etc.]?" in order to rank each of the attributes in relation to each of the goods and services previously listed.

From this it was possible to determine which attribute (sex, race, single parenthood, and so on) the women perceived as causing the greatest difficulty in reaching goals (decent housing, good jobs, and the like). It was also possible to obtain an overall picture of which attribute was perceived as the most influential in preventing achievement of all of the goals. Finally, it was possible to compare the perceptions of black and white women.

The women indicated that certain of the attributes were more salient in regard to some goals than to others. While having a low income affected their ability to obtain decent housing, to get into training programs, to obtain a good education, to receive credit or loans, and to be valued and respected, educational background and sex were the strongest factors hindering them from finding a good job and getting promotions or raises.

When black and white respondents were compared, blacks were found to rank race the most potent discrimination attribute overall, while whites ranked race/ethnicity as the least potent. In fact, the white respondents reported an overall, though small, advantage because of their race. However, if race is excluded from the ranking, both black and white women rated the remaining attributes in precisely identical order. Excluding race for each group of respondents, low income was the most salient discrimination attribute with sex, single parenthood, and educational background in descending order of importance. Both the convergence in perception on the other four attributes and the agreement that black women suffer and white women are ahead of the game because of their respective races are striking results of this investigation.

It is also evident that women who are discriminated against for a variety of reasons suffer from a perverse "Catch-22" situation in which the barriers caused by discrimination because of one attribute compound the problems associated with each of the other attributes. Thus, low income makes it more difficult to get a good education, and limited educational attainment prevents a woman from getting a good job and thus raising her income. Feagin and Feagin (1978) refer to this cyclical effect of discrimination as "side-effect discrimination" because the discriminatory actions in one area clearly influence the discriminatory actions in another. The more stigmatized status attributes a person possesses, the more difficult it must be to overcome the discrimination barriers associated with any one attribute. The effect of discrimination on the multiply stigmatized appears to be more than the sum of discriminatory actions based on each variable alone. As Gordon (1965) expressed it:

> Being both poor and black means that one's movement in the world—physically, socially, psychologically—is doubly circumscribed. When one adds the status of woman, it is a world with tight steel bands around it [p. 37].

THE EXPERIENCE OF DISCRIMINATION

Respondents were asked to describe incidents of discrimination they had experienced or that had been experienced by those close to them. Incidents of discrimination were reported to have occurred in all the familiar and important institutions of urban life, from restaurants to welfare offices, from schools to hospitals. Frequently named discriminators included welfare department workers, rental agents, employers, restaurant employees, policemen, school personnel, salespersons, and taxi drivers.

White men were by far the most frequent discriminators reported. Both black and white women reported more incidents of discrimination by white people than by black people. Blacks were named more often than whites as the victims of discrimination, as shown in Table 8.1.

Discrimination sometimes ocurred even "before the fact." One woman said that the schools "draw conclusions before they see you—IQ you out!" Another said, "I am divorced, [a] single parent and on welfare—you're labeled." However, there were differences in the way discrimination was experienced by whites and blacks. For whites discrimination was most often linked to class status (for example, being denied credit in a store). For blacks discrimination was a result of, first, their race and, second, their economic and/or social position.

Many blacks experienced discrimination as they went about their daily lives: shopping, going out to restaurants, or walking down the street. Several black respondents mentioned being closely watched while shopping in stores. Ms. Houser stated: "From the time you walk in the store, it's the security guard, he's following you everywhere you go." Another respondent told about being denied service in a restaurant.

> I sat down, and I don't know how long, and those people didn't ever wait on me. So I just got up and left. I felt like they didn't want to be bothered. And everybody [white] would come in, and they would sit down, and they would get served. And to me it looked like they didn't want to wait on me.

Ms. Sawyer spoke of almost casual abuse from strangers.

> More than a couple of times going about my daily business in the downtown streets of Boston I've been called "Nigger" here and "Nigger" there, and people have allowed the doors they have opened to fall in my face.

TABLE 8.1   Race of Person(s) Discriminated Against

Blacks	58%
Whites	39%
Blacks and Whites together	2%
Other races	1%
Total	100%

Sometimes discrimination happened within ethnic groups. Two black women reported the particular pain of experiencing discrimination by other blacks who had a different class status. For example, Ms. Walker talked about some blacks who "consider themselves to be a bourgeoisie black class of people." She felt that such people set themselves apart from other blacks because they have some money and have established themselves with academic credentials. She commented on her disappointment in discovering that "a little money, a little power, [a] little prestige can take people into—a whole [new thing]. They always identify that they're black, but they are not identifying too. . . . Their whole attitude is saying, 'I'm black, but you know I'm not into what you're into and I'm above you.'" Ms. Sawyer believes that white people mistakenly think that blacks "automatically turn around and help their so-called 'own.'"

> Blacks are not better than whites when it comes to being in a higher position and giving a helping hand to those who have not been able to climb that so-called social-economic ladder . . . even though a few of us have had the decency, heart, and humanity to turn around and give a helping hand, we don't see that at this time. I feel that it is inexcusable, really, because we haven't even had the opportunity to hardly touch the ladder, let alone get on it. I think any normal black person who has had the opportunity to get on the ladder owes it to the people of his community to turn around and give a helping hand in some way.

Linked to class discrimination, both black and white respondents spoke about the difficulties they experienced because of their limited educational attainments. Many such incidents concerned employment. Ms. Franklin said: "There have been several places I went for appointments that said that because I have no more than a high school diploma they'll not give me a chance." Ms. Monroe has had similar difficulties. After applying for a job at a supermarket and at a department store, she concluded, "now I think you can't get a job unless you go to college."

Other incidents related to educational attainment involved the experience of not being respected. Ms. Rand, a white respondent, told about an old friend whom she had known since she was four years old. They parted as friends at high school because "she thought she was better than me, because she was going to college, and there was a different type of people. But they weren't really different. It was just that they were learning. . . . I was learning, but I was learning in another manner. But, I mean, she thinks she is better."

DISCRIMINATORY VIOLENCE

Other incidents of discrimination were life threatening for the victims. Most of these (75 percent) involved violence against black people. Several white respondents told of instances in which violence was directed against blacks who had moved into predominantly white neighborhoods. Ms. Paine described how her stepfather, who is black, was forced to move after shootings and threats of violence. While his furniture was being moved, "there were a few people who showed up with handguns. They showed to say it is good that you are leaving." Similarly, Ms. Ramsey spoke of her black friend: "Bricks were thrown at her house until she was forced to leave the building, and they set fires in front of her house." Ms. Marshall told of the harassment to which black families who were residents of her housing project had been subjected. She spoke of windows being broken and of a car being destroyed. She went on to relate the outcome of an incident in which white teenagers attacked a black resident's apartment in the housing project.

> She was expecting a baby at the time . . . They almost cost her and the baby's [life]. Her blood pressure shot up sky high. They had to take her out that night in the ambulance. And she was in intensive care due to all the harassment they were causing her. She just had to leave the apartment. She did come home to another apartment over there and then, finally, they must have started again. . . . They moved out. They couldn't stand it anymore, and moved.

In one instance, Ms. Franks, a black respondent, told about her two uncles (one of whom had just returned from 16 months in Vietnam). It was the day before Christmas and they were on the way to visit their mother. Two policemen, one white and one black, stopped them as they walked down the street looking for a cab and demanded to know what they were looking for. A fight ensued and the uncles were arrested—for resisting arrest. When then respondent's family protested the arrest to the NAACP and other community agencies, the case was dismissed for lack of evidence.

In another incident a black respondent told of being attacked and brutally beaten by several white men. She and her boyfriend and two other friends had simply stopped for food at a take-out restaurant.

RESPONSES TO DISCRIMINATION

The women responded to acts of discrimination in various ways, depending upon the circumstances and those involved. Responses ranged from confrontation with the discriminator and active protest to an outside agency or community group to the decision to ignore the incident, to put it aside.

An example of both confrontation with the discriminator and active protest to others resulted when a black respondent was denied credit to purchase furniture. At first the store approved her credit, saying that she could pay for the furniture in installments, as she had a good job at the time and money in the bank to pay for whatever she bought. When she returned to the store to check on the delivery date, the manager had changed his mind and told her that the store needed to ask her more questions. It was implied that the respondent could not be trusted to pay her bill because, "when your children get sick you'll be paying the hospital bill instead of us." The respondent asked for her deposit back and filed a complaint against the store for discrimination. "I wanted society to know that these people discriminated." The store was investigated, and not only did the respondent have her money returned but she also received a check for $100.00 and a written apology from the assistant manager of the store.

However, such active strategies did not always produce results. When Ms. Smith's brother was attacked by a group of white youths in front of a police station, he was arrested and the white youths were not. Her brother was badly beaten and the police refused him any medical treatment. Ms. Smith's grandmother contacted a local radio station for support. However, even after involving the radio station and complaining directly to the police, Ms. Smith's brother never saw a doctor until after his release. She said, "When I saw him his face was swollen and all black and blue. He was hurt bad."

Discrimination was more likely to be put aside or tolerated when needed services were involved. Ms. Hill, a white respondent, stated that when professionals such as doctors treat her in a condescending manner, she tries to ignore their behavior. "I just walk away, or I don't come back, and they can't affect me."

Some respondents feel they cannot get the service they need unless they submit to discrimination. When a dentist at a dental school clinic was inappropriately "friendly" toward Ms. Ross, a white respondent, she felt that there was not much she could do because she wanted the work on her teeth done well and had few options of other dentists. But, she said, "I remember thinking about it and being sort of angry."

Some situations seem to offer only "no-win" solutions. Some involve the choice to do without a life-saving service rather than be subjected to discrimination. Ms. Palmer, a white respondent, told about black friends who hesitate to call the fire department because they believe that the firemen are destructive of property belonging to blacks. If the fire is small, neighbors often try to put it out themselves instead of calling the fire department.

HELPING VICTIMS OF DISCRIMINATION

Respondents also reported incidents in which they helped others who had suffered discrimination. Sometimes they helped family members or friends, and sometimes they helped total strangers. For example, Ms. Stevens, a black respondent, told about a friend's daughter who received a school assignment notice informing her that she would be bused to a predominantly white high school. Scrawled on the busing notice was the insult, "Bring your black ass on out here, nigger." Ms. Stevens went with her friend to the NAACP to file a complaint. In another instance, Ms. Palmer, a white respondent, told of trying to help a black friend who felt discriminated against by the police because they often failed to respond when called. Ms. Palmer offered to call the police when her friend's stereo was stolen because she thought they might respond if they heard a white voice.

A white respondent told of two instances in which she helped blacks she did not know. Once when she was out driving she saw two young black boys being attacked by several white teenagers. She stopped her car and intervened when she realized that this was not a game, and that one of the boys was calling for help. When she learned that the black children had been accused of stealing a bicycle, she advised the white teenagers to contact the police. She told them, "You have no business taking things into your own hands." She took the two black children to their homes. Another time when the same respondent worked with a tenants' union, she spent the night in the apartment of a black family who had been subjected to racial harassment. However, despite her efforts, the family eventually moved.

CHILDREN AS VICTIMS

When the respondents' children were victims of discrimination, the respondents' reactions appeared to vary with the age of the perpetrator and with the amount of control perceived. In instances in which an adult mistreated a child, the parent often intervened and directly confronted the discriminator. For example, Ms. Sawyer, a black woman, learned that her nine-year-old son had been in a school lunchroom fight with another child. A school aide had stopped the fight and had "put [Ms. Sawyer's son] on the floor and stepped on his private parts." Ms. Sawyer arranged for a child advocate to go to the school with her for a conference with the principal and the aide involved.

When children discriminated against other children, the parents' responses varied. Ms. Wood's daughter had trouble with some black children both in school and on the school bus. She told her daughter that she should learn to fight to protect herself, if necessary.

A different approach was taken by Ms. Lewis when other children would not play with her daughter because of her color.

> I went to the kids and they changed their attitudes. . . . Instead of ignoring, I think you have to talk about it and do something about it. I was pleased with the way it worked out.

A third approach was taken by Ms. Walker when her daughter experienced discrimination in first and second grades at school. Ms. Walker did not intervene directly. "I didn't give her any advice because I didn't want to tell her what to do. I gave her moral support."

It is possible that the different approaches taken by these mothers reflect the extent of their perception of their real power to influence the different situations involving their children. Ms. Lewis was able to meet the neighborhood children personally who had rejected her daughter, and this encounter was effective in ending the painful discrimination her daughter had experienced. Problems with other children in school or on the school bus may not be so amenable to parental involvement. In such cases, a parent may have to resign herself to providing support for her child rather than intervening directly.

EFFECTS OF DISCRIMINATION ON
CHILD-REARING STRATEGIES

While parents can protect, advise, and support their children in many ways, they must also prepare their children to face life on their own. According to several respondents, discrimination has had a strong effect on child-rearing strategies. This was especially true for black respondents.

> That's a very hurting thing. The kinds of things that they need to know to protect themselves, and even though they are real tiny sometimes you need to have to come out and tell them 'cause their skin is not a certain color, they cannot do what other children whose skin is light can do.

> Yes, being black, I am forced to do and say things that I do not want to do and say. . . . I have to tell my children that there are certain things they cannot do because they are not white, and even though those signs of discrimination are not up there "NO BLACKS ALLOWED IN THE BATHROOM" and "DRINK AT THE FOUNTAIN," and so forth, the fact is that there are invisible signs and the children have to be protected from this. And when you know that the children stand a chance of discrimination occurring you have to try to condition their thoughts as gentle as you can due to the fact that there are a lot of ignorant people in the world.

> And I find as a black mother, it is most disheartening and frightening to raise black male children—especially in this kind of environment where they're always under suspicion.

THE EMOTIONAL TOLL OF DISCRIMINATION

The emotional consequences of discrimination are immense. The women reported that the stress caused by discrimination was often severe, lasting for months and, in some cases, even years. For blacks, the stress was significantly greater than for whites (as measured according to the eight-point scale used in the Life Events Interview).

The feelings the women expressed about discrimination are a further indication of its toll on their lives. They said they were "angry," "bitter," and "frustrated" whenever they or anyone they knew had been a victim of discrimination. It seemed to make no difference whether the discrimination was based on race, ethnic background, class, or some other attribute. The women were upset that they or those close to them had been treated unfairly.

When Ms. Daily lost her job as a nurse's aide in a hospital because she was unjustly accused of stealing, she was "bitter and hurt." When Ms. Moore was a child her Protestant family moved to an all-Catholic neighborhood and the children called her names, threw dirt at her, and refused to play with her. When they teased her, she said, "I used to think that was the most awful thing . . . and my whole family felt so bad for me. But they couldn't do nothing." Because she had no friends, she tried to play by herself. "I used to cry all the time," she remembered.

When Ms. Charles was hospitalized with one hand completely bandaged and the other connected to an intravenous solution so that she could not care for herself in any way, she was totally ignored by the nursing staff. "It look like they didn't want to take me in that part of the hospital. . . . I think when you go to those kinds of places, look like they would try to help you. But . . . they try to . . . drive you crazy. If you didn't have strong will power, they will get you crazy. You feel like . . . you want to get up and kill yourself, the way they treat you."

Cause for concern comes from those feelings that expressed a change in the victim's attitude toward society as a whole. A number of women reported that the incidents of discrimination had caused them to feel antagonistic toward people in general. This was especially true of incidents of ethnic and racial discrimination. One black respondent stated, "for a long time I didn't like people after that. If they didn't like me, I didn't like them. . . . I almost thought about going out and getting some white people . . . but, I said that wasn't going to solve nothing." Another respondent told of her experience in a southern jail when she was arrested for participating in a civil rights march. "I grew to hate when I should have been loving."

Thus it is clear that discrimination causes the women intense and long-lasting pain. On an institutional level, discrimination serves to perpetuate the inequalities of our society by denying equal opportunities for advancement to all citizens. As awful as the act of discrimination can be for the individual victim, its ramifications go far beyond the act itself. Discrimination against the poor, for instance, serves to keep its victims from participating fully in the benefits society has to offer. It perpetuates poverty because its victims often cannot attain a decent education and, in turn, cannot then qualify for well-paying jobs that would enable them to improve their lives. They cannot afford better housing in neighborhoods in which their children could benefit from improved public education. And thus, the cycle continues for future generations.

REFERENCES

Brandwein, R., Brown, C., & Fox, E. Women and children last: The social situation of divorced mothers and their families. *Journal of Marriage and the Family,* 1974, *36,* 3, 498-514.

Dion, K. L., & Earn, B. M. The phenomenology of being a target of prejudice. *Journal of Personality and Social Psychology,* 1975, *32* (5), 944-950.

Feagin, J. R., & Feagin, C. B. *Discrimination American style: Institutional racism and sexism.* Englewood Cliffs, NJ: Prentice-Hall, 1978.

Glass, D. C., & Singer, J. E. *Urban stress: Experiments on noise and social stressors.* New York: Academic Press, 1972.

Gordon, J. The poor of Harlem: Social functioning in the underclass. Report to the Welfare Administration, New York, 1965.

Gornick, V., & Moran, B. *Women in sexist society: Experiments on noise and social stressors.* New York: Basic Books, 1971.

Rosaldo, M., & Lamphere, L. *Women, culture and society.* Stanford: Stanford University Press, 1974.

Staples, R. *The Black woman in America: Sex, marriage and the family.* Chicago: Nelson Hall, 1976.

Willie, C. B., Kramer, B. M., & Bertram, S. *Racism and mental health.* Pittsburgh: University of Pittsburgh Press, 1973.

9

THE POLITICS OF THE POOR

ELIZABETH GREYWOLF

"Politicians believe poor people don't vote," said Ms. Page, one of the women interviewed. This belief has been shared by other segments of American society and often extends to a broader view that the poor are politically inactive in all areas of politics. Miller (1968) stated that "usually, the long-term economically depressed are unlikely candidates for a dynamic political movement" (p. 144), and that there are a number of obvious roadbocks to cohesive action by urban low-income women, as well as other disadvantaged groups. Kimball (1972) hypothesized that "a feeling of separation from the mainstream of American life, coupled with a sense of political powerlessness, is a potent combination working against political participation by the urban poor" (p. 21). This sense of powerlessness is a common emotional component of the lives of many of the women interviewed in the Stress and Families study. If the poor do participate less often in political activities, and if a sense of personal powerlessness contributes to noninvolvement, then the roadblocks to empowerment need to be examined and overcome before the democratic ideals of this country can be fully realized.

The poor, perhaps more than any other group in America, often find their crucial life issues decided in the political arena. Without their participation in deciding those issues, resolutions will inevitably reflect an imbalance of power. To examine how deeply a sense of political disenfranchisement may be experienced by low-income women, the respondents were asked a number of questions regarding current political issues which directly affect their lives. They were questioned regarding any contacts attempted with their local political representatives, about their voting behavior, their opinions about government-sponsored work programs, about abortion funding restriction for women on welfare, and about "the system" in general.

The women's responses varied tremendously. While their overall opinions of "the system" were expressed through anger, skepticism, and disillusionment, a surprising number of the women regularly vote in local, state, and national elections. A large proportion of them had, at one time or another, attempted to solve personal, family, or community problems with the help of their local representatives. However, the majority of these attempts were unsuccessful and seemed to contribute additional feelings of powerlessness and cynicism about political practices.

CONTACTING LOCAL REPRESENTATIVES

One might hypothesize at least two forces at work in motivating an individual to attempt to contact a local political representative. First, an issue of sufficient concern arises which is felt to be beyond individual control. Second, there exists some belief that the representative of the system has the power to help solve the problem. In addition, one may or may not feel that the representative is really concerned (for whatever reasons) with matters affecting his/her constituency.

In some cases it may be that contact with a local politician simply satisfies a need for voicing one's opinion. But there is cause for belief that the respondents who tried to interact with their local representatives did so not for cathartic effect but actively to seek help with their life problems. Thirty-three women were questioned as to whether they or someone they know had ever gone to an elected representative with a problem. Ten women answered that they themselves had done so; 12 women had friends or relatives who had attempted to solve problems in that manner. One should bear in mind that many respondents indicated feeling not only a lack of control over their lives because they were receiving AFDC payments, but also sometimes fear stating their true feelings on issues because of possible reprisal from "the system." It appears most likely that this action-initiating group of women had to overcome that apprehension as well as initial reluctance and inertia which any individual might feel at attempting to get help through an unfamiliar system. It was hypothesized that highly educated women might be more likely than others to contact a local representative. Two of the ten women had some college experience; however, four of the women who had contacted their representatives had less than a ninth-grade education.

Half of the women contacted their representatives on concerns directly related to their children. These concerns involved attempts by the mothers to deal with schooling issues, such as trying to get a child into a better school or improving a child's school experience. This finding gives additional weight to the view of Brager and Barr (1967) that while low-income parents are often charged with disinterest in their children's schooling, studies show the reverse to be true. Four other contacts had to do with neighborhood or housing concerns (which may have also been motivated, indirectly, by concern for their children's care and safety). One woman made concerted efforts (ultimately unsuccessful) to dispute a parking ticket.

While a few attempts at seeking political aid were successful, the majority of women in this sample who made attempts failed to gain the responses they were seeking. Eight of the women who have firsthand experience with local politics have been left with negative impressions. Ms. Ross, for example, contacted her local representative on a day care issue but said the next time she would probably "contact community people I trust" instead. Ms. Stevens tried to find help about her son's schooling and said she "called for three months before they got around to responding and by then he had been placed in a school." Perhaps that is why, when asked if she would make that attempt again, she responded, "No, because you can't find them." Ms. Charles indicated that she had at one time gone to her City Hall about fires in her neighborhood to see if she could get someone to "come and check it out, but they never did." When asked if she would try again, she said, "What for? So he could tell me something and don't stick to it?"

Four of the 19 women who indicated they definitely would not try to solve a problem with the aid of a politician spontaneously expressed their belief that politicians are too inaccessible. Three of the women felt politicians were *physically* inaccessible. Ms. Ansel, for example, says she literally cannot find her representative. But Ms. Irby feels a class barrier which prevents her access to political aid; she said she "wouldn't know how to talk to them, they are out of my class."

VISIBILITY AND IMPACT OF
LOCAL REPRESENTATIVES

Respondents were asked whether they ever heard about the local politicians who were supposed to represent them and, if so, whether they felt those politicians affected in their lives. In line with the political disenfranchisement which Kimball (1972) believes is a potent factor in the feelings of powerlessness among the poor, 20 of the 34 women who responded said they do not hear about their representatives at all (except, a few commented, "if they want to push something," or "only before elections"). Of the 11 women who indicated they did hear about their representatives, 10 said they believed their lives were affected by them. Only one woman, however, mentioned being affected in a *positive* way.

VOTING BEHAVIOR

When questioned about their voting practices in national, state, and city elections, the respondents for whom we have data were split almost evenly between those who generally vote and those who generally do not. Three of the women who do not vote, however, told interviewers they had voted in the past. One woman had just registered but had not had the opportunity to vote at the time she was interviewed.

Interestingly, the group of 10 women previously mentioned as having contacted their local representatives on various issues were exactly divided: five do not vote and five still do. In addition, one of the two women who indicated some positive results from representative contact always votes; the other never votes.

The Survey Research Center at the University of Michigan, which has studied voter turnout since 1952, has found that there is a high correlation between voting behavior and feelings of a sense of political efficacy (Kimball, 1972). Do the poor generally feel that as individual voters they can help to bring about social and political change? Kimball believes the answer is no. In his work on voter participation, he found that "the feeling of powerlessness among the urban poor is often an accurate reflection of institutional bias actually at work in our political system. . . . That structure discriminates most particularly among the poor" (p. 2). The pervasive sense of disenfranchisement, which many low-income women feel, is not based on illusion. All too often they have come face to face with the reality of a system which seems to mock its political mottos. Responses from this sample, however, indicate that slightly more than half of these women are still exercising their right to make a statement of their positions at the polls in national and local elections. The proportion indicating they usually vote in state elections is comparable to the average for the state: according to the election division figures of the Office of the Secretary of State, 48.3 percent of those persons of voting age in Massachusetts actually voted in the November 1978 state election.

Some women, however, have become convinced they are politically ineffectual. Cause for concern may be found in the statements of the women who have previously voted but do not do so now. Ms. Marcus, for instance, indicated she used to vote in another state but does not vote now in Massachusetts. Ms. Paine indicated that she doesn't vote because "My vote doesn't mean a damn thing." Ms. Sanders, a widow who once contacted her representative about a housing problem and received no help, said she also once voted but no longer does so. These women may have lost faith in the democratic system and/or now feel they have lost control over their lives.

WORK PROGRAMS FOR WELFARE RECIPIENTS

The issue of work programs is one which we believed might be particularly stressful for low-income mothers. At the time of the interviews, proposals for mandatory "workfare" for welfare recipients was a controversial news item. Also, a form of workfare had recently been put into effect in Massachusetts. A total of 32 women were asked for their opinions of government work programs. While five respondents did not believe they had enough information to make informed judgments, the remaining 27 women gave responses which were subsequently categorized as negatively inclined to such programs, positively inclined, or ambivalent.

It was immediately apparent that the group had little firsthand knowledge about government work programs. Much of the information offered was based on hearsay from friends or the media. Only one woman mentioned having been given firsthand information from the welfare department. Of the 15 women who indicated some opposition to the programs, at least three based their judgments on extremely limited information. This lack of information was even more apparent for 6 of the 9 women who were coded as positively inclined. Another 3 women were ambivalent about the issue.

The 9 women who were positively inclined toward government work programs frequently commented on what they saw as the *potential* of work programs, not on how well they actually function at present. The work ethic appeared to play a large role in their thinking. "I like them because I think every adult should work to help themselves. Sitting home waiting for a check every two weeks, you can't be out doing something constructive with your body and mind. You feel more independent working for something instead of sitting on your butt and letting it come to you." This comment, and several others, seemed to reflect the high value placed by the respondents on work itself, or the opportunity to work, rather than approval of any specific program.

Low pay, uninteresting jobs (and lack of training), and being forced to work are the main reasons given by 15 respondents for dissatisfaction with existing work programs. Seven women mentioned the lack of a salary incentive. Two women voiced the general sentiments of this group: "It's wrong because no one in their right mind is going to work for the government for free. Why can't the government switch it around? Why can't they make up a proposal for the poor that want to work and give them in their working wages enough to live on and then they'll no longer need welfare?" Another woman said: "One person I know on CETA got welfare and Medicaid benefits taken away and is still making $5.00 less than when [she was] on welfare."

The lack of financial incentive, coupled with the general impression that the jobs offered are the most menial possible, may set up a series of resistances to the whole image of work programs. Four women mentioned the types of jobs offered as those least appealing within society. One woman spoke of welfare fathers getting menial "teenage type" jobs. Another said, "If they had training programs, halfway decent jobs besides cutting grass, clipping hedges or painting fences, I would like it. If there was a training program, something to make it constructive in some field of work." While many women feel work plays an important part in contributing to self-esteem, this last comment indicated awareness of the need for growth and challenge in a job setting.

Two other negative aspects of the programs were mentioned: the difficulties inherent in getting into a program (one woman made this point) and lack of trust in government-related projects (several women raised this objection). This lack of trust in programs or persons representing the system is also mentioned in other contexts.

As previously indicated (see Chapter 1), the 43 Stress and Families respondents include a greater proportion of more highly educated respondents than is found in the low-income population from which the respondents are drawn. Because of this, one might expect that, overall, these women would be somewhat better informed than many low-income mothers about the specifics of programs which directly affect their lives. The general lack of awareness is, therefore, surprising. It suggests a real lack of communication between the welfare department and welfare recipients; between policy intent and bureaucratic followthrough.

ABORTION FUNDING RESTRICTIONS

Historically, the issue of abortion has been complicated and emotional. Gilligan (1977) recently documented the complexity of decision making involving abortion. The question is intensely personal for many women, involving social, familial, and religious expectations. For low-income women the question of abortion is further complicated by economics and politics. Women on welfare who cannot personally pay for an abortion need the sanction of the government in the form of Medicaid funds. Not only are churches, families, personal feelings, and frequently the disapproval of friends, husbands, or boyfriends involved, but society in the larger sense must also give its legal permission and approval to a low-income woman's decision to seek abortion as a solution to an unwanted pregnancy. Many women believe this is yet another example of discrimination against women, especially poor women.

Some of the women interviewed are in conflict about the question of government restrictions of funds to pay for abortions. Thirteen percent responded ambivalently, with comments such as: "I don't really know. Maybe they should pay for it to keep people from having kids they don't want but I don't believe in taking a human life." However, when asked for their opinions about the "bill the Massachusetts legislature is considering which would prevent the use of Medicaid funds to pay for abortions for low-income women in the state," 60 percent of the 40 women questioned were opposed to the proposed restrictions. Four respondents were either neutral or were too unfamiliar with the issue to comment. Seven women (18 percent) agreed with the proposed restrictions.

The majority of women who agreed with restriction proposals, however, also indicated that they were either religiously or ethically opposed to abortion. The issue for them was abortion itself, whether or not the government provided funds for the procedure. As Ms. Olson, a Catholic said, "I have my religious beliefs about abortion. I feel that if it's for a woman's health then that's OK. There are some cases where it's necessary. . . . I feel with all the contraception available that nobody who doesn't want a baby doesn't have to get pregnant."

Ms. Sawyer is a Christian Scientist with six children. She says she realizes "some people become very desperate if they're expecting a child and can't take care of it. But I am definitely against killing life and to me from the very conception of a child that's life; an abortion is just a legal term for murder." Her comments are particularly interesting because she is extremely well acquainted with the "bleakness" of living in poverty and yet she still maintains "no matter how little money I have personally, no matter how little, how bleak my future looks, I always feel that my child born in this country . . . can always be taken care of."

The average number of children in the families within this pro-restriction group is five, compared to an average of 1.4 children in the families of the majority of women who oppose restriction of funds for abortions.

Because women on welfare need governmental approval in order to secure abortion payment, many women feel there is a built-in inequality regarding access to this medical procedure. Some women expressed the outrage they feel at the possibility that their already overburdened lives might be further complicated and even endangered. The question of restricted fundings is a vital issue which necessitates dealing intricately and emotionally with the system in order to get what other women who are more economically secure can acquire with few or no problems.

On June 12, 1979, the governor of Massachusetts signed into effect a bill which restricts Medicaid funds for welfare recipients to those women whom physicians certify as requiring abortions "to prevent the death of the mother." It was an act indicative of a current national trend. Now women on welfare have only three options open to them if they find themselves pregnant with an unplanned for child and cannot borrow enough money for an abortion: they can try to find an unlicensed practitioner and risk damage, infection, or death; attempt to induce an abortion themselves and face the same possible medical consequences; or compound their economic and emotional entanglements by having a child they do not want and/or cannot afford. Some women feel the system is trying to punish them. Some feel, understandably, that they will be held responsible for an action for which more privileged women are not held accountable. As Ms. Patterson put it,

> Everyone I know thinks that it's stupid to restrict government funds for abortions. Women are going to get abortions anyway. Poor women are either going to have illegal abortions or have babies they don't want and that is such a mess in terms of abused children and women stuck on welfare. . . . I mean what the politicians usually are into is saving money, which they do by supporting abortions rather than supporting the kids for twenty years and in punishing welfare people. I don't see how denying welfare people abortions, I mean yes, it's punishing them, but you're cutting off your nose to spite your face.

Ms. Palmer related one account of the extreme pressure a welfare mother underwent when she was pregnant and was unable to secure an abortion: "I went to the abortion hearings at the State House. Women [there] were desperate. One women . . . said her husband was leaving her and she was pregnant and tried to kill herself. Someone found her and then she was allowed to have an abortion. That's what she had to do!"

Comments by two other women emphasize the class discrimination they feel is at the heart of abortion restrictions. Ms. Ross feels that "many operations such as tubal ligations [sterilizations] that are done that the government pays for are controls over poor people. The government should *also* pay for abortions." Ms. Page is even more vehement:

> I think that's disgusting. You know how I see it? I see it as an overall plan. They start restricting abortions—only in certain instances can you get them. . . . It makes me laugh, a provision I read—three doctors have to write things . . . to save the health of a mother. How long will it take you to find three doctors? About eight months.

> Then I see President Carter start saying things like, "We should subsidize women to have children." What I see it as is . . . poor women have to have babies for the middle class to adopt.

Two recurring themes about which the respondents spoke were the potential for child abuse if mothers are forced to have children they don't want, and the additional economic hardship it entails. On the question of child abuse, Ms. Marks voiced the sentiments of several women: "If a person resents being pregnant, why keep an unwanted child and abuse its well-being?"

Five women specifically mentioned that part of their decision regarding the need for abortion funding involved the economic cost Ms. Oliver spoke of: "If funds are cut off it will cost more to finance another child. The money for needs and added expenses could be put to better use if the mothers didn't have to spend it for the abortion." Another variation on this theme came from Ms. Paine: "I feel the government is wrong in restrictions. [It] just adds another kid to the rolls. The ones bitching about it are the ones who can afford it."

Currently the abortion funding issue continues to be as heatedly debated as any restriction related to AFDC. It is an issue, as has been noted, which is affected by religious, ethical, and personal feelings. It is also the issue most profoundly affecting the individual women and their families who suffer the consequences of unwanted children. In the long run, most women seem to feel they, their families, and taxpayers all lose when an unwanted pregnancy adds, as Ms. Paine said, "another kid to the rolls."

OPINIONS OF "THE SYSTEM"

When asked, "Generally speaking, what do you think about this political system?" 29 women gave negative responses; 6 felt they were too uninformed to make an opinion; 4 indicated there was something positive about the system; and 3 women were "in between." None of the positive responses came from women with personal experience with the system, and none was emphatically positive (for example, "I think it works . . . well it can work, it has worked, it takes participation. If you don't participate you can't expect to get much out of it." "I think it's good but I don't really know that much about it.").

Not surprisingly, several women who had dealt personally and unsuccessfully with their representatives were the most dissatisfied. In fact, even the two women who had received some positive feedback from the system were unhappy with it. Ms. Hill, who praised one particular representative for fulfilling a promise to have traffic on her street restricted to one way after she procured the required number of signatures on a petition, still feels that overall "it (the system) sucks. I couldn't phrase it any better. The rich pigs try to speak for and control the poor." And Ms. Newman, politically active in several areas with a moderate degree of success, said, "I could almost go to socialism, but then you're afraid of communism. Being that it is the only political system that we have to work with, I'll use it."

The other women who have had no luck in communicating with their representatives were even more vehemently opposed. Ms. Ross indicated she is "extremely dissatisfied. The government benefits a select few with power and money." Ms. Frazier feels that "all politicians are out for themselves. They don't care about the people."

The idea of corruption within the political structure was a major theme. In fact, one-third of the women said they believe that, generally, politicians are not to be trusted. Repeatedly the women said, "It's who you know" or "Every time you turn around somebody is stealing money but they're not often prosecuted," The observations mentioned next most often were the lack of control respondents feel as low-income citizens and the belief that politicians never keep promises. Sometimes the implication was that politicians do not have to keep promises to the poor or average citizen, but that "the rich get richer" and the "poor have things taken away from them."

SUMMARY

The majority of the women interviewed have strong, though negative, opinions about many aspects of the political system in the United States. A surprisingly large proportion of them vote and have attempted to take some positive action by seeking out their local representatives to improve their own and their children's lives. These efforts have been mainly concerned with educational opportunities for their children and with securing decent housing and safety in their neighborhoods.

While 7 of the 40 women questioned are in favor of restrictions on abortion funding, the majority of women are strongly opposed to government restrictions. They believe it makes no sense for the government to withhold relatively small amounts of funds for abortions which will ultimately force poor women either to seek dangerous, illegal abortions or to bear unwanted children who may suffer years of child abuse and deprivation. Several women would welcome training and employment opportunities through the welfare system because they believe work is an essential part of life, but few women cite existing programs as functioning satisfactorily. Fifteen of the women who voiced opinions of work programs (almost 50 percent) are opposed to current programs for welfare recipients because they disagree with the mandatory aspects of the programs, especially for mothers with young children. They also believe the programs offer only uninteresting, undervalued, and underpaid jobs which do nothing to educate welfare clients or train them for desirable positions. In addition, there is a distressing lack of available information about work programs. The comments underline the need for possible restructuring and improved information dissemination (through welfare offices or elsewhere) that must take place before work programs can begin to fulfill the needs of those citizens for whom they are designed.

A few women have positive feelings about the political system in this country, but the majority express a marked distrust of politicians in general and dissatisfaction with local politicians in particular. Corruption, selfishness, disinterest in the plight of poor people, and the inclination to make promises which are not kept were frequently cited as characteristics of politicians.

It is also interesting to note that all of the women who have had direct contact with representatives of the political system feel negatively about the system. Frequently they voiced much stronger criticisms than women who are relatively more politically naive. Apparently their personal involvement with their local representatives has not been reassuring and may, in fact, have created an even more negative impression of how the American political system works.

NOTE

1. The Institutions Interview was written by Kristine Dever, Elizabeth Neustadt, and Polly Ashley.

REFERENCES

Brager, G. A., & Barr, S. Perceptions and reality: The poor man's view of social services. In G. A. Brager & F. P. Purcell (Eds.) *Community action against poverty*. New Haven: College & University Press, 1967.

Gilligan, C. In a different voice: Women's conceptions of the self and of morality. *Harvard Educational Review*, 1977, *47*, 481-517.

Kimball, P. *The disconnected*. New York: Columbia University Press, 1972.

Miller, S. M. Poverty, race and politics. In C. I. Waxman (Ed.) *Poverty, power and politics*. New York: Grosset and Dunlap, 1968.

PART IV
RELATIONSHIPS

10

SOCIAL TIES AND SOCIAL SUPPORT

DEBORAH BELLE

In recent years social isolation has received considerable attention as a risk factor for mental health problems and poor family functioning, while the benefits to be derived from social bonds have been widely heralded (see Cobb, 1976; Unger & Powell, 1980). Brown, Bhrolchain, & Harris (1975) found that when women experienced difficult life circumstances and suffered important losses, the availability of a confidant was an effective buffer against depression. Pearlin and Johnson (1977) reported that women who lived in the same neighborhood for a while, had really good friends close by, and belonged to voluntary associations were less likely than those without such social ties to report themselves depressed. Social isolation has been found to afford a context in which child abuse is more likely to occur when a parent is under a great deal of stress (Garbarino, 1977). Social support, defined as emotional and instrumental assistance from others, has been credited with substantial stress-buffering power.

Social support has often been measured by proxy variables such as number of friends or relatives, membership in organizations, or marital status (Dean & Lin, 1977; Eckenrode & Gore, 1981). Those who have certain kinds of social relationships have been presumed to receive more emotional and instrumental assistance than those who lack such social relationships. However, not all investigations have confirmed the dangers of social isolation or the advantages of social involvements. Andrews, Tennant, Hewson, & Vaillant (1978) reported that neighborhood interaction and community participation were not associated with superior mental health. Straus (1980) found that physical violence between husband and wife was actually more common among couples who had many relatives nearby than among those with few nearby kin. Cohler and Lieberman (1981) discovered that for middle-aged women in certain ethnic groups, extensive social ties were associated with psychological distress. Such findings suggest that social relationships may not guarantee social support and that the disadvantages of social relationships deserve attention along with the advantages.

This chapter first considers the types of support, such as child care assistance and emotional support, which are related to good mental health among the respondents. Then specific sorts of relationships are investigated: those with friends and relatives the respondent describes as important to her, and those with neighbors. The social support provided by resident husbands and boyfriends is considered separately in the following chapter.

Interviews with the Stress and Families Project respondents reveal that these women draw many crucial forms of social support from their interpersonal relationships. Yet social ties also bring additional stresses into women's lives, and in many relationships women appear to provide more support to others than they receive in return. The social relationships of low-income mothers do not automatically constitute a social *support* system for them. Instead, the costs of social ties must be weighed against their benefits to gain a complete picture of their importance for low-income women.

RECEIVING SOCIAL SUPPORT FROM OTHERS

Since child care responsibility was something all the respondents had in common, each respondent was asked whether there was anyone she could count on to take care of her children in case of sickness or some other emergency, and whether there was anyone who could be counted on to take care of the children if the respondent wanted to go out for a while or do something for pleasure. Responses to these questions were rated for the extent of *emergency* and *nonemergency child care assistance* they reflected. The respondents were also asked whether they received help with any of 10 day-to-day concerns, such as household work and repairs. The number of these concerns for which help was received formed the *day-to-day assistance* score. As a measure of *emotional support* each respondent was also asked how often she felt there was no one to tell how she was really feeling. Each indicator of instrumental or emotional support was scored so that higher scores indicated greater support.

As Table 10.1 shows, the social support respondents received is strongly reflected in their emotional well-being. Women with more adequate child care assistance in emergency situations had superior mastery scores, and

TABLE 10.1 Correlations Between Support and Emotional Well-Being

	Depression	Anxiety	Mastery	Self-Esteem	Stability of Self-Esteem
Day-to-day assistance	−.18	−.16	−.41**	−.27*	−.06
Emergency child care	.06	.02	−.37**	.07	.13
Nonemergency child care	−.26*	−.38**	−.42**	−.30*	−.29*
Someone to tell	−.26*	−.35**	−.29*	−.19	−.10

* p < .05
** p < .01

women with more adequate child care assistance in normal times experienced better mental health according to each of the five indicators we used. The amount of day-to-day assistance women received was associated with both mastery and self-esteem. The more help a woman received, the more she felt that she exercised control over what happened in her life and the more highly she esteemed herself. Women who reported more often having someone to confide in reported fewer symptoms of depression and anxiety and greater mastery over their lives than did women who more frequently lacked such a confidant.

These findings show that receiving help with commonly experienced needs, having someone to turn to, and feeling confident of child care assistance in day-to-day and emergency situations are associated with good mental health. Of these types of social support, nonemergency child care help is most consistently related to emotional well-being among the women studied. Sense of mastery was the most consistent correlate of the forms of social support studied, suggesting that women who receive more support from others feel more in control of their own lives. Finding basic security in other people does not appear to sap individual strength—quite the opposite.

THE NATURE OF WOMEN'S SOCIAL TIES

While all of the SFP respondents live in a densely populated urban area, each woman's personal social world is different. Some women are deeply involved with members of their extended families: mothers, sisters, brothers, in-laws. Other women have little or no involvement with kin. Some women share their households with husbands or boyfriends, others with a sister or a brother or adult children, and other women live with no other adult in the household. Some women socialize with their neighbors virtually every day, while other women have little to do with their neighbors.

THE SOCIAL NETWORK

Each woman in the study was asked to name the people who were most important to her, including relatives and friends. For the purposes of this discussion, this list of important others will be considered the *social network*. In naming the people most important to them, all the respondents living with husbands or boyfriends listed these men, and most women listed their children. We believe women decided whether or not to list their children for reasons connected to their interpretations of the instructions, rather than for any substantive reason, and therefore for further analysis we excluded the respondent's children from consideration as part of the network. Even so, for seven respondents the network was composed entirely of relatives, and, on average, over half of all network members named were relatives.

Twenty-four respondents named their own mothers as one of the people most important to them. This figure is particularly impressive, since only 35 respondents had mothers living, and half of these resided outside the Boston area. The importance to adult women of their own mothers has been noted in countless investigations (for example, Young & Willmott, 1957; Firth, 1956; Cohler & Grunebaum, 1981) and is once again confirmed.

The average size of the network, excluding the respondent's children if she named them, was between seven and eight persons. The great majority of these people lived within the Boston area, although an average of only one or two network members lived within the block where the respondent lived, and only about three network members lived within walking distance. Network members who had been known to the respondent less than one year were rare, and even relationships of less than five years' duration were a small minority. Most network members were seen at least a few times a month, and over half were seen at least once a week. Networks also generally were tight-knit, in that most network members knew each other. For over a third of the respondents the network was very tight-knit: over 80 percent of the possible pairs of network members knew each other. Thus, the social networks of these low-income mothers are characterized by "strong ties" rather than "weak ties" in the sense that many, if not most, network members were relatives or old friends who knew each other as well as the respondent, lived in the same urban area, and saw the respondent frequently (Granovetter, 1973).

Benefits of Network Ties. Some of the benefits of a relatively extensive, nearby, frequently contacted social network are seen in the extent of help and emotional support women receive from their networks (Table 10.2). Women who named more network members reported more child care in emergency situations. Those with more network members in the Boston area more often had someone to tell how they were really feeling. Women with more network members within walking distance had more day-to-day assistance, and women who frequently saw network members reported increased child care assistance in emergency and nonemergency situations. All but one of the

TABLE 10.2 Correlations Between Social Network Characteristics, Support, and Stress

| | Support Variables | | | | Stress |
	Day-to-Day Assistance	Emergency Child Care	Nonemergency Child Care	Someone to Tell	Relatives and Friends Stress
Number of network members:					
Named	.24	.30*	.13	.25	.34*
Living in the Boston area	.22	.24	.18	.27*	.31*
Living within walking distance	.31*	.16	.24	.03	.33*
Living within a block	.18	.10	.11	-.15	.45**
Seen at least a few times a month	.13	.33*	.09	.07	.27*
Seen at least once a week	.12	.37*	.07	.08	.32*
Seen at least a few times a week	.20	.29*	.29*	.16	.35*
Seen everyday	.25	.25*	.43**	.01	.28*

* p < .05
** p < .01

137

associations in the table are positive, and many of the correlations achieve statistical significance. Thus, the importance of social networks for instrumental assistance, particularly child care, and for emotional support are strongly demonstrated.

Costs of Network Ties. While interpersonal relationships provide mental health-sustaining forms of support, such relationships can also bring distress and pain, as many respondents told us. Ms. Webb, for instance, spoke of her mother, who is her major confidant and provider of daily assistance. However, Ms. Webb's mother drinks heavily and has been raped while incapacitated by alcohol. The mother's drinking and its consequences in the dangerous neighborhood where they live are constant sources of worry and distress to Ms. Webb. As she told the interviewer, "I will have a breakdown with all the problems with my mother! She is always asking me to do all kinds of things for her . . . and she has so many problems! She always gets into trouble."

Husbands and boyfriends were frequently described by respondents as a mixed blessing. Physical abuse and unmet expectations for help during a crisis were among the most serious problems women reported. While the respondents reported that they were more likely to tell good news to their husbands or boyfriends than to anyone else, women were not so likely to confide in these men when they had personal problems. Nor were they so likely to feel that their partners understood them better than anyone else did. As one respondent who is now single told us, "I consider myself much more free of stress and strife as a single parent, even though I would like the help of a supportive husband. I also consider myself fortunate to be out of the physical abuse. I consider myself lucky to be by myself."

Respondents also told us of distress when an old friend betrayed a confidence and "put my business out in the street," when family members turned their backs because of a divorce, and when relatives sided against a respondent who wanted to leave her physically abusive husband. Other women suffered when those close to them—husbands, mothers, or friends—experienced illness or other serious problems. Many respondents told us they provided more instrumental and emotional support to others than they received in return.

To assess the costs of network ties, we asked respondents to rate subjectively the extent of their worries and concerns about their friends and relatives. Each woman chose a number between 1, standing for no worries, concerns, or problems, and 100, standing for severe problems, worries, or difficulties all or most of the time. These ratings were made as part of the interview on stressful life conditions, which is discussed fully in Chapter 3. Women rated separately the stresses they experienced concerning friends and relatives, and these scores were averaged to provide a single score reflecting the costs of social ties to both friends and relatives.

The costs of network ties can be seen in Table 10.2. Greater network size, propinquity, and interaction level are associated with a higher level of stress (worries, upset, and concern) felt by the respondent about her relatives and friends.

Network Ties and Emotional Well-Being. Since members of the social network bring with them both support and stress, one might hesitate to predict whether characteristics of the social network are themselves associated with depression. Analysis reveals that women with large social networks, women who live in proximity to network members, and women who interact frequently with network members are neither more nor less likely than socially less involved women to experience depressive symptoms or high symptom scores on any of the other indicators of mental health (anxiety, mastery, self-esteem, stability of self-esteem).

THE NEIGHBORHOOD

While relatives and close friends were particularly important to the respondents, their social contacts were, of course, not limited to these individuals. Many women socialized and exchanged babysitting assistance, food items, and other forms of aid with their neighbors. We therefore investigated the neighborhood as a context for such sociability and exchange.

We found that while almost half (44 percent) of the respondents were originally from outside the Boston area, most had moved to their current neighborhood from a nearby Boston neighborhood or from another section of the Boston area. The median length of residence in the neighborhood was slightly over four years. Six women had lived in their current neighborhoods less than one year, six for more than 15 years. Four women had lived in their present apartments or houses 10 or more years, and one woman had lived in her current apartment 29 years.

When asked why they had moved to their current neighborhoods, many women spoke merely of the affordable rents or of the relative disadvantages of their previous apartments or neighborhoods. One respondent noted that her rent was cheap, and "they don't care if you're on welfare or how many kids you have." Another mentioned the "rough situation" in her last apartment, which was also too expensive. Women also had moved because of a fire in the last house, problems with landlords or fellow tenants, heating problems, and because their former house was sold. In evaluating their current neighborhoods on such attributes as personal safety, quiet, protection of property, and sense of community, respondents rarely chose the highest rating (very good). The average rating for each community characteristic hovered between "not so good" and "good."

Most respondents got together at least occasionally with their neighbors to chat and have coffee and to help each other out. Half of the respondents reported babysitting for each other's children more than once a month, and half reported borrowing or lending food items that frequently. The exchange of things like irons and snow shovels was not so frequent, and there was little exchange of small sums of money. Almost half the respondents got together for coffee with the neighbors at least once a month, and a third got together for coffee at least once a week.

With longer residence in the neighborhood came more neighborhood sociability and exchange. Long-time residents were more likely to borrow or loan small amounts of money, to borrow or lend food items and to help each other in other ways. However, staying longer in the same neighborhood was not associated with a more positive view of the neighborhood.

In most research which examines this issue, long-term residents of a neighborhood are found to rate that neighborhood more positively than recent arrivals, as Fischer, Jackson, Stueve, Gerson, & Jones (1977) report in a review of the literature on this topic. The lack of such a relationship in the present study can be viewed as evidence that the low-income respondents we interviewed were not able to exercise much choice about moving to a preferred neighborhood. In support of this interpretation, it should be noted that having lived longer in the neighborhood was marginally correlated with having less income ($r = -.25$, $p < .064$) and less education ($r = -.22$, $p < .078$).

Just as women appeared to choose their neighborhoods without great enthusiasm and without real alternatives, many women in the study appeared to engage in frequent interactions with their neighbors as a matter of necessity rather than free choice. Respondents with more difficult life situations, as measured by the Life Conditions Stressor Score, reported more frequent exchange of food items and small sums of money with neighbors, more frequent shopping for one another, more mutual assistance, and more sociable get-togethers over a cup of coffee than did respondents with less difficult life situations. Similarly, respondents who experienced more stress in their lives, as measured by the Life Conditions Stress Score, reported more exchange of small sums of money, more mutual assistance, and more frequent get-togethers (see Table 10.3). Thus, the most hard-pressed women in the study were the women who involved themselves in the most extensive neighborhood sociability and exchange.

A similar phenomenon was reported by Jeffers in her participant observation study of poor families in a housing project (1967). Jeffers noted that families with particularly "inadequate and uncertain incomes" and those for whom "the task of keeping a roof over their heads and food in their children's mouths occupied much of their time" were among those families with "the

TABLE 10.3   Correlations Between Life Situations and the Frequency of
Neighborhood Sociability and Exchange

	Life Conditions Stressor Score	Life Conditions Stress Score
Babysit for each other's children	.16	.22
Borrow or lend food items	.26*	.11
Borrow or lend things like irons	.13	.11
Borrow or loan small amounts of money	.29*	.39**
Do shopping for each other	.31*	.10
Help each other in other ways	.32*	.44**
Get together for a cup of coffee	.20*	.28**
Chat with neighbors	.05	.03
Children play with neighbor's children	− .17	.02

* p < .05
** p < .01

most extensive communication network in the project" (p. 19). Mutual assistance with neighbors made it possible to survive the worst times.

While the women who involved themselves extensively with their neighbors undoubtedly received crucial benefits, such involvement was *not* associated with overall measures of social support. The extent of neighborhood involvement did not predict the level of day-to-day assistance, emergency or nonemergency child care assistance, or the availability of confidants. Only two respondents ever named a neighbor as a potential confidant. Perhaps women turn to neighbors for mutual aid when other helpers are unavailable to them, or perhaps mutual aid with neighbors is a tenuous system in which women cannot feel great confidence. For whatever reason, the women who involved themselves the most with their neighbors were not among the best-supported women in the study. Nor did women who involved themselves a great deal with neighbors show mental health advantages over women who avoided such involvement. This is hardly surprising, since involvement with neighbors was associated with stressful life circumstances and not with social support. For the low-income mothers we interviewed, extensive involvement with neighbors occurred when women were in particularly difficult circumstances. Such involvement appears to be a useful survival strategy, one which is practiced by the most desperate of low-income mothers.

DISCUSSION

For the low-income mothers who were interviewed for this study, social ties proved to be a two-edged sword, associated with important forms of assistance and emotional support and yet also associated with troubling worries, upset, and concern. Other researchers have also described the social ties of low-income women as involving both costs and benefits. In her powerful account of social networks among low-income black mothers, Stack (1974) describes how the women she studied created informal exchange networks to help each other when the inevitable crises arose. The prolonged and essentially involuntary interdependence of friends and kin led to bitterness and hostility, as well as to love and trust. Stack also notes that those in a position to do without the exchanges of the network because of their greater access to economic resources tended to opt out of the mutual obligations such exchanges entailed. Thus, economic resources allowed women greater freedom of choice about interpersonal relationships, and economic stress reduced options and essentially coerced some women into relationships which they might otherwise avoid. Fischer et al. (1977) found that *"degree of choice* was usually the most critical determinant of whether people would be affected negatively or not by conditions many assume to be universally detrimental" (p. 199; italics in original), such as place of residence or proximity to kin. The reduction in a woman's ability to choose whether or not she will enter or maintain a particular relationship can thus be seen as one of the consequences of poverty. Among the low-income mothers interviewed for the Stress and Families Project, financial limitations made the degree of choice about where to live and among whom to live painfully small.

Collins and Pancoast (1976) have noted that "natural helpers" are generally those who are "free from drain" themselves. They are "sufficiently on top of their own life situations" to help others without fear of depleting their own "emotional and physical resources" (p. 28). It would appear from our work and from the work of Stack and Jeffers that the mutual aid networks formed by the most hard-pressed of low-income mothers do not conform to this principle. Instead, it is the mothers who are least "free from drain" who must band together for their own survival and that of their children. The woman who lends her neighbor a pint of milk also needs that pint of milk, and the woman who tends her neighbor's children for an afternoon expends energy and attention on these children that she may well need for her own young ones. A woman provides such aid because in return she can then request such assistance when she needs it badly. Yet the costs of such giving should not be underestimated.

CONCLUSION

A one-sided concentration on the advantages of social connections has been misleading in its characterizations of both the isolate and the socially enmeshed person. In order to understand the implications for well-being of a woman's social involvements we need to explore both the costs and the benefits of these involvements, and we need to consider the pressures which lead to involvements with an unfavorable cost-benefit ratio. While many researchers have attempted to abstract social support from the human beings who provide that support, one cannot receive support without also risking the costs of rejection, betrayal, burdensome dependence, and vicarious pain. This is probably especially true among the poor, whose relatives, friends, and neighbors are likely to be stressed and needy themselves.

This finding should not be taken to mean that it makes no difference to a woman whether or not she is involved in a dense network. The woman who is enmeshed in a dense, often supportive, but also often demanding circle of friends has different problems and different resources than the woman who lacks the support and the demands as well. We can conclude, however, that a dense network is not in itself protective of the mental health of the low-income mothers we have studied.

We can also conclude that for women who lack nearby relatives and friends, the provision of help with important daily concerns such as child care could be productive of better mental health. For women who already have such support, the opportunity to find relief from the pressures of intensive social involvements could be productive of better mental health. A woman who relies on kinfolk and friends for crucial needs because she cannot afford paid help has no way of reducing the stress that comes with enforced dependence. A woman who has enough money to pay a babysitter suddenly has a greater ability to moderate the stress in her life.

NOTE

The Social Network Interview on which this report is largely based was written by Deborah Belle and Cynthia Longfellow and includes questions based on the work of Virginia Abernethy, Laura Lein and her colleagues at the Working Family Project, Elizabeth Bott, Leonard Pearlin, Marie Peters, Rachelle Warren, and the University of Michigan-Wayne State University Detroit Unemployment Study. In addition, suggestions for this interview were received from participants in a study group on social support which included John Eckenrode, Susan Gore, Joan Liem, Marie Killilea, David Jacobson, Heather Weiss, and Alice McLerran. Stress and Families Project staff members also contributed many valuable suggestions to the interview and to the data analysis.

REFERENCES

Andrews, E., Tennant, C., Hewson, D., & Vaillant, G. Life event stress, social support, coping style, and risk of psychological impairment. *Journal of Nervous and Mental Disease,* 1978, *166* (5), 307-316.

Brown, G., Bhrolchain, M. & Harris, T. Social class and psychiatric disturbance among women in an urban population. *Sociology, 1975, 9,* 225-254.

Cobb, S. Social support as a moderator of life stress. *Psychosomatic Medicine,* 1976, *38* (5), 300-314.

Cohler, B., & Grunebaum, H. *Mothers, grandmothers, and daughters: Personality and child care in three generation families.* New York: John Wiley, 1981.

Cohler, B., & Lieberman, M. Social relations and mental health among three European ethnic groups. *Research on Aging,* 1981, *3.*

Collins, A., & Pancoast, D. *Natural helping networks.* Washington, DC: National Association of Social Workers, 1976.

Dean, A., & Lin, N. The stress-buffering role of social support: Problems and prospects for systematic investigation. *Journal of Nervous and Mental Disease,* 1977, *165* (6), 403-417.

Eckenrode, J., & Gore, S. Stressful events and social supports: The significance of context. In B. Gottlieb (Ed.) *Social networks and social support.* Beverly Hills, CA: Sage, 1981.

Firth, R. (Ed.). *Two studies of kinship in London.* London: University of London, Athlone Press, 1956.

Fischer, C., Jackson, R., Stueve, C., Gerson, K., & Jones, L. *Networks and places: Social relations in the urban setting.* New York: Free Press, 1977.

Garbarino, J. The human ecology of child maltreatment: A conceptual model for research. *Journal of Marriage and the Family,* 1977, *39,* 721-735.

Granovetter, M. The strength of weak ties. *American Journal of Sociology, 1973, 78* (6), 1360-1380.

Jeffers, C. *Living poor: A participant observer study of choices and priorities.* Ann Arbor: Ann Arbor Publishing, 1967.

Pearlin, L., & Johnson, J. Marital status, life-strains and depression. *American Sociological Review, 1977, 42,* 704-715.

Stack, C. *All our kin: Strategies for survival in a black community.* New York: Harper & Row, 1974.

Straus, M. Social stress and marital violence in a national sample of American families. *Forensic Psychology and Psychiatry, Annals of the New York Academy of Sciences,* 1980, *347,* 229-250.

Unger, D., & Powell, D. Supporting families under stress: The role of social networks. *Family Relations,* 1980, *29,* 566-574.

Young, M., & Willmott, P. *Family and kinship in East London.* London: Routledge & Kegan Paul, 1957.

11

FATHERS' SUPPORT TO MOTHERS AND CHILDREN

SUSAN ZUR-SZPIRO AND CYNTHIA LONGFELLOW

Interest in the role of fathers in running a household and raising children has heightened as both men and women begin to break down the barriers of the roles to which they have traditionally been assigned. It has been the father's role to provide financial support for his family, while that of the mother has been to raise the children and to take care of the household. The increasing number of women (including those with families) joining the paid labor force and the changing configuration of American families has resulted in less clear role delineation for men and women.

Despite the increased participation of women in the paid labor force, there has been only minimal change, if any, in men's roles in the family (Lein, 1974, 1979; Pleck, 1976, 1979). This has resulted in increased role demands or role "overload" for employed wives. The study of men's roles is thus important for the study of sex role changes in general, but also, more specifically, to assess the impact men's involvement in the family has on the well-being of its members.

Several studies have found that the father who is emotionally supportive of his wife and involved in his children's upbringing enhances his wife's feelings of competence as a mother (Abernethy, 1973) and increases her enjoyment in and responsiveness to their child (Feiring & Taylor, n.d.; Aug & Bright, 1970). Children may benefit in a number of ways from their father's involvement. One study found that boys who had frequent interaction with their fathers (more than two hours per day) scored better on a number of cognitive measures than did boys who had infrequent interaction with their fathers (Blanchard & Biller, 1971). In fact, children of low-involved fathers scored no better on the achievement tests than did children who had no fathers living with them. Rutter (1971) found that children who had a supportive relationship with their mother or their father were protected from stress which might otherwise result in behavioral problems.

This chapter examines the contribution made by fathers to the home and family front and assesses the importance of these contributions to the well-being of mothers and their children. We found enormous variation in the extent to which fathers were involved in the round of family life. Whatever help the father gave was support for the mother and children and contributed to their well-being.

In our sample there were 22 families in which the woman lived with a man, either a husband or a boyfriend. Regardless of marital status, we called all of these men "fathers" for the sake of simplicity, since very few of the families were organized according to the stereotypical model of a legally married couple with children, all of whom are biologically related to both parents. In some families the resident man was the biological father of some but not all of the children; in other families he was not the biological father of any of the children; some children had two fathers: one who lived with them but was not biologically related, and one who was their blood relative but not a co-resident. Here we will consider only support from resident fathers.

A series of interviews with each mother provided data on the extent of the father's contribution in four major areas: (1) financial support, (2) help with child care, (3) help with household tasks, and (4) emotional support. While we relied on the mother for a measure of the father's various types of support, the data were obtained from many different interviews, and questions were asked in a variety of contexts. Many of the questions asked were informational, not evaluative. For example, we obtained a great deal of information about the father's support with child care tasks from the interview on daily routine in which mothers were simply asked to account for each household member's time and activities. Other interviews asked more specifically from whom a woman received certain forms of support. For these questions we noted whether respondents spontaneously mentioned their partners. Other questions asked directly about the father's contribution: how much of the household's income was earned by him; what sorts of things he did with the children; whether he was someone with whom the respondent could talk things over.

We assessed the significance of the father's support to his family by correlating it with indices of well-being for both mothers and children. For the mothers we used scores on the depression scale and her stress ratings in the areas of parenting, intimate relationships, and money (see Chapter 2 and

3 for a complete description of these measures). For children, we used a self-report measure of their reliance on the father for help and support. The measure asked the child to whom she or he turned if feeling upset, frightened, happy, or in need of help, and we counted the number of times the father was mentioned. (For a full description of the interviews with children see Chapter 12.)

FINANCIAL SUPPORT

The traditional contribution of the father has been to provide financial support to his family. We assessed the father's role as economic provider by examining the mother's report of the breakdown of family income by source and amount. Full details on income were available for only 16 of the 22 families. (In some cases, respondents did not wish to supply specific information about their partner's income; in other cases, erratic work patterns or major illnesses of the partner prevented making an accurate estimation of his contribution.) On average, the fathers contributed slightly more than 50 percent of the household's income; their support ranged from 0 (two of the men were unemployed) to 94 percent of the family's total income.

Mothers were also asked how they felt about the man as a wage earner. An analysis of their responses indicated a certain degree of ambivalence about his performance in these roles: most (82 percent) of the 22 women with partners said that he was a good wage earner and that he spent money wisely (64 percent), but most of them also said that they and their partner held different views about the way money should be spent (82 percent). Furthermore, almost half of the women said their men had money problems, (43 percent) and the same percentage (41 percent) said their partners had work problems.

The partner's contribution to family finances was related to the level of stress the respondent reported in her relationship with her partner. As shown in Table 11.1, the more per capita income her partner contributed, the less stress the mother felt about her relationship with her partner. Furthermore, she was more likely to regard him as a good wage earner ($r = .50$, $n = 16$, $p < .10$), and in general her view of him was more positive ($r = .47$, $n = 16$, $p < .05$). There was no association between the amount of financial support and the child's view of the father as a source of nurturance.

CONTRIBUTIONS TO CHILD CARE

Data about the father's participation in child care were obtained from questions that asked specifically about the father—for example: "What sorts of things does your husband/boyfriend do with the children?" "What things

TABLE 11.1   Correlations Between Types of Support from Fathers and Outcomes for Mothers and Children

Type of Father's Support	Maternal Depression[a]	Mother's Parenting Stress[a]	Mother's Intimate Relationship Stress[a]	Mother's Money Stress[a]	Child's View of Father's Nurturance[b]
Financial support[c]	−.09	.22	−.36†	−.12	.30
	(16)	(15)	(15)	(15)	(11)
Child care support[c]	−.45*	−.57*	−.12	−.31	.45*
	(19)	(19)	(19)	(19)	(15)
Support with household tasks[c]	−.31†	−.45*	−.52*	−.51*	.13
	(19)	(19)	(19)	(19)	(15)
Emotional support[c]	−.40*	−.36†	−.27	−.17	.47*
	(22)	(21)	(21)	(21)	(16)
Positive view of partner[c]	−.40*	−.13	−.47*	−.09	.63*
	−(22)	(21)	(21)	(21)	(16)

NOTE: Numbers in parentheses indicate number of families for whom correlation was computed.
   a. High scores indicate higher levels of stress or depression.
   b. High scores indicate child names father more often as a source of nurturance.
   c. High scores indicate more support.
†p < .10
*p < .05

does he do especially well?" Other data were provided by more general questions about who was responsible for doing certain tasks for the five- to seven-year-old child in the family, who gave help with the children when the respondent wanted to go out or do something for herself, and who provided help on weekends or in an emergency. A child care support score was compiled by assigning a point to the father for each task area in which he was said to provide assistance. This scoring method permitted us to assess the father's overall contribution in this area and to identify the tasks in which he was most frequently involved.

All fathers made some contribution to their children's care, but there was enormous variation in the extent to which the fathers were involved. The maximum possible score on the support measure was 17; the scores of the fathers ranged from 2 to 13, with an average of 8.5. One mother described the degree of her partner's involvement with the child as follows: "He entertains her. [She] likes to jump in his lap. He's company for her." At the other extreme, another mother said that her husband "shares in the whole process of bringing the kids up." Over half of the men were reported to participate in play and recreation; discipline and supervision; and routine child care, such as bathing the children, putting them to bed, and fixing meals. The tasks least often done by fathers included tending to the children's health needs and taking care of them in an emergency or if the mother simply wanted to get out of the house for a while.

Although our analysis of the mother's responses to numerous questions revealed that all fathers were indeed making some contribution to the care of the children, when asked outright, "Who is helpful to you as a parent?" only eight mothers spontaneously mentioned their partners. When mothers were asked what they wished the fathers would do that they were not already doing, less than a quarter said there was nothing more to be done, about half suggested one potential improvement, and the remaining fourth had several complaints. The complaint most frequently lodged by the mothers was that the fathers should be more involved in disciplining the child. Discipline was also the issue about which mothers said they and their partners were most likely to disagree.

As shown in Table 11.1, the extent of the father's contributions to child care was found to be highly correlated with the measures of well-being for mother and child. Mothers who had helpful partners were less depressed and reported less stress about parenting. Children whose fathers were more actively involved in their care more often named the father as someone to whom they would turn for nurturance and help.

CONTRIBUTIONS TO
HOUSEHOLD MAINTENANCE

Fathers were less involved in household tasks than they were in child care tasks. Information about this type of help was obtained from the interview on daily routine and other spontaneous mentions of the father in response to questions about help with various tasks. For this type of support we simply scored "yes" or "no" depending on whether the father was said to provide any help with household maintenance.

Only 10 fathers were reported to do any type of housework. In general, the burden of these tasks seemed to rest with the mother and older children. When fathers did provide assistance, it was with tasks like washing dishes after dinner or with tasks done on an irregular basis. The father's contribution to housework was related to all of the mental health outcomes for the mother, as shown in Table 11.1. Women whose partners helped around the house were less depressed and stressed. Children's view of their father's nurturance did not depend on this type of support.

EMOTIONAL SUPPORT

In addition to providing for the family financially and helping in the care of the children, men are often an important source of emotional support for women, providing companionship, affection, and intimacy. A number of questions were asked to assess the quality of the relationship between the respondents and their partners and to determine whether the respondents turned to their partners for emotional support. In describing their relationships with their partners, most women agreed that their partner was affectionate, that he helped with problems in the family, that she could talk to him about important things (particularly good news), and that he was one of the four most important people in her life. Women also agreed that the major advantage of living with a man was the companionship he provided and the general help he offered. Nevertheless, when asked directly, "Who do you turn to for help with personal problems?" the majority of women did *not* name their partner.

Two indices of emotional support were computed. One reflected the degree to which the mother turned to her partner when in need of emotional support—for example, when she felt down or needed to talk over problems. The second index was developed from a series of questions about the characteristics of the partner—for example, "my partner is affectionate," "he appreciates me," "he doesn't act like he's the only one around." This second index reflected how positive a view the mother had of her partner.

Women who described their partners in more positive terms scored lower on depression and reported less stress in their relationships (see Table 11.1). The extent to which a woman reported turning to her partner for help with personal concerns was also related to her well-being: the more support a partner gave, the less depressed she felt, and the less stressed she felt about her parenting situation. There was also a clear association between a mother's positive view of her partner and her child's reliance on him as a source of nurturance. We found that women who turned to their partners for emotional support had children who turned to these men for nurturance (see Table 11.1).

SUMMARY AND DISCUSSION

These findings suggest that the support provided by fathers is related to reduced stress and depression among mothers, and to the children's view of their father as a nurturant person. It appears that for the mother, beneficial effects existed for all types of support from her partner. If his financial contribution to the household was substantial, she felt more positive and less stressed about their relationship. When his participation in child care was extensive, she felt less stress in her role as parent and less depressed. If a woman could turn to her partner for emotional support, she also experienced less stress and depression. Even his support with household maintenance tasks, which seemed limited even for the most helpful partners, was related to all mental health outcomes for the mother. For children, too, emotional support and involvement of their fathers in their care were closely related to their view of him as a nurturant person—someone to turn to in time of emotional need.

Although there are several ways in which the father's support may benefit his family, these findings do not indicate the nature of this process. It is most certainly the case that financial support and help with child care and household tasks ease burdens in these areas and therefore may remove some of the sources of a mother's stress and depression. Some researchers have suggested that support serves to validate a person's efforts in coping with various situations (Caplan, 1974; Weiss, 1974). Others have argued that support leads to successful role adaptation. For example, when the father is involved in child care and household tasks, he is sharing with the mother in a very concrete sense certain values and behavioral norms. The sharing of norms and behaviors validates the individual's performance in this role (Abernethy, 1973; Cochran & Brassard, 1979). The child's view of his/her father as nurturant is probably equally dependent on the father's physical and emotional involvement with the family. Since young children's conceptions of the parental role are largely based on the notion that parents provide for them physically (Saunders, 1979), the father's active involvement in their care would seem essential for them to view him as a nurturant parent.

We have no way of knowing whether the fathers in our sample, compared with other American men, were exceptional or simply average in their participation in family life. Time-budget studies indicate that men's family role is rather limited, averaging about 1.6 hours per day for all family work and 0.25 hours a day in child care. By contrast, employed wives spend an average of 4 to 5 hours a day in family work and 0.6 hours a day in child care. Nonemployed wives spend a total of 8 hours per day in family work and 1.5 hours a day in child care (Walker & Woods, 1976; Robinson, Juster, & Stafford, 1977; Pleck, 1979).

Why men have persisted in making only limited contributions to family life despite the dramatic changes in women's roles has been subject to speculation. Nye (1976) suggested that even though women's roles have been changing (as far as employment is concerned), men and women's attitudes and values about running a household and raising children have changed more slowly. He found that the majority of men and women in his study believed that women should have the primary responsibility for child care (and, in fact, more women than men held this view). Rubin (1976) found that both low-income and middle-income men and women agreed that it was a woman's job to take care of the household. The issue for them (even if the wife was working), was whether the man should help her with it. "With only a few exceptions, when a man does anything around the house that falls within the domain traditionally defined as the woman's, it is spoken of also as 'helping her' and is almost always at the wife's instigation" (p. 103).

Lein (1979) suggested that it is not that men perceive the work of the home as demeaning, but that they feel an inconsistency between the family's expectations of their involvement and the ridicule and stigma from friends and members of their peer groups for being active in family work. Furthermore, these fathers do not view paid work as an activity removed from the family, but rather as the primary male contribution *to* the family. Effort expended in home life is often perceived as energy diverted from the primary effort of breadwinning.

Leibow found that unemployment or erratically employed black men spent few of their many free hours participating in family life. Leibow suggests that "the greater is his public and private commitment to the duties and responsibilities of fatherhood . . . the greater and sharper his failure as the provider and head of the family. To soften this failure . . . he pushes the children away" (1967, p. 86).

These studies thus suggest that fathers may avoid involvement with child care and housework not because they lack commitment to their families but because of sex-role stereotypes. Some men seem to be held back, not by their own attitudes, but by the ridicule of friends and relatives who continue to have a traditional outlook, particularly by other men who feel threatened in their own positions by the active participation of other men.

Bernard (1981) has argued that men's "traditional" role as sole economic provider arose as recently as the 1830s and is already in decline. Our own study shows that there is much to be gained as men move away from this tradition and participate in other aspects of family life. In families where the father's contribution was greatest, mothers experienced less stress and depression and children were more likely to turn to their fathers for support and nurturance. Recent studies suggest that increased involvement in family life has payoffs for men as well: men reported that they expect to derive their greatest feelings of happiness and satisfaction from their families and not through their work (Pleck, 1979), and fathers who were more involved in the care of their infants were also more satisfied with their marriages than men who were less involved (Cowan & Cowan, 1981). Thus, greater participation of men in family life provides psychological benefits for all family members.

REFERENCES

Abernethy, V. D. Social network and response to the maternal role. *International Journal of Sociology of the Family*, 1973, *3*, 86-92.

Aug, R. G., & Bright, T. P. A study of wed and unwed motherhood in adolescents and young adults. *Journal of the American Academy of Child Psychiatry*, 1970, *9*, 577-592.

Bernard, J. The good-provider role: its rise and fall. *American Psychologist,* 1981, *36* (1), 1-12.

Blanchard, R. W., & Biller, H. B. Father availability and academic performance among third-grade boys. *Developmental Psychology,* 1971, *4* (3), 301-305.

Caplan, G. *Social support systems and community mental health.* New York: Behavioral Publications, 1974.

Cochran, M., & Brassard, J. Child development and personal social networks. *Child Development,* 1979, *50,* 601-616.

Cowan, C., & Cowan, P. Couple role arrangements and satisfaction during family formation. Paper presented at the Biennial Meetings of the Society for Research in Child Development, Boston, Massachusetts, April, 1981.

Feiring, C., & Taylor, J. The influence of the infant and secondary parent on maternal behavior: Toward a social systems view of infant attachment. Unpublished paper, University of Pittsburgh, n.d.

Lein, L., & the Working Family Project. *Work and family life: Final report.* National Institute of Education Project No. 3-3094. Cambridge, MA: Center for the Study of Public Policy, 1974.

Lein, L. Male participation in home life: Impact of work, social networks and family dynamics on the allocation of tasks. *Family Coordinator,* 1979, *28.*

Liebow, E. *Tally's corner: A study of Negro streetcorner men.* Boston: Little, Brown, 1967.

Nye, F. I. *Role structure and analysis of the family.* Beverly Hills, CA: Sage, 1976.

Pleck, J. Men's new roles in the family: Housework and child care. In C. Safilios-Rothschild (Ed.) *Family and sex roles,* 1976.

Pleck, J. The work-family role system. *Social Problems,* 1977, *24,* 417-427.

Pleck, J. Men's "family work" role: Three perspectives and some new data. *Family Coordinator,* 1979, *28,* 481-488.

Robinson, J., Juster, T., & Stafford, R. *Americans' use of time: A social-psychological analysis.* New York: Praeger, 1977.

Rubin, L. *Worlds of pain: Life in the working class family.* New York: Basic Books, 1976.

Rutter, M. Parent-child separation: Psychological effects on the children. *Journal of Child Psychology and Psychiatry,* 1971, *12,* 233-260.

Saunders, E. Children's thoughts about parents: A developmental study. Unpublished thesis, Harvard Graduate School of Education, 1979.

Walker, K., & Woods, M. *Time use: A Measure of household production of family goods and services.* Washington DC: American Home Economics Association, 1976.

Weiss, R. S. The provisions of social relationships. In Z. Rubin (Ed.) *Doing unto others: Joining, molding, conforming, helping, loving.* Englewood Cliffs, NJ: Prentice-Hall, 1974.

12

PARENTING PHILOSOPHIES AND PRACTICES

PHYLLIS ZELKOWITZ

Parental beliefs and attitudes toward child-rearing issues have long been of interest to social scientists. The influence of these attitudes on the personality and behavior of children is a persistent theme in the study of parent-child relationships. Child-rearing philosophies do not emerge in a vacuum. In conjunction with the personal history of the parents and their experience in raising their own children, the culture and environment in which the parents live serve to shape their views about child-rearing practices.

In this regard, many studies have documented social class differences in parenting attitudes and behavior. Interviews with parents have indicated that low-income parents tend to be more punitive and restrictive and less warm than their middle-class counterparts (Bronfenbrenner, 1958; Sears, Maccoby, & Levin, 1957). Preferred techniques of punishment are also said to differ: lower-income parents rely on physical punishment, while middle-class parents use "love-oriented" techniques, such as withdrawal of affection or reasoning. Low-income parents have been found to place greater value on conformity to external authority (Kohn, 1959); further, they stress such "traditional" values as neatness and obedience to adults, as opposed to the "developmental" values of self-reliance, eagerness for learning, and growth as a person (Duvall, 1946).

Observational studies of mother-child interaction in a laboratory setting have found low-income mothers to be more authoritarian, in that they make commands without explaining the reasons for them, expecting their children to do as they say because they say so (Hess & Shipman, 1965; Kamii &

Radin, 1967). In contrast, middle-class mothers are inclined to be more affectionate with their children, more responsive to their children's requests, and more likely to consult their children than to issue commands. They make more appeals to conscience—attempts to modify the child's behavior by referring to hurt feelings or behavior worthy of a "good" child.

The use of social class as an explanatory variable is somewhat simplistic, since it is not one variable but many. It can encompass differences in income, education, housing, the quality of schools, and the safety of the environment, among others. In the current study we sought to pull apart the variable of social class in order to examine how the life circumstances of low-income women affect the parent-child relationship. We wished, first, to discover how our low-income sample perceived the issues of parenting: for example, dependence, maturity demands, aggression, and discipline. Further, assuming that there would indeed be variation within the sample with respect to child-rearing beliefs and practices, we investigated whether such variation could be explained, at least in part, in terms of the stress experienced by the mothers and the feelings of anxiety and depression hypothesized to be concomitant with such stress.

This chapter reports on an exploratory investigation of these issues. It is the first of two chapters which discuss the impact of life situations and maternal mental health on the parent-child relationship. In this chapter the impact of stress and depression on parenting philosophies and self-reported parenting practices is examined. In the following chapter mothers' observed child-rearing behavior and the children's assessments of the parent-child relationship are considered in relation to stress and depression.

Each woman in the sample was asked a series of open-ended questions concerning parenting philosophies and practices, with particular reference to the target child (the child between five and seven years of age who was the focus of the behavioral observations). The responses to these questions were categorized using a coding system which was derived inductively through content analysis.

The reliability of the coding system was tested by having two persons code six interviews. Agreement between the two coders ranged from 81 to 89 percent, with an average of 85.2 percent. This level of agreement was deemed acceptable.

Each woman's responses to questions on a particular topic were coded for as many of the categories as were present. For example, there were four categories under "views of the maternal role"—ensuring personal growth, physical maintenance and care, satisfying emotional needs, and inculcating socially appropriate behavior. A woman's response could be coded for none, one, or as many as the total number of categories.

The chi-square statistic was used to test for differences in the use of the various categories. A cutoff point of $p = .10$ was used in testing for statistical significance.

Analysis of the material from the parenting interview indicates, first and foremost, that the fact of low income does not in itself result in a single set of child-rearing beliefs and practices. There was great variation within the sample in their views concerning a whole range of parenting issues: for example, views about the maternal role, expectations regarding obedience, techniques of discipline, and attitudes toward dependent or aggressive behavior in their children. Indeed, many of the mothers reported attitudes and techniques generally associated with middle-class parents: they saw their role as fostering personal growth in their children, and they used reasoning and emotional appeals when their children were disobedient. Furthermore, on such issues as the satisfactions or dissatisfactions of parenthood, the responses of the mothers in our sample were very similar to those of a national sample of parents (Hoffman & Manis, 1978).

However, a certain pattern of responses was characteristic of mothers experiencing stress, depression, and anxiety. These mothers espoused child-rearing practices which discouraged dependence while promoting self-reliant and responsible behavior. They also placed great emphasis on obedience and "good" behavior.

In the following sections we shall examine how certain child-rearing attitudes and values appear to be common among parents of young children, while others seem to reflect the stressful life circumstances faced by many low-income mothers.

VIEWS OF THE PARENTAL ROLE

There was a high degree of consensus within the sample with respect to the nature of parental responsibilities. First and foremost was the provision of physical maintenance and care (feeding, clothing, ensuring physical safety and cleanliness), mentioned by 87 percent of the mothers. The importance of satisfying emotional needs, such as providing love and understanding, was noted by almost two-thirds of the mothers. Instilling socially appropriate behavior (such as good manners and good citizenship) was a concern of 60 percent of the mothers, while half the mothers also saw it as their responsibility to ensure personal growth for their children (that is, fostering self-reliance, self-esteem, or imparting abstract values such as a knowledge of right and wrong).

When asked about the satisfaction of being a parent, nearly two-thirds of the mothers mentioned the fact that children provided amusement and companionship. In terms of dissatisfaction, the most common responses were the restriction of freedom and the fact that children were a source of worry.

These types of responses were also predominant in a national sample of married couples in the United States (Hoffman & Manis, 1978).

Thus, the views of the parental role expressed by the mothers in our sample seem to be typical of parents with young children and bore no relationship to any of the mental health indicators under study.

ATTITUDES TOWARD DEPENDENCE

Most of the mothers in our sample made certain maturity demands upon their five-, six-, and seven-year-old children. All but one of the mothers in the sample said that their children had to take care of their own rooms and belongings and to pick up after themselves. In addition, half the mothers expected their children to perform such routine household chores as doing dishes, taking out the trash, caring for pets, dusting, or sweeping. Mothers experiencing higher stress and depression were somewhat more likely to assign such chores ($x^2 = 2.73$, df = 1, p < .10, and $x^2 = 3.43$, df = 1, p < .10, respectively).

About a fourth of the mothers assigned what might be deemed fairly responsible household chores for five- to seven-year-old children. These included errands away from home, care for younger siblings, or meal preparation. Once again, mothers reporting greater stress were more likely to assign such chores ($x^2 = 4.50$, df = 1, p < .05).

When asked whether they would help a child do something which they felt he or she was able to do alone, all but one of the mothers said they would do so at least sometimes, and two-thirds (65 percent) said they would *always* help. Mothers with lower anxiety scores were more likely to say they always helped ($x^2 = 7.63$, df = 2, p < .05), as were mothers reporting less parenting stress ($x^2 = 5.09$, df = 2, p < .10).

Thus, while all the mothers in the sample expected their children to participate in household maintenance, mothers under greater stress demanded more extensive involvement and placed greater responsibility on their children. Further, while most mothers expected their children to be able to care for themselves and their belongings, those who were less anxious and stressed expressed a greater willingness to provide assistance if necessary.

Tolerance of attention-seeking behavior was another aspect of the mother's attitude toward dependence which tended to vary with the mother's level of stress and depression. Few mothers were unfailingly responsive to their children's bids for attention, though about 70 percent said that they would comply at least some of the time. Typically, mothers said they were unlikely to react favorably to their children's requests for attention when they were busy with housework, child care, or school work. This was particularly true of working mothers ($x^2 = 5.02$, df = 1, p < .05) and mothers of young families (whose oldest child was seven or younger: $x^2 = 4.59$, df $= 1$, p $<$ .05). It was more common for mothers of small families (that is one or two children: $x^2 = 2.98$, df $= 1$, p $< .10$), and mothers experiencing less parenting stress ($x^2 = 4.51$, df $= 1$, p $< .05$) and less anxiety ($x^2 = 2.72$, df $= 1$, p $< .10$) to say that they would not give attention when they were doing something for themselves, such as reading, sewing, or entertaining guests. These mothers thus seemed to be able to carve out some time for themselves during the day, either because fewer demands were placed upon them or perhaps because they insisted on preserving something for themselves despite their children's demands.

Although most mothers claimed to be understanding of their children's attention-seeking bids, a few reacted negatively. Six mothers (or 17 percent) said that they yelled or chastised their children, and four (11 percent) said they punished such behavior. Mothers of young families (where the oldest child was seven or younger) were more likely to punish bids for attention ($x^2 = 3.18$, df $= 1$, p $< .10$) , as were more depressed and anxious mothers ($x^2 = 2.98$, df $= 1$, p $< .10$, and $x^2 = 3.68$, df $= 1$, p $< .05$, respectively).

The difficulty depressed mothers have in dealing with their children's demands for attention is graphically illustrated in Ms. Chapman's response to the questions, "What does your child do when s/he wants some attention?" "What do *you* do?":

> He gets loud. He will do things that are totally ridiculous. Sometimes he whines. Usually I get aggravated, and I have to count to 10 and say to myself not to get too upset. Sometimes I beat him.

Ms. Stevens, who was not suffering from depression, was far more tolerant of her son's dependent behavior:

> He starts acting out either babyish-like or being bad. Or just in general talking a lot. . . . This means something so I usually set him down and talk to him and try and find out what the problem really is, and he usually cools down afterwards.

Many of the depressed mothers were acutely aware of the effects of their psychological state on their reactions to dependent behavior. Describing her response to her son's attention-seeking bids, Ms. Ramsey said, "I do the wrong thing. When I'm O.K., I give him attention. When I'm not, he gets punished."

ATTITUDES TOWARD OBEDIENCE AND DISCIPLINE

In addition to making greater maturity demands on their children, mothers under stress also placed great emphasis on socially appropriate behavior in their children. In other words, they were very much concerned that their children be obedient and well-behaved. Mothers reporting high stress and many depressive symptoms were more likely to see their role as inculcating socially appropriate behavior ($x^2 = 3.33$, df $= 1$, p $< .10$, and $x^2 = 6.52$, df $= 3$, p $< .10$, respectively). This was also true of single mothers and mothers of young families (those whose oldest child was aged 7 or younger: $x^2 = 3.96$, df $= 1$, p $< .05$, and $x^2 = 2.99$, df $= 1$, p $< .10$). Assuming that single mothers and mothers of very young children are over-burdened in terms of child care responsibilities, it is understandable that these women emphasize obedience and good behavior.

In keeping with their concern about obedience and "good" behavior, mothers suffering from stress, anxiety, and depression tended to demand immediate compliance from their children. When asked whether they ex-pected their children to comply immediately with their requests, nearly one-half (49 percent) of the mothers said no, while 31 percent said yes and 20 percent said that they sometimes did so. Mothers reporting a greater number of stressors and those experiencing more anxiety and depression were more likely to expect immediate compliance from their children ($x^2 = 6.96$, df $= 2$, p $< .05$; $x^2 = 7.46$, df $= 2$, p $< .05$; $x^2 = 6.74$, df $= 2$, p $< .05$, respectively). Mothers not suffering from these problems appeared to be more flexible, in that they expected compliance only sometimes.

Mothers were also asked whether they would follow through on their requests if their children did not comply. Nearly one-third (32 percent) said they did so all the time, and an additional 52 percent said they sometimes did so. The remaining 16 percent said they never did so. Mothers with high anxiety were more likely to be among the latter group ($x^2 = 5.51$, df $= 2$, p $< .10$). Thus, while mothers suffering from stress, depression, and anxiety had high expectations regarding compliance, they were inconsistent in fol-lowing through.

The presence of mental health problems also had an effect on the kinds of punishments mothers used. More anxious mothers tended to yell or strike back at their children. Similarly, depressed mothers tended to yell, to retali-ate, and to use physical punishment, while their less depressed counterparts relied more on reasoning and loss of privilege. Mothers reporting many stressors and experiencing greater stress were more likely to retaliate when their children engaged in hurtful or annoying behavior. This is particularly true of women reporting high parenting stress.

We cannot draw any conclusions about the relative effectiveness of these differing strategies from the available data. However, research evidence does suggest that while in the short term the use of verbal punishment such as shouting and yelling does result in compliance, eventually such sanctions lose their deterrent effect and may well serve as reinforcement for attention-seeking behavior (Martin, 1975). In other words, given the fact that mothers under stress are less likely to be responsive to attention-seeking behavior, their children may attempt to provoke them in order to gain the attention, albeit unpleasant, which is likely to accompany misbehavior.

In reading the interviews, one gets the sense that many of the mothers who said they shouted at their children realized that this was quite ineffectual. It seemed as though these mothers were exasperated and lacked the emotional resources to devise more successful means of disciplining their children. For example, Ms. Wood reported her annoyance at the fact that her child did not clean his room properly. When asked what she did about this, she replied, "Nothing—I just screamed." Similarly, in describing her response to an incident in which her son was acting out, she stated that she did "nothing—just yelled. But it doesn't help."

Reliance on physical punishment as a disciplinary technique may not have the consequences desired by mothers concerned with "good" behavior. Parents who use physical punishment frequently may be providing their children with a model of aggressive behavior and, indeed, are likely to have children who behave aggressively (Martin, 1975). Furthermore, these children are less likely to internalize standards of behavior than are children whose parents use reasoning in discipline (Maccoby, 1980). Thus, children who are provided with reasons for their behavior are more likely to develop self-control than are children accustomed to physical punishment for misbehavior.

DISCUSSION AND CONCLUSIONS

While the parenting philosophies expressed by the mothers in our sample reflected a range of opinions and views, stress, depression, and anxiety did have an impact on maternal attitudes. When mothers were experiencing such problems, they tended to make greater maturity demands on their children: they were more likely to demand that their children take a greater share in the running of the household, were less likely to assist with tasks they felt their children should be able to handle on their own, and were less tolerant of bids for attention. In addition, while all the mothers in the sample were concerned to some extent about socially appropriate behavior, the stressed, anxious, and depressed women placed great emphasis on this issue. They expected immediate compliance with their requests, though they could be inconsistent in following through. In the face of misbehavior on the part of their children, they were inclined to shout or to use physical punishment.

An examination of the life circumstances of low-income mothers may help us to account for the emergence of this particular constellation of attitudes. Two factors seem to be at work here. First, we may view the parenting attitudes of mothers under stress as adaptive to their environment.

For example, emphasis on the issue of obedience may well be related to very real concerns about the safety of the neighborhood. Kriesberg (1970) found that low-income mothers who lived in what they perceived to be very dangerous neighborhoods were less likely to believe in reasoning as a technique of control; they were more inclined to believe in spanking. Single mothers were more likely to overcontrol their children in more dangerous neighborhoods. Similarly, Silverstein and Krate (1975) have speculated that low-income Black mothers insist that their children obey them unquestioningly because of the difficult and dangerous circumstances in which they live. The mother's actions are motivated by the concern for the welfare of her children, and there is no room for discussion or compromise.

Second, the stress associated with low income may severely limit the emotional energy mothers can invest in parenting. Lacking adequate financial resources, the low-income mother is faced with a constant struggle to ensure the basic necessities of life for her family. Jeffers (1967) argued that in allocating scarce resources of time and energy, the low-income mother must give precedence to the provision of food, clothing, and shelter. This may leave her little time or inclination to respond to attention-seeking behavior or to engage in affectionate interaction with her children.

Mothers under stress may insist on greater self-reliance among their children in order that they might devote their attention to the youngest ones (Jeffers, 1967; Silverstein & Krate, 1975). Similarly, the assignment of household responsibilities to her children may also serve to alleviate a part of the burden shouldered by the low-income mother under stress.

In a study of maternal adequacy in a low-income population, Giovannoni and Billingsley (1970) noted that stress factors such as single parenthood, large family size, marital disruption, and inadequate housing are likely to affect a mother's ability to meet the dependency needs of her children, particularly in the area of emotional nurturance. In the current study, we have found that such difficult life circumstances take their toll on women's mental health. In turn, her feelings of stress, depression, and anxiety not only may diminish a mother's willingness to be responsive to her children's dependent behavior, but also may affect her disciplinary behavior. Such a mother often chooses to employ verbal and physical punishment, which result in compliance initially but which may eventually lose their effectiveness. Thus, the stressed, anxious, or depressed mothers might be using disciplinary techniques which are counterproductive, given their great concern with obedience.

Zussman (in press) has coined the term "minimal parenting" to describe the behavior of parents in the face of competing demands for their time and attention. In these cases, parents curtail warmth and responsiveness and engage in more punitive and critical behavior. Zussman explains the use of these disciplinary techniques as those seen to be the most effective at gaining compliance with the least expenditure of effort. The reliance of the stressed, depressed, and anxious mothers in our sample on verbal and physical punishment would seem to exemplify a minimal parenting strategy.

Despite the difficult circumstances under which the women in our sample were bringing up their children, many of the mothers mentioned marriage and family life when asked about their aspirations for their children. This was especially true of single women and women reporting high stress and depression. The joys of parenthood clearly have not escaped these mothers, who are faced with the grim realities of raising their children in poverty.

REFERENCES

Bronfenbrenner, U. Socialization and social class through time and space. In E. E. Maccoby, T. M. Newcomb, & E. L. Hartley (Eds.) *Readings in social psychology* (3rd ed.). New York: Holt, Rinehart & Winston, 1958.

Duvall, E. M. Conceptions of parenthood. *American Journal of Sociology,* 1946, *52,* 193-203.

Giovannoni, J. M., & Billingsley, A. Child neglect among the poor: A study of parental adequacy in families of three ethnic groups. *Child Welfare,* 1970, *49,* 196-204.

Hess, R. D., & Shipman, V. C. Early experience and the socialization of cognitive modes in children. *Child Development,* 1965, *34,* 869-886.

Hoffman, L. W., & Manis, J. D. Influences on marital interaction and parental satisfactions and dissatisfactions. In R. M. Lerner & G. B. Spanier (Eds.) *Child influences on marital and family interaction: A life-span perspective.* New York: Academic Press, 1978.

Jeffers, C. *Living poor.* Ann Arbor: Ann Arbor Publishers, 1967.

Kamii, C. K., & Radin, N. L. Class differences in the socialization practices of Negro mothers. *Journal of Marriage and the Family,* 1967, *29,* 302-310.

Kohn, M. L. Social class and parental values. *American Journal of Sociology,* 1959, *64,* 337-351.

Kriesberg, L. *Mothers in poverty: A study of fatherless families.* Chicago: AVC, 1970.

Maccoby, E. E. *Social development.* New York: Harcourt Brace Jovanovich, 1980.

Martin, B. Parent-child relations. In F. D. Horowitz (Ed.) *Review of child development research* (Vol 4). Chicago: University of Chicago Press, 1975.

Sears, R. R., Maccoby, E. E., & Levin, M. *Patterns of childrearing.* Evanston, IL: Row, Peterson, 1957

Silverstein, B., & Krate, R. *Children of the dark ghetto.* New York: Praeger, 1975.

Zussman, J. U. The overloaded parent: Results and reasons in family size effects on parenting. In B. C. Rollins (Ed.) *Family structure and process in the socialization of children.* Provo, UT: Brigham Young University Press, in press.

13

THE QUALITY OF
MOTHER-CHILD RELATIONSHIPS

CYNTHIA LONGFELLOW, PHYLLIS ZELKOWITZ, AND
ELISABETH SAUNDERS

As evidence accumulates on the adverse effects of stress on the emotional well-being of the adult, particular concern is raised over the plight of women with families. Having young children by itself is a significant source of stress (Pearlin & Johnson, 1977; Brown, Bhrolchain, & Harris, 1975), and the stress factor is compounded by the fact that the mother of young children herself is usually young, often poor, and, in a growing percentage of cases, shouldering parental responsibilities alone. Our own findings and those of other researchers show that stress produces an increased vulnerability to depression and other mental health problems (Brown et al., 1975; Dohrenwend & Dohrenwend, 1969; Pearlin & Johnson, 1977). The fact that low-income families with young children represent a sizable portion of the population means that a large number of children are growing up under stressful conditions that pose a mental health risk not only for their mothers but perhaps for the children themselves.

Substantial research exists on the effects of stress on children, much of which has examined children's reactions to particular stressful events such as divorce, death, separation from a parent, or hospitalization. For example, children whose parents have divorced have more behavioral difficulties than children from nondivorced families (Felner, Stolberg, & Cowen, 1975; Hetherington, Cox, & Cox, 1978; Tuckman & Regan, 1966). Other research focuses on the effects of particular life conditions on children's development. For example, one of the most damaging experiences for children is living in a conflict-ridden home where serious marital tensions exist between the parents (McCord, McCord, & Thurber, 1962; Nye, 1975; Rutter, 1971). In many cases, living with a single parent can be stressful for the young child: children from single-parent homes have two to four times the admission rate to psychiatric outpatient services than do children from two-parent homes (Belle, 1980).

Maternal mental illness is also known to pose a threat to the child's adjustment. Children who live with emotionally ill parents compared to those who live with parents without psychiatric problems are more likely to have behavioral or emotional problems (Rutter, 1966; Rutter, Tizard, & Whitmore, 1970; Rolf, 1972), perform less well in school (Rolf & Garmezy, 1974; Weintraub, Neale, & Liebert, 1975), and have more impairments in their relationships with their classmates (Rolf, 1972, 1976; Weintraub, Prinz, & Neale, 1978). There is some evidence that a child whose parent suffers from depression has more problems than a child whose parent has some other form of mental illness (Rolf, 1972; Cohler, Grunebaum, Weiss, Garner, & Gallant, 1977; Baldwin, Kokes, Harder, Fisher, Littlefield, Perkins, Schwartzman, Cole, & Baldwin, 1979).

In much of this research there is an assumption, implied or asserted, that life stressors or parental mental health problems give rise to some form of disturbance in the parent-child relationship, which in turn results in adjustment or developmental problems for children. Although little research has directly tested this assumption, there does appear to be some justification for this claim. For example, observations of families struggling to adjust to a divorce show that compared to married mothers, single mothers are less successful in gaining compliance from their preschool youngsters, are less affectionate, and use harsher, more authoritarian strategies for controlling their children (Hetherington et al., 1978). Clinically depressed mothers compared to normal mothers are less involved with and less affectionate toward their children and are less likely to meet their children's demands for attention and communication (Weissman & Paykel, 1974). Interviews with children show that they sense this diminished affection when their mothers are stressed or depressed (Zill, 1978).

This chapter investigates the vulnerability of the mother-child relationship to the effects of stressful life conditions and maternal depression. The previous chapter on parenting philosophies found that mothers' self-reported styles of parenting were affected by stress and depression. This chapter pursues the issue by focusing on the mother-child relationship from two other vantage points—naturalistic observations of children with their mothers and interviews with the children themselves. Over 70 children spanning the ages of infancy to adolescence were growing up in the homes of the 43 study respondents. Both the interviews with the children and observations of daily interactions revealed that a warm, nurturant relationship between mother and child was difficult to maintain when a mother was highly stressed or depressed.

ASSESSING MOTHER-CHILD INTERACTIONS

Interactions between mothers and their children were recorded during six half-hour nonparticipant observations in the family's home. One child in each family aged between five and seven was designated the "target" child and was the focus of the observations. During each half-hour session an observer made a written record of the target child's activity with particular attention to his/her social behavior. Mothers were asked to be at home while the observations were made, but no further control was attempted on the presence of other family members or friends.

Each running record was coded using a modified version of the Transcultural Code for the Social Behavior of Children developed by Whiting (1968). The coding scheme focuses on dyadic interaction. Its basic premise is that persons engaged in interaction have certain goals or intentions involving an exchange of resources, both material (for example, food) and social (for example, approval or comfort). The attempt by one individual (the subject) to change the behavior of another (the object) in order to realize a goal is called a *mand*. Each mand may be classified in terms of the interpersonal goal, the resource to be exchanged, and the beneficiary of the exchange. A mand may benefit the subject, the object, both of them, or the social group (such as family or society) to which they both belong. Because the coding system requires that a person's intentions and affect be inferred from verbal and gestural cues witnessed during the observation session, running records were coded by the observer who made them.

The running record was divided into units called *interacts,* which included the following elements:

(1) the initiator of the interaction (*subject*);
(2) the subject's goal or intention (*mand type*);
(3) the behavioral strategy employed to effect the desired change in behavior (*mand style*);
(4) the person whose behavior is to be changed (*object*);
(5) the response of the object (*compliance* or *noncompliance* to the mand); and
(6) the behavioral strategy used by the object in responding to the mand (*style* of *compliance*).

Although each target child was observed for approximately the same amount of time, the absolute number of interacts coded between targets and their mothers varied greatly. In order to create variables of maternal behavior that would be comparable for all families (that is, that would control for the variations in frequency of mother-child interactions from one family to the next), proportion scores were calculated describing the percentage of all interactions between mother and child that were of a certain mand type or that used a certain style of interaction. The particular maternal behaviors that were analyzed are described below.

MATERNAL MANDING BEHAVIOR

When mothers initiated interactions with their children, their mands tended to be one of three types: (1) *Nurturant mands* included mothers' offers of food, comfort, attention, and other material and emotional resources to their children. (2) *Prosocial mands* reflected mothers' instructions and prohibitions to their children regarding socially appropriate conduct in various situations, such as table manners, chores, school behavior, and behavior with friends and family. (3) *Dominant mands* were attempts by the mother to control the behavior of her child simply for the sake of exerting her will over her child. Dominant mands were distinguished from prosocial mands in that the latter were legitimate requests or commands which benefited both the mother and the child (by teaching the child the rules of behavior in different settings), whereas dominant mands were simply attempts to control for the sake of control.

MATERNAL STYLES OF INTERACTIONS

Since the overwhelming majority of interactions initiated by mothers were coded as using a neutral behavioral style (which included direct verbal requests, commands, questioning, and explanations), it was decided to focus on the more extreme styles of behavior—one positive and one negative. *Friendly-affiliative mand styles* were coded when mothers initiated interactions using physical affection, smiling, humor, friendly conversation, or positive affect. *Hostile-dominating mand styles* were coded when mothers yelled, scolded, threatened, or physically or verbally abused their children. It was also of interest to document the style of behavior a mother used when responding to her child's requests. *Positive response styles* meant a mother was responding to her child in a manner that conveyed positive affect (humor, smiling, affection) or in a manner that appealed to the child's sense of reason or fairness (for example, intellectual exchange, offering an alternative, reasoning and explanation). *Negative response styles* included the use of hostile-dominating styles described above and a particular style of noncompliance to the child's requests—ignoring.

MATERNAL COMPLIANCE TO DEPENDENT MANDS

A percentage was calculated for the number of times a mother complied with her child's dependent mands—requests for emotional and material resources such as food, attention, help, and comfort.

RELIABILITY AND VALIDITY

Reliability was established among five staff members who supervised the training and checked the coding of all fieldworkers. Percentage of agreement between pairs of coders ranged from .76 to .91. A question of validity is always raised about the effects of an observer on the family's behavior. There is no doubt that families were aware of the observer, and that they altered their behavior in some way while they were being observed. Because we spent a good deal of time in the families while written observations were *not* being done, it was possible to compare the official running record to our informal observations. In no case did we feel that a family was carrying on an elaborate charade for our benefit. The mother who avoided contact with her children during the observations tended to interact infrequently with them at other times, preferring to retreat to the quiet of her own room. The target child who was extremely dramatic (and who loved being observed) was a prima donna even when the observer did not have her pad in hand.

Because the coding scheme required observers to make inferences regarding the intention of family members, an observer bias may have been introduced into the observations. The hazards involved in making inferences are reduced if the observer is a socialized member of the culture of the persons being observed and thus is privy to the culturally shared meanings of behavior. All our families and the vast majority of observers were American-born and raised. Although we made every effort to assign observers to families on the basis of race, half the black families were observed by white researchers. Comparisons indicated that white observers in black families did not view the family's behavior in ways consistently different than black observers in black families.

MOTHERING UNDER STRESS AND DEPRESSION

Our observations of the mothers with their children showed that parenting suffered under the effects of stress and depression. We examined the correlations between the eight behavioral variables and the mother's level of depressive symptomatology, the extent of the difficult life conditions she experienced (life conditions stressors), the amount of stress she reported feeling about her life situation (life conditions stress), and the amount of stress she experienced over recent life events (life events stress). (See Chapter 3 for complete descriptions of the stress and stressor measures.) Mothers who scored highest on the measures of depression and conditions stress were the ones whose behavior with their children was most troubled. Neither life events stress nor the amount of life conditions stressors was a very good predictor of maternal behavior (see Table 13.1). It was the mother's subjec-

TABLE 13.1   Correlations of Maternal Behavior with Events Stress, Life
Conditions Stressor Score, Life Conditions Stress, and Depression

	Events Stress	Conditions Stressor Score	Conditions Stress	Depression
Dominant mands	−.24*	−.16	.04	.19
Nurturant mands	.00	−.22†	−.38**	−.36**
Prosocial mands	.16	.30*	.39**	.34**
Compliance to child's dependent mands	.04	−.30*	−.45**	−.52***
Hostile and dominating mand styles	−.04	.03	.12	.44**
Friendly-affiliative mand styles	.13	−.06	−.05	.00
Positive response styles	.10	−.11	−.19	−.35*
Negative response styles	−.24†	.08	.32*	.37*

†p< .10
*p< .05
**p< .01
***p< .001

tive state—feeling stressed or depressed—that was most clearly linked to her parenting techniques.

The pattern of behavior of stressed and depressed mothers was most notable for its lack of responsiveness to the children's dependency needs. Children's bids for attention, help, and even food were not granted and often ignored. By the same token, stressed or depressed mothers were less likely to direct nurturant mands to their children. Instead, when they initiated interactions with their children, it was usually for prosocial reasons—for example, to issue warnings, reminders, and commands to their children about correct behavior.

[Mrs. C is a highly stressed and depressed woman. She has five children, three of whom are home on the day of this observation, which takes place around noontime. Her six-year-old son, Charlie, is the target of the observations.] Charlie and his sister have been roughhousing in their rooms. His mother, who is in the living room, calls to them to cut it out. They don't and continue their playing. In a short time they come into the living room, and Charlie asks his mother if he can have a glass of water. She says no. He goes into the kitchen and he looks around and asks again if he can have some water. Mrs. C says no. Charlie plays some more with his sister—in sight of his mother, he calls to her to tell her that his sister has hurt him. His mother looks at him briefly but says nothing. Charlie continues to play with his sister. Mrs. C tells Charlie to get dressed and go outside. Charlie says he is hungry and asks his mother to fix something for him to eat. She ignores him. As he leaves the kitchen, Mrs. C tells him again to get dressed and go outside and pulls his hair as she tells him this.

While some behaviors were linked to both stress and depression, other styles of interaction were associated only with depression. Depressed mothers were much more likely to use hostile and dominating styles both when initiating behavior to their children and when responding to their children's requests. Typically they yelled at their children or threatened them. When a child made a request to a depressed mother, she/he ran the risk of getting no response at all or getting a harsh, negative one.

[Mrs. P has one of the highest depression scores in the sample. Her six-year-old son, Teddy, is the target of the observations. They are observed here at the supper table.] Teddy asks his mother, "Hey, Ma, it's good, right? I pressed down on my fork and it broke." (He is referring to a croquette.) Mrs. P responds with, "Get your fingers out of your mouth. Somebody better start eating!" Teddy adds, "Even this—" Mrs. P interrupts with, "I don't want to hear a word out of you!" Teddy returns to slowly eating his food and remains silent for the rest of the observation.

Depressed mothers compared to nondepressed mothers were much less likely to use styles that conveyed warmth, affection, or positive affect. Attentiveness, responsiveness, and warmth were observed much more often in the families where the mother was not depressed.

[Mrs. A has a low depression score. In this observation, she is with her three children, a one-year-old infant, an eight-year-old boy, and Paul, the five-year-old target child.] Mrs. A and Paul are sitting at the kitchen table discussing which valentines to send to which of Paul's friends, and what to say on them. The other two children are in an adjacent room. Mrs. A tells Paul where and how to write one of the names. She spells the name for him. Paul resists some of his mother's advice, but Mrs. A explains that he needs to write the whole name on one line. Paul works at it and then says to his mother, "I think I made a mistake." Mrs. A reassures him that he did it just right. Paul complains that he's not sure if it's right, but his mother quickly reassures him that it is fine. Paul continues working while his mother watches. She comments, "Paul, you surprise me with how smart you are sometimes." She shows him some new letters and asks Paul if he has made them in school. He continues working while his mother gives him lots of praise, encouragement, and specific advice about how to make the letters.

The effects of depression on maternal behavior were present regardless of other important background characteristics of the family. The same was not true for the impact of stress. Two groups of mothers were particularly vulnerable to the effects of stress—single mothers and mothers with large families. For both of these family types a pattern of nonnurturant, nonresponsive, and negative behavior was associated with the mother feeling a high degree of stress about her life situation. The behavior of coupled mothers and mothers with small families was not affected by the amount of stress the mother felt about her life situation (see Tables 13.2 and 13.3).

In sum, stress and depression appeared to take their toll on some of the more positive aspects of the mother-child relationship. Nurturing behavior, which requires anticipation of the child's needs and simply having the time

TABLE 13.2   Correlations of Maternal Behavior with Conditions Stress for Single and Coupled Mothers

	Single (n=20)	Coupled (n=20)
Dominant mands	.13	−.26
Nurturant mands	−.62**	−.27
Prosocial mands	.62**	.36†
Dominating-hostile styles	.46*	.06
Friendly-affiliative styles	.09	−.22
Compliance to child's dependent mands	−.70***	−.05
Positive response styles	−.55**	−.01
Negative response styles	.52**	−.18

†p< .10
*p< .05
**p< .01
***p< .001

TABLE 13.3   Correlations of Maternal Behavior with Conditions Stress for Small and Large Families

	Small Family[a] (n = 24)	Large Family[b] (n = 16)
Dominant mands	−.47***	.17
Nurturant mands	−.02	−.50*
Prosocial mands	.16	.43*
Dominating-hostile styles	−.15	.47*
Friendly-affiliative styles	−.02	.06
Compliance to child's dependent mands	.20	−.73***
Positive response styles	.15	−.61**
Negative response styles	−.15	.52**

a. One or two resident children under 16 years.
b. Three or more resident children under 16 years.

* p < .05
** p < .01
*** p < .001

and energy to pay attention to the young one's demands, represented a smaller proportion of the depressed mother's interactions with her child than of the nondepressed or nonstressed mother. Instead, the stressed or depressed mother spent proportionately more of her time issuing warnings, prohibitions, reminders, and general instructions. It is easy to see that the depressed woman's feelings of helplessness, hopelessness, and lack of energy would make her less likely to initiate nurturant interactions with her children. In the same way stress—a state of emotional arousal—would also divert a mother's attention from her children except when their behavior (or misbehavior) requires immediate attention—usually an instance requiring a prosocial mand. It is interesting to note that stressed and depressed mothers did not interact less frequently with their children than did nonstressed or nondepressed mothers. They simply attended to different aspects of their maternal responsibilities.

In other ways, depressed and stressed mothers interacted with their children in ways that could be considered more negative. They used more dominating and hostile styles and were less responsive to their children's dependency requests. Also, when they responded they used proportionately more dominating response styles and were more likely to ignore their children's requests than were nondepressed mothers. Depressed and stressed mothers also used relatively fewer friendly and affectionate styles of behavior when responding to their children.

Our observations are consistent with what other investigators of depressed women have learned through interviews. The most comprehensive of these studies, that by Weissman and Paykel (1974), found that depressed mothers had difficulties communicating with their children, felt a lack of affection toward their children, and expressed a considerable amount of overt hostility toward their children. Other researchers have also found that emotional detachment from one's children and feeling resentful and openly hostile toward one's children characterize the depressed mother's parenting (Cohler et al., 1977; Rutter, 1966). Links between depression and child abuse further point to the degree of hostility that may exist between a depressed mother and her child (Kinard, 1980).

Our observations of the mothers' behavior corroborate the women's own reports about their parenting practices that were described in the previous chapter. Depressed mothers reported less tolerance for dependent behavior, which corresponds to their lack of responsiveness to their children's dependency requests. The greater emphasis stressed and depressed mothers said they placed on socially appropriate behavior was reflected in the greater proportion of socializing and disciplining behavior we observed among them. Furthermore, the mothers recognized that depression affected their relationships with their children. We asked each woman what she found hardest to do when she felt depressed. The most frequent responses concerned housework and "getting going," but the next most frequent response concerned interacting with the children. One woman said, "I have less patience with the children." Another said it is "hard to get activities going for the kids." Other women cited "play [the] mother role," "handle the kids," "coping with [my daughter]," and "patience with the child" as the things they found hardest to do when they were depressed.

THE CHILDREN'S VIEW

We completed our investigation of the impact of stress and depression on the mother-child relationship by asking children for their view. All children over the age of five[1] were administered three self-report scales that assessed the quality of their relationships with their mothers (or both parents when both were present in the house). The Swanson Parent-Child Relationship Scale (Swanson, 1950) included 50 statements describing various feelings which a child might have about his/her parents—for example, "my parents are my friends." Children were asked to indicate whether these statements reflected their true feelings about their parents. The Nurturance Scale, designed for this study, consisted of nine questions asking the child to whom she or he would turn in times of upset, worry, fear, or other needs. The scale was scored for the number of times a child mentioned his or her mother as a source of support. The Punishment Scale was taken from Bronfenbrenner's Questionnaire for Children Concerning Parental Behavior (Siegelman, 1965). It contained 11 statements describing various kinds of punishments, such as "I get sent out of the room" or "my parents nag me." The children were asked to indicate on a rating scale how frequently they experienced these kinds of punishments. Their answers were interpreted as indicating the children's appraisals of the punitiveness of their parent(s) rather than as factual information about the frequency with which they were punished.

Correlations were computed between the mothers' scores on the conditions stress and depression measures and the responses of the youngest child interviewed in each family.[2] Thus, the views expressed here are those of 31 children ranging in age from five to eight years. We found that children of stressed or depressed mothers were less likely to view their family life as a happy one compared to children whose mothers had lower stress or depression scores (see Table 13.4). The children's view of their mothers as nurturant and nonpunitive was not dependent on her level of stress or depression. Young children were likely to turn to their mothers for support regardless of her self-reported emotional state (see Table 13.4). Both coupled status and family size were related to children's view of their home life. Children of single mothers were less likely to depend on their mothers for

TABLE 13.4   Correlations Between Mothers' Stress and Depression Scores and Children's Questionnaire Scores (n = 31)

	Parent-Child Relationship Scale	Nurturance Scale	Punishment Scale
Conditions stressors	.25	−.06	.06
Conditions stress	.35*	−.05	−.04
Depression	.34*	−.23	.03

* p < .05

nurturance than were children whose mothers were coupled. Less favorable views of the parent-child relationship were held by children from large families compared to children from small families. Children's reports concurred with our observations that large families and single parenthood can lead to strained relationships between mother and child.

The views of the Stress and Families Project children correspond with those of seven- to eleven-year-old children interviewed in a nationwide survey (Zill, 1978). The survey found that mothers' anxiety, depression, and negative attitudes toward parenthood were related to children's reports that their parents neglect and belittle them. The study also found that children living with two happily married parents or with a widowed mother reported happier relationships with their parent(s) than did children living with two unhappily married parents or with a divorced or a never-married mother.

Our findings suggest that children are sensitive to their mother's emotional state and that they experience her depression in the form of a less satisfying family life. Two children whose mothers had very high depression scores commented that the way to make their mothers happy was to "leave her alone" and to "get out of the house." It has been suggested that the heightened sensitivity to their parents' emotional states displayed by children whose parents are separated or divorced is a positive step toward growth and maturity (Weiss, 1979). Our findings suggest that such an awareness has a painful side as well. Even more poignant is the fact that as troubled as their relationships with their mothers might be, youngsters still turned to them for nurturance and understanding.

CONCLUSIONS AND DISCUSSION

Our findings confirm what many other researchers have suspected: the quality of the mother-child relationship suffers when a mother feels stressed or depressed. The highly stressed or depressed mother is likely to behave in a way that is unresponsive, inattentive, and even hostile toward her children, and her child's sense of security in their relationship is shaken.

That the effects of stress and depression so completely permeate family life is cause for concern, particularly for the children. The importance of a good relationship with at least one parent has been identified as a protective factor which buffers children from the potentially adverse effects of life condition stressors such as marital discord, parental mental illness, and social disadvantage (Rutter, 1979). The children in our sample all lived in poverty, and many of them faced multiple life stressors. Thus, their need for a supportive relationship with their mothers was even greater if they were to withstand the adverse effects of their life situations. However, as Chapter 3 reports, adverse life situations were strongly correlated with maternal feelings of stress and depression, which, in turn, we found to detract from a positive parent-child relationship. It would be a no-win situation except for the fact that life condition stressors—the root of many maternal mental health problems—were not related to children's feelings about home life, nor were they as closely associated with maternal behavior as were stress and depression. Thus, children's relationships with their mothers were not directly threatened by an adverse life situation but were jeopardized by their mother's emotional state. If we can buffer a mother's mental health from the ill effects of life condition stressors, then we can protect the supportive relationship between mother and child.

Although our findings point to the importance of the mother's emotional state in providing a nurturant, supportive environment for her children, we do not wish to leave the impression that depressed and stressed mothers are inadequate or uncaring parents. The women in our study expressed a great deal of concern for their children. The mothers were faced with parenting young children under trying life conditions, and many verbalized the difficulties they had in giving their children the kind of care and upbringing they wanted them to have. The women who were rearing their children under less difficult life conditions were better able to be the kind of parents they wanted to be. Thus, efforts to improve the life situations of low-income mothers through economic security, assistance with child care, and improved access to medical care could also alleviate the emotional problems that erode the quality of the mother-child relationship.

NOTES

1. We originally excluded children under age six because we believed they would not understand the questions. Subsequently we decided to try interviewing five-year-olds and were able to complete the questionnaires with many of them successfully.

2. In 12 of the families no child was interviewed.

REFERENCES

Baldwin, A. L., Kokes, R., Harder, D., Fisher, L., Littlefield, N., Perkins, P., Schwartzman, P., Cole, R., & Baldwin, C. The relation of mental illness of the parent to the social competence of the child. Symposium presented at the Biennial Meeting of the Society for Research on Child Development, San Francisco, 1979.

Belle, D. Who uses mental health facilities? In M. Guttentag, S. Salasin, & D. Belle (Eds.) *The mental health of women.* New York: Academic Press, 1980.

Brown, G. W., Bhrolchain, M. N., & Harris, T. Social class and psychiatric disturbance among women in an urban population. *Sociology,* 1975, *9,* 225-254.

Cohler, B., Grunebaum, H., Weiss, J., Garner, E., & Gallant, D. H. Disturbances of attention among schizophrenic, depressed and well mothers and their young children. *Journal of Child Psychology and Psychiatry,* 1977, *18,* 115-135.

Dohrenwend, B. P., & Dohrenwend, B. S. *Social status and psychological disorder: A causal inquiry.* New York: John Wiley, 1969.

Felner, R. O., Stolberg, A., & Cowen, E. L. Crisis events and school mental health referral patterns of young children. *Journal of Consulting and Clinical Psychology,* 1975, *43,* 305-310.

Hetherington, E. M., Cox, M., & Cox, R. The aftermath of divorce. In J. H. Stevens, Jr., & M. Mathews (Eds.) *Mother/child father/child relationships.* Washington, DC: National Association for the Education of Young Children, 1978.

Kinard, E. M. Child abuse and depression: Cause or consequence? Paper presented at the annual meeting of the American Public Health Association, Detroit, Michigan, October 1980.

McCord, J., McCord, W., & Thurber, E. Some effects of paternal absence on male children. *Journal of Abnormal and Social Psychology,* 1962, *64,* 361-369.

Nye, F. I. Child adjustment in broken and in unhappy unbroken homes. *Marriage and Family Living,* 1957, *19,* 356-360.

Pearlin, L., & Johnson, J. Marital status, life-strains and depression. *American Sociological Review,* 1977, *43,* 704-715.

Rolf, J. The social and academic competence of children vulnerable to schizophrenia and other pathologies: Current status. *Journal of Abnormal Psychology,* 1972, *80,* 225-243.

Rolf, J. Peer status and the directionality of symptomatic behavior. *American Journal of Orthopsychiatry,* 1976, *46,* 74-87.

Rolf, J., & Garmezy, N. The school performance of children vulnerable to behavior pathology. In D. F. Ricks et al. (Eds.) *Life history research in psychopathology* (Vol. 3). Minneapolis: University of Minnesota Press, 1974.

Rutter, M. *Children of sick parents: An environmental and psychiatric study.* Institute of Psychiatry Maudsley Monograph No. 16, London: Oxford University Press, 1966.

Rutter, M. Parent-child separation: Psychological effects on the children. *Journal of Child Psychology and Psychiatry,* 1971, *12,* 233-260.

Rutter, M. Protective factors in children's responses to stress and disadvantage. In M. W. Kent & J. E. Rolf (Eds.) *Primary prevention of psychopathology. Vol. III: Social competence in children.* Hanover, NH: University Press of New England, 1979.

Rutter, M., Tizard, J., & Whitmore, K. *Education, health and behavior.* New York: John Wiley, 1970.

Siegelman, M. Evaluation of Bronfenbrenner's questionnaire for children concerning parental behavior. *Child Development,* 1965, *36,* 163-174.

Swanson, G. W. The development of an instrument for rating child-parent relationships. *Social Forces,* 1950, *29,* 84-90.

Tuckerman, J., & Regan, R. A. Intactness of the home and behavioral problems in children. *Journal of Child Psychology and Psychiatry,* 1966, *7,* 225-233.

Weintraub, S., Neale, J. B., & Liebert, D. E. Teacher ratings of children vulnerable to psychopathology. *American Journal of Orthopsychiatry,* 1975, *45,* 839-845.

Weintraub, S., Prinz, R. J., & Neale, J. B. Peer evaluations of the competence of children vulnerable to psychopathology. *Journal of Abnormal Child Psychology,* 1978, *6,* 461-474.

Weiss, R. S. Growing up a little faster: The expereince of growing up in a single-parent household. *Journal of Social Issues,* 1979, *35,* 97-111.

Weissman, M. M., & Paykel, E. S. *The depressed woman.* Chicago: University of Chicago Press, 1974.

Whiting, B. A transcultural code for the social behavior of children. Unpublished paper, Harvard University, 1968.

Zill, N. Divorce, marital happiness and the mental health of children: Findings from the Foundation for Child Development National Survey of Children. Unpublished report, 1978.

PART V
WELL-BEING

14

THE CHALLENGE OF COPING

DIANA DILL AND ELLEN FELD

The preceding exposition of the stress-provoking conditions with which low-income mothers must cope naturally leads one to ask how these women experience and manage stress, with what impact on their lives and their mental health, and what differentiates those women who survive stressful conditions from those who succumb. The following pages will examine the process of experiencing and managing stress, a process which mediates the associations we find between stressful living conditions and poor mental health outcomes. This process is revealed in the ways these women talk about their lives. In the two quotations below, we can observe how women perceive their problems, try to make sense of them, and try to manage them successfully:

> I'm beginning to learn that no matter what happened in your past, you have to keep pushing today. I've learned through experiences and won't repeat mistakes. There are concrete reasons why I'm 27 and just getting a B.A. I cope by thinking that the way I've done this makes sense because I was ready for all this at a later time. When I was in college and my father couldn't help pay tuition and then I got pregnant, I really had no choices. Now that I'm older and understand more, there's no question that I can be responsible for myself. I

AUTHOR'S NOTE: Portions of this chapter were reprinted from "The Impact of the Environment on the Coping Efforts of Low-Income Mothers," D. Dill, E. Feld, J. Martin, S. Beukema, and D. Belle, in *Family Relations,* October 1980, pp. 503-509. Copyright 1980 by the National Council on Family Relations. Reprinted by permission. The authors would like to thank Jacqueline Martin for writing the Coping Interview from which material for this chapter was drawn, as well as Stephanie Beukema for helping with data analysis.

turn to myself rather than to others. Things happen, like my daughter gets hurt, or I get behind in school and don't recover. I used to have the illusion that people would help. It's clear now that if I don't do it, it won't get done. You get better as each emergency comes up. If I relinquish too much control, I'm afraid I'll use it as an excuse to avoid facing up and getting things done. Like when you know how to control money, you are not depressed by it. Sometimes I feel deprived, but I'll go out and buy something and feel better. I can afford it—I just have to let a bill go. I don't buy anything ridiculous, like a car. Things may be difficult, but I've gained a sense that I'll always get by—always get under the wire. My survival is directly proportionate to how angry I can get.

The car broke down last summer, my medical bills and Christmas, all three situations affected our finances. When the car [essential to her husband's home-based business] broke down, I kept saying "tomorrow it will be fixed." At the end of two months I couldn't stand it any longer and it got fixed. It will change tomorrow. It won't stay this way forever. Things turn out well. We take responsibility faster. We tighten our belts. We were overspending. There are always ways of cutting down. I cut the brillo pads in half and used liquid detergent for shampoo. It makes you appreciate shampoo when you have it. Finances are the biggest problem in my life. I was going to get a small store. My philosophy is that this is not my time in life. It doesn't mean it wasn't a good idea: maybe next year will be a better time. That philosophy usually works.

For most people, the word "coping" conjures up a wide range of ideas regarding human functioning. "Coping" is most frequently associated with ways people adapt or adjust to stress. It has also been used to describe day-to-day problem solving, mastery efforts, and normal ego functioning. Given the seeming lack of consensus in the literature regarding how coping is to be defined and what function it serves, one is likely to encounter a comparable range of ideas regarding what domain of human functioning should be studied, whether behavior, thought, affect, or physiology. Bypassing these debates for the time being, we set out to discover empirically how low-income mothers experienced and dealt with problematic situations, using as data what they knew consciously about their experiences. What we found was not only evidence of extraordinary resourcefulness, ingenuity, and flexibility, but also evidence of evolving belief systems, such as those contained in the words of the two women above, according to which the women constructed and negotiated their experiences. Philosophies such as "I'll always get by . . . my survival is directly proportionate to how angry I can get" and "This is not my time in life . . . next year will be better" suggest that something more profound is occurring beneath the surface of negotiating daily life or emergency situations. It seemed as if a motivational urge toward consistency of experience served to guide these individuals through troublesome or uncharted terrain. That is, not only did they try to cope with the immediate implications of a current situation, they also tried to make meaning of it in terms of how it could be integrated into their ongoing lives.

We also found that respondents engaged in a multiphasic process of "digesting" and responding to environmental stressors. Although the forms of "digestion" and response differed, we found a similarity in the structures of these processes. That is, once something has been recognized as threatening, the process of coping follows an identifiable path. Other chapters in this book have highlighted the detrimental effects of stressful living conditions—predicated by low income—on women's mental health. What we focus on in this chapter are the processes by which stressors are digested and managed.

In order to understand the relationship of stress-provoking conditions to mental health, we need a model of coping, a model which is true to the phenomenological experiences of these women. This chapter develops such a model of coping, one which considers the interplay of the person's unique phenomenology with her life context as she attempts to understand and come to grips with stressful experiences. This model represents an integration of various threads of current coping theory with respondents' descriptions of how they experienced 128 different stressful situations. We end by discussing how this model can help us understand the detrimental impact of stressful conditions on mental health.

THE PROCESS OF COPING

Traditional coping research has tended to focus on coping *strategies*, for the purposes of identifying and evaluating either strategies used by individuals across situations or strategies used in certain types of situations across individuals. The first type of research attempts to identify generalized coping styles. An example of this is the simple model of coping styles proposed by Byrne (1964) and Lefcourt (1966), who suggest that individuals tend toward either repression of or sensitization to stress-provoking stimuli. The second type of research identifies coping strategies particular to specific types of stress. Pearlin and Schooler (1978), for example, assessed the efficacy of different coping strategies used to address problems within broad life areas such as occupation, parenting, and marriage. While such research is useful in defining more clearly specific components of the coping process, the focus on the coping strategy alone may define coping too narrowly. It neglects the cognitive processes and environmental contingencies which precede and follow the implementation of a coping strategy.

Only recently have coping researchers attended to the cognitive mediation of stress experiences. Lazarus, Averill and Opton (1974) initiated this approach, describing three cognitive processes involved in coping: first, the recognition and interpretation of a threat inherent in a situation, second, the perception and appraisal of possible coping strategies, and, third, a reconsideration of the initial appraisal of the situation. We have adapted and expanded the cognitive mediation model of coping proposed by Lazarus et al. to illustrate more fully the phases through which coping proceeds.

The impact of environmental contexts on coping has been neglected in coping theory as well. Our work with low-income mothers has dramatically demonstrated the undeniable effects of environmental contexts on the coping process. Most models of coping emphasize instead personality traits or processes. The "sources of variance" model of coping, developed by Lazarus et al. (1974), is unique in coping research in allowing for the analysis of situational effects. To date, however, we have no model of coping which systematically describes the various mechanisms by which the person's environment affects the process of coping. Our work represents a step toward elaborating these effects. If we conceive of coping as a process of sequential phases in which the person and her environmental context carry out some transaction, we can describe the nature of the person-context transactions which occur at each phase.

In our schematic model of coping, a single coping episode consists of four phases. A situation is perceived as something with which the woman must cope. She then searches for a means of coping with it. The coping is put into effect and its outcome is observed. Outcomes are evaluated in terms of the success of the chosen coping strategy and in terms of their implications for the self. Based on these evaluations, new coping strategies may be initiated. (See Figure 14.1 for a schematic representation of this process.) This is a simplified structural model of a single coping episode. Coping is rarely this simple, however. Stressful situations often involved multiple threats, and multiple coping strategies may be used. Also, environmental feedback and cognitive restructuring of a situation tend to be more fluid and ongoing than we have conceptualized them here. This structural model, however, allows us to schematize what occurs as a person copes with a single threat, with one coping strategy, and a clear direct outcome of that strategy.

In this chapter we will use the single coping episode model to illustrate the process of person-environment transactions at each phase, particularly as they are experienced by low-income mothers. We will focus on the interplay of the effects of living environments common to this group of women with women's idiosyncratic values, expectations, and beliefs.

INITIAL APPRAISAL

"Primary appraisal" (Lazarus et al. 1974) consists of the recognition of a threat to oneself, which initiates a coping cycle. The person recognizes this threat in her unique way, assessing the threat in terms of both its immediate

FIGURE 14.1   Schematic Representation of the
Process of Person-Environment
Transactions in a Single Coping Cycle

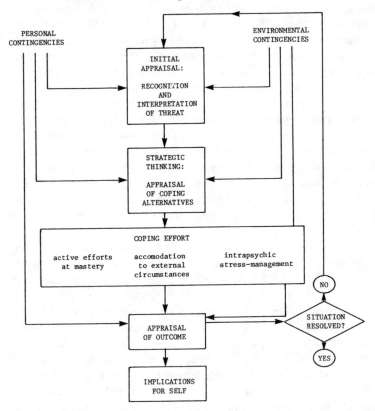

danger and its potential effect on her ongoing life. The threat may arise from external sources or from within the self, and may contain pleasant or challenging aspects as well as threatening aspects, but there is a point at which the individual recognizes this threat as a situation with which she must cope. Cues from both the immediate situation and her ongoing life context are used in this assessment.

As has been shown in the preceding chapters, stressors impinge on the lives of low-income mothers from a multiplicity of sources. For instance, life events which require change and readjustment are one potent source of threat. On a checklist of 91 life events, Stress and Families Project respondents reported a mean of 14.1 events during the previous two years in which they had been the central figure (Makosky, this volume). In contrast, most community surveys report an average of one or two events a year (Coates, Mayer, Kendall, & Howat, 1976; Dohrenwend, 1973). Many of the reported events required major readjustment. Reporting on events which had occurred in the two years preceding the interview, 26 respondents (62 percent) reported deaths of family members or friends, 16 (38 percent) reported illnesses or accidents which required hospitalization or surgery, 24 (57 percent) respondents reported 41 instances in which they had been a victim of a crime, and 15 (36 percent) reported large drops in income. In 37 reported incidents, respondents were victims of violence.

Ongoing conditions which make continuing demands on the individual's resources are another powerful source of threat. Compared to national averages, all of the respondents lived in high-density, high-crime neighborhoods. Only half (58 percent) of the respondents knew a month ahead of time how much money they would have coming into their households. One-third of the respondents said they did not have enough money to buy adequate food for their families. Twenty-three percent rated their health as poor or very poor. Forty-eight percent reported that at least one child had problems in school.

Life events and life conditions such as the above severely threatened the well-being of the women we interviewed. One of the women, quoted at the beginning of this chapter, detailed the multiple concurrent stressors typically experienced by this group. Her husband supported the family, which included seven children, through a home-based business for which the family car was essential. The car broke down at a time when the children were expecting new boots, and one daughter needed expensive dental treatment. The respondent, who was epileptic, learned that she had also developed rheumatoid arthritis. The family was not supported by welfare and not eligible for Medicaid benefits, and their medical bills precluded fixing the car. The family business came to an effective halt and financial crisis ensued.

Another woman discussed her mental health. She had lost her mother when she was a young child, and three of her own children had died young. In the three years preceding the interview, her father, the father of her children, and her sister all died, and her son was sent to jail. So many losses had precipitated severe depression.

A widow who supported two young children on an annual income of $5500 was slowly going blind. Her husband had recently died and the family income plummeted. Her blindness, not yet severe enough to make her eligible for benefits for the blind, and her children's regression into constant quarrelling compounded this woman's troubles.

Another woman could have been speaking for many when she said: "My life has always been a matter of coping with one thing or another. I get through one crisis to find another coming up. Sometimes it feels as if everything is caving in all at once."

Despite having in common a dramatically high level of environmental stressors, low-income mothers were seen to vary widely in the ways these threatening situations were appraised. One major source of variation is found in differences in life contexts on which superficially similar threats impinge. For instance, three respondents who had recently returned to school discussed problematic pregnancies. These women differed in life circumstances and, as a result, differed in how they expected their pregnancies to affect their lives. One woman had been intimidated by her college experiences and wanted to enjoy her life more. Her grandmother, however, was very ambitious for her and insisted that she complete her education. Pregnancy gave this woman an excuse for leaving school which her grandmother would accept. Another woman became pregnant unexpectedly. Education and family life were equally important to her. She wanted to bear the child but worried that the newborn child would interfere with her schoolwork and the happiness of her other children. Her decision was further complicated by her partner's increasing job responsibilities, which made him less available to share household duties and child care than he had been previously. The third respondent, a single woman, felt already overstressed by lack of income and by conflicting responsibilities at work, at school, and at home caring for a young daughter when she became pregnant. She did not want to make a commitment to the father of this child, and carrying the pregnancy to term would have meant interrupting her education, which was central to her self-esteem.

Apart from the impact of high stressor levels and varying life contexts on women's initial appraisal of situations, a woman's belief system acts as a filter on stressors. Some potential stressors, such as the death of an intimate, are universally stress-provoking. Other situations do not affect every person in the same way. Often a situation is appraised as threatening because it calls into question a woman's central beliefs. A woman who believes, for instance, that hard work will be rewarded will be threatened if she fails to win recognition for a particular effort, while a woman who believes that awards can be expected only from friends will not be threatened in the same way when her efforts are not recognized, for instance, by a welfare bureaucrat. One respondent's worries about her daughter centered on her fear that her daughter would repeat her own mistakes, and that she could do nothing to prevent this. The belief implicit in this appraisal was that she was in some way responsible for her daughter's behavior. Other women did not interpret their children's misbehavior in this way. Rather than considering it a threat to the self, misbehavior was considered a threat to the child's well-being or to family harmony. Another respondent, a licensed practical nurse, was threatened by a doctor's assumption of her ignorance. This woman took pride in her training. For her it represented an entry, albeit insecurely held, into the valued world of the educated. She expected the doctor to respect her judgment regarding her child's illness. Other mothers believed they were ignorant about their children's illnesses or injuries. Therefore they felt no threat when doctors assumed their ignorance. In cases like this what is threatened is the woman's self-esteem. Depending on what one believes oneself to be like, and on what one values in oneself, vulnerability to stress in certain situations could vary greatly. Environmental context and personal belief systems determine not only whether a situation is experienced as stressful, but also the nature of the threat. That is, they determine what in the person is threatened and how.

One may have one's own beliefs about the nature of certain situations; these beliefs constitute one's personal phenomenology. One is also, however, susceptible to the influence of others, who provide alternate interpretations of situations. Social influence is here considered part of the environmental context's effect on initial appraisals of threat. While both intimates and the larger cultural setting can aid a person in making sense of a situation, this influence is not always without cost. For instance, several respondents mentioned, as additional stressors to already stressful situations, the arguments they had with others about how to interpret a situation. One woman believed that her son's emotional problems derived from a frightening encounter with another child. Her social worker, however, attributed her son's troubles to the respondent's deficient parenting. Other women reported feeling troubled by their intimates' lack of concern about situations which they felt represented significant threats. These difficulties in gaining support for one's efforts to make meaning out of situations posed additional threats in calling into question the person's meaning-making process itself.

The recognition and interpretation of threat within a situation initiates the need to neutralize the threat in some way.

STRATEGIC THINKING

In response to the perceived threat, the person searches for means to overcome it. We have called this second phase, the search for a means of coping, "strategic thinking." This effort is not necessarily conscious or sustained. What it means is that there has been prior learning about what coping strategies are appropriate in given situations and what outcomes may be reasonably expected from a given strategy. These values and expectations limit the range of perceived coping strategies. For each individual faced with problematic circumstances, the universe of potential strategies for mastering these problems is limited—first, by how the threat was interpreted. Just as a newspaper selects and reports only a portion of the events which finally appear as a news story, so do each of us limit our perception of events to those features which are personally salient. Thus we respond to the event-as-perceived rather than to the total stimulus field. The person then searches for means of coping with what *she* perceives as stressful in the situation.

The universe of potential strategies is then further limited by inner constraints. For instance, one resists coping in ways which conflict with one's values. The woman who believes that divorce is morally wrong may only reluctantly consider separating from an abusive husband. The woman who believes that authority should be respected might find it difficult to argue her point of view against a welfare or public housing or Medicaid administrator.

In addition, potential coping strategies are further limited by one's inner resources. In strategic thinking, one cannot consider coping in ways that draw on personal resources one does not have. A depressed woman, for instance, finds it difficult to sustain persistent efforts toward reaching a long-term goal. Coping strategies of choice are those that are consonant with who one knows oneself to be. One woman in this group called in a news spotlight team to demonstrate her flooded basement as a way of getting the housing authority to pay attention to her case. While this strategy may be effective, others might not have the self-confidence to carry it out.

Personal predispositions like those mentioned above can limit one's choice of coping strategy, but the environment may also effectively limit options for addressing a problem. One respondent wanted to work. She hoped that working and being useful would make her feel more worthwhile as a person. She also wanted to increase her family's income. She found, however, that potential employers would not consider her. They gave as reasons her lack of references, her unsteady work history interrupted by childbirth, and her child care responsibilities, which they assumed would conflict with her work. She would have had to demonstrate her working ability in order to get a job. Another woman, separated from her husband and left with a very low income, articulated the dilemma she faced in attempting to "become [her] own woman":

> I thought that working and having my daughter in school was the solution to my problems. But it is not because I don't make enough. The main reason I went back to work was to stimulate myself, to get on my own, and to feel independent. My job is comfortable, but not exciting in any way. If I were making enough money, I could sit back and stay there. So in a way I am glad I'm not. I have no choice but to look at alternatives. The reason I decided to make a decision is because I can't make ends meet on $80 a week. I can't even pay a babysitter. I was as well off not working full-time [while on welfare] but working part-time, if not better. I went to work in the first place because welfare is degrading.

Sometimes the most obvious coping strategy becomes incredibly complicated, full of costs to the respondent which may finally outweigh the benefits she hopes to gain. Washing machine repairs involve welfare vouchers for which payment may take many months. Attempts to address children's behavior problems quickly involve the school system, health and mental health services, and social workers, and women must weigh the costs of humiliating intrusions against the likelihood that their child will eventually be helped. Experience with such intrusion has led at least one woman to consider that option closed. Another woman mentioned that she would not seek counseling for her own emotional problems because she was afraid that her children would be taken away from her. What these women are learning is that certain potential strategies will not have the desired results.

Options for coping effectively with some problems may simply not be available to a woman already hampered by inadequate financial resources and lacking the power, status, language, information, or appropriate advocates to move institutions in her favor. The strategy with which a woman eventually addresses a problem will often be a compromise between what the environment allows and what she wants and is capable of accomplishing. Thus her performance may not accurately reflect her ability.

COPING

In the third phase, the person actively copes. This can take many forms, which have boggled researchers who have attempted to create taxonomies of coping strategies. Coping forms may include active problem-solving efforts (which may themselves require several subphases), denial of the problem and other defenses, managing the subjective feelings of stress which have resulted (as by taking sedatives or giving vent to one's feelings), and accommodating oneself to changed circumstances—for instance, by changing what one expects from an intimate relationship.

Coping is the actual efforts made to solve a problem, to manage the stress that results, or to accommodate oneself to a situation perceived to be resistant to change. Problem-solving efforts are the easiest of these to describe and range from calling a plumber to improving one's education. Other situations did not easily lend themselves to these kinds of coping strategies. In situations involving marital discord, arguments with friends, deaths of intimates, worries over children, or concern about their own worth, women tended to use strategies directed toward keeping the stress from reaching unbearable proportions. Mourning women found ways to live with their grief: making funeral arrangements, crying, talking to other intimates, drinking, or blocking it out of their minds. Broken attachments were often followed by attempts to understand the situation one had left in new ways. For instance, one woman left her mother, who had beaten her often and tried to kill her. We can hear her attempting to reconstruct this situation when she says:

Up 'til then, I was completely blinded by devotion. Up 'til that time I put up with a lot from her. This was the last straw. All the years she kept beating me and all the love I gave her. I would fight back now. A month after the fight I felt a great relief that I didn't have to live under her pressure.

COPING OUTCOME

The coping effort is made, and, in the fourth phase, its results are observed, with consequent reflection on its implications for the self and for one's initial assessment of the situation. Many factors influence this appraisal. First, outcomes may be attributed to several possible causes. Fate, others' intercession or lack of it, or the immovability of an external problem are attributions which have implications for the person very different from attributions to the success or failure of one's own efforts. The latter can reflect negatively on the self. Second, an outcome may be successful in an objective sense but costly to the person in terms of embarrassment, loss, time, or expense, as will be seen in the examples below. A person may feel that a problem has been solved, but the process of coping in itself may lead to greater stress than was initially experienced. Third, situations may resist resolution despite a woman's best efforts. When the situation has not been satisfactorily resolved, other efforts will be considered and initiated and their outcome observed in turn.

The environment can oppose or facilitate the person's efforts to cope with the threatening situations, whether by response to direct problem-solving efforts or by providing a set of common interpretations of situations which help the person to comprehend what is happening to her. Situational outcomes and the environmental response then affect the person's motivation, self-esteem, and the coherence of her understanding of the world in which she lives.

Low-income mothers constitute a special group, in that they depend heavily on public institutions for support and basic services. This particular social environment has a powerful capacity to affirm or deny a woman's efforts to master stressful circumstances. Respondents provided us with numerous examples of how public institutions, primarily the public welfare system, were unresponsive to their efforts to cope with adverse situations. Attempts to alter situations directly were frequently met with resistance or resulted in little, if any, improvement, with the unfortunate result that women felt they had little control over the forces and policies which determined their lives and the lives of their children.

One respondent discussed the frustration of trying to get appropriate help for her young son who was dyslexic and emotionally disturbed. She tried and failed to get him an early learning abilities evaluation through his school. She also tried and failed to have her son placed in a Big Brother program, in after-school day care, and in a special school for the learning-disabled. Because she was not able to obtain the help she needed from these institutions, through no failure of effort or imagination on her part, she felt guilty and inadequate as a mother and worried that her son's problems, left untreated, would get worse. When another woman, as mentioned previously, sought psychiatric help for her child, her social worker was more concerned about her capacity to mother than about her worry over her son. She did not receive the help she had sought and finally enlisted legal aid to resist the invasion of her privacy which resulted from her efforts.

A third respondent waited six months to get welfare approval of the furniture voucher and the assistance with her utilities bills which had been promised to her. During the six-month period, she repeatedly visited the welfare office without receiving any information on her case. She hired a lawyer, who finally determined that her caseworker had been laid off several months before. A black woman's three sons were bused to school in a white community which has been the scene of interracial violence. Her sons were afraid to go to school and complained that they weren't being taught anything. She tried many times, without success, to transfer them to another school district. Finally she considered sending them to live in another city, where she felt they could go to school without fear. Another woman, as mentioned previously, has had her apartment ruined by leaking water. Public health officials declared the apartment unsafe, but the public housing authority never came to make repairs. She appealed to everyone she could find to listen to her case, even calling in the local media for an expose. Her suit is now pending in court, while water continues, years later, to leak into her apartment.

In these examples, persistent, energetic, and imaginative strategies were used to alter threatening situations. These strategies were ineffective, not because they were inherently deficient, but because the institutions simply would not respond.

MULTIPLE THREATS AND
MULTIPLE STRATEGIES

We often found that what a respondent construed as a single situation involved threats to several aspects of her life at once. As an example, one woman reported about her adolescent daughter's "change in attitude"; she became disobedient and intolerant of her younger siblings. This situation also involved her daughter's antagonism toward the respondent's sister, who had joined the household following the death of their mother. The circumstances surrounding the mother's death had led the respondent to feel both responsible for and disappointed by her younger siblings and her family in general. When the respondent took a stricter approach toward her disrespectful daughter, the daughter's behavior deteriorated. The respondent worried that trouble at home might keep her from her plans to look for work. She reported feeling that the integrity of her family, her relationship with her daughter, her daughter's well-being, and her own pursuit of employment were simultaneously threatened. These were perceived as interlocking parts of the same situation and yet were construed as separate "fronts" which needed to be addressed in different ways. In such situations, we find that coping efforts may be addressed to threats on several fronts simultaneously, or to each front in sequence.

We also found that coping efforts may themselves have negative repercussions with which respondents must also cope. The respondent discussed above, for example, tried to cope with her daughter's change in attitude by making stricter demands on her. She found, as a result, that her daughter would no longer confide in her, and the original threat to their relationship intensified. In order to find another way of coping with the situation, she had to reconstrue the nature of the threat. She tried, instead, to understand the problem as her daughter's lack of privacy, caused by the addition of a new member to the household.

In addition to having negative repercussions, coping efforts may be unsuccessful or only partially successful. These experiences usually result in a reformulation of the problem with which one is coping and a reconsideration of coping strategies.

If we conceive of [Perception of threat → Strategic thinking → Coping effort → Appraisal of outcome] as a single coping "cycle," as represented in Figure 14.1, then we find that a single situation may consist of several simultaneous and/or sequential cycles of coping, as represented schematically in Figure 14.2. These graphic representations form the broad structure of what we call "coping processes." Again, it should be emphasized that this model attempts to simplify coping processes so as to make them more understandable. Yet in reality these processes are not necessarily experienced as separate cycles with distinct subphases.

THE PERSON-ENVIRONMENT TRANSACTION

The most important theoretical conclusion that can be drawn from the above discussion is simply that coping cannot be reduced to a single event in which a stressful stimulus calls forth a given response. That is, if one attempts to "freeze" and analyze a segment of what unfolds after a threat has been perceived by the individual, one can identify a series of exchange events occurring between the individual and the environment. Lazarus (1978) has described these exchanges as "transactions," whereby the person affects the environment and the environment affects the person. These transactions, he argues, are constantly changing over time, depending on what

FIGURE 14.2   Possible Combinations of
             Coping Cycles

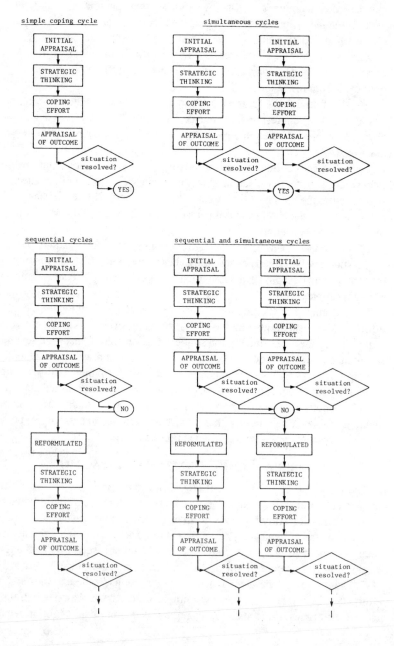

happens in the environment and within the individual. Also suggested in the above discussion is that environmental factors not only represent sources of threat with which the individual must cope but also continue to influence coping from beginning to end. Thus, transactions occur throughout the coping process and are altered as much with each change in the environment as with each change in the person.

The model described in the preceding pages schematizes what, in fact, is being transacted or exchanged between the individual and her environment. At the environmental end, externally imposed stressors present themselves in the forms of particular events or conditions, such as a child's misbehavior or the high cost of repairing a broken washing machine. Once a source of stress has been recognized as such by the individual, the process of coping begins to unfold. In what transpires after the initial appraisal of threat, environmental characteristics such as the availability of social or material resources come into play. We have seen that environmental factors may limit the individual's range of options for taking action; may inhibit her efforts, once in effect, to resolve the problem; and may provide little or negative reinforcement for those efforts after the fact.

The idea that environmental factors continue to play an important role in the direction coping takes, by facilitating or inhibiting processes along the way, is not well developed or empirically supported in the clinical and research literature on stress and coping. Researchers have only recently begun to address the coping "experience" as being inextricably tied to environmental contingencies and thus as being changeable and continuous (Antonovsky, 1979; Lazarus, 1978). We have seen that stressful aspects of the individual's social environment not only call forth coping initiatives but also become salient factors throughout the coping process. The path an individual takes initially in coping and the ultimate outcome may be dramatically altered with the introduction of new variables, such as social support, material resources, or a lack of such resources.

At the individual end of the person-environment exchange, personality characteristics such as motivation or maturity are embodied in the unique way the individual constructs or makes meaning of experience. With regard to coping, the individual responds to events perceived as stressful in ways that reflect her particular phenomenological or belief system. Initially, information, such as a demand made by a family member or a physician's remark, is actively construed by the individual as threatening. The formulation of threat has been referred to as the cognitive "assimilation" or "mediation" of objective stress (Haan, 1977; Lazarus et al., 1974). Both Haan and Lazarus also regard the affective component of the response to stressors as a *product* of cognitions, rather than as generating cognitions.

Next, options for coping are strategically appraised by the person as possibilities and then pursued if judged to be feasible. The appraisal of options and limitations has been likened by Haan (1977) to the Piagetian notion of "accommodation" and "the development of a motive plan" (p. 170). Both may be regarded as the adaptational work engaged in by the individual once a situation has been perceived as threatening. Just as the individual constructs her world around her, she constructs a repertoire of ways to cope, however varied or limited in scope.

Motivating these assimilative and accommodative processes is, we believe, what Antonovsky (1979) refers to as the urge toward a "sense of coherence." "Coherence" is defined as "a global orientation that expresses the extent to which one has a pervasive, enduring, though dynamic, feeling of confidence that one's internal and external environments are predictable and that there is a high probability that things will work out as well as can reasonably be expected" (p. 123). We believe coping is motivated by the urge to (and thus serves to) preserve this sense of coherence—that is, to preserve the belief that one's world is predictable and benevolent. This idea is conceptually consistent with what Piaget (Flavell, 1963) called "equilibration," whereby the individual attempts to make her cognitive frame of reference consistent with her experiences. Coping involves not only dealing with the immediate stress of a situation but also making sense of it. This requires either using existing cognitive frameworks or adapting them to fit discrepant experiences. The inability to achieve and maintain a sense of coherence may seriously jeopardize the balance necessary for emotional well-being.

IMPACT ON MENTAL HEALTH

The experiences of low-income mothers are characterized, as we have seen, by an unusually high level of stress-provoking situations, many of which are unresolvable or out of their immediate control, by limited options for coping effectively, and by difficulty in achieving the desired outcomes of coping efforts. The coping model we have illustrated allows us to examine possible pathways by which stressful environmental contexts lead to poor mental health. We suggest that the difficulties low-income mothers experience in coping lead, in many cases, to beliefs that they lack control over their environment and that their environment is unpredictable. These beliefs, in turn, erode the woman's motivation and sense of coherence.

By looking at the nature of the person-environment transactions which occur at each phase of coping, we can better see how this may happen. First, the stressful situations to which low-income mothers are subject can themselves affect well-being. In this sample, reported stressful situations were often both unexpected and of relatively long duration. The respondents as a group suffered from chronic stressful conditions from multiple sources. Various researchers have suggested mechanisms by which such conditions lead to poor mental health outcomes. Wortman and Brehm (1975) predict that repeated exposure to innumerable and continuous stressors that are objectively beyond the individual's control would undermine the individual's sense of self-determination and, thus, lead to lowered motivation, passivity, and, ultimately, to depression. The posited mechanism for deteriorating well-being is the erosion of the belief that one is in control. Haan (1977) believes that chronic stress precludes both assimilation and recovery by leaving the individual little time to appraise or make sense of experience. Seligman (1975) suggested that the unpredictable occurrence of stressors leads to anxiety. In these two hypotheses, well-being deteriorates as a result of the lack of coherence of experience.

Second, options for coping effectively were limited in this sample, and mechanisms by which this can affect well-being have also been suggested in the literature. Schneiderman (1964), for instance, argues that with limited opportunities for mastery, individuals learn to devalue their capacity for mastery and to relinquish control to external forces. Similarly, Seligman (1975) and White (1959) contend that opportunities for mastery are a necessary precondition to developing a belief that one is able to control what happens to oneself. In other words, without being able to perceive options for coping, and lacking opportunities to initiate coping strategies, one is less likely to believe one is *able* to cope effectively. Motivation is thereby diminished when one consistently perceives limited options for coping.

Finally, we have noted the difficulties these respondents experienced in achieving the desired outcomes of their coping efforts. This is a third theoretical source of poor mental health outcomes related to coping, which has also received support in the literature. Seligman (1975) and his colleagues have popularized the notion of "learned helplessness," in which the lack of contingency between the person's response to a stressor and the perceived outcome teaches the person that she does not have control. With repeated experiences of response-outcome noncontingency, the belief that one is helpless becomes generalized. When helplessness occurs repeatedly in traumatic situations, the person exhibits many symptoms of depression. Kohn (1976) suggests a different mechanism by which lack of response-outcome contingency affects mental health. When individuals repeatedly experience a lack of connection between their efforts and the outcomes of their efforts, in response they come to internalize what is perceived to be devaluative feedback. In other words, they come to believe that their relationship to their social world is insignificant. As was mentioned previously, Antonovsky suggests a third mechanism by which unpredictable outcomes to coping efforts detract from mental health. He suggests that unpredictable outcomes to one's efforts erode one's confidence in the predictability of events in general and in the probability that things will work out, thus eroding one's sense of coherence.

The coping experiences of these low-income mothers lead us to believe that chronic and unpredictable stressors, limited options for coping, and unreliable outcomes of coping efforts overdetermine symptoms of poor mental health. Any of these factors alone can erode the individual's belief that her world is consistent and that it allows her to act effectively upon it. These beliefs have been regarded by many, including those mentioned above, as essential to emotional well-being. The psychological burden such coping experiences impose over time has led many respondents to call into question the validity of their lives. One woman said: "I constantly worry about my own worth. I begin to question my role here on earth." We can hear in this statement what happens when life experiences are difficult to digest, and antidotes for the "poisonous" experiences are not available. The resultant erosion of sustaining beliefs is analogous to the breakdown of the body's natural immunosystem, in that the person's capacity to cope is diminished.

REFERENCES

Antonovsky, A. *Health, stress, and coping.* San Francisco: Jossey-Bass, 1979.

Byrne, D. Repression-sensitization as a dimension of personality. In B. Maher (Ed.) *Progress in experimental personality research.* New York: Academic Press, 1964.

Coates, D., Mayer, S., Kendall, L., & Howat, M. Life-event changes and mental health. In I. Sarason & C. Spielberger (Eds.) *Stress and anxiety.* Washington, DC: Hemisphere Press, 1976.

Dohrenwend, B. Social status and stressful life events. *Journal of Personality and Social Psychology,* 1973, *28,* 225-235.

Flavell, J. *The developmental psychology of Jean Piaget.* New York: Litton, 1963.

Haan, N. *Coping and defending.* New York: Academic Press, 1977.

Kohn, M. The interaction of social class and other factors in the etiology of schizophrenia. *American Journal of Psychiatry,* 1976, *133,* 177-180.

Lazarus, R. The stress and coping paradigm. Unpublished manuscript available from Department of Psychology, University of California, Berkeley, 1978.

Lazarus, R., Averill, J., & Opton, E. The psychology of coping: Issues of research and assessment. In G. Coelho, D. Hamburg, & J. Adams (Eds.) *Coping and adaptation.* New York: Basic Books, 1974.

Lefcourt, H. Repression-sensitization: A measure of the evaluation of emotional expression. *Journal of Consulting Psychology,* 1966, *30,* 444-449.

Pearlin, L., & Schooler, C. The structure of coping. *Journal of Health and Social Behavior,* 1978, *19,* 2-21.

Schneiderman, L. Value orientation preferences of chronic relief recipients. *Journal of Social Work,* 1964, *9,* 13-19.

Seligman, M. *Helplessness.* San Francisco: W. H. Freeman, 1975.

White, R. Motivation reconsidered: The concept of competence. *Psychological Review,* 1959, *66,* 297-333.

Wortman, C., & Brehm, J. Responses to uncontrollable outcomes: An integration of reactance theory and the learned helplessness model. In L. Berkowitz (Ed.) *Advances in experimental social psychology.* New York: Academic Press, 1975.

15

MENTAL HEALTH PROBLEMS
AND THEIR TREATMENT

DEBORAH BELLE, DIANA DILL, ELLEN FELD,
ELIZABETH GREYWOLF, MAUREEN FOLEY REESE,
AND EMILIE STEELE

The Stress and Families Project respondents, like the population of low-income mothers which they represent, experience a high rate of depressive symptoms and other mental health problems. The extent of depressive symptomatology among the research sample was not only alarming to the researchers, it was also of concern to the respondents. When the respondents were asked if anyone they know had ever had an emotional problem, two-thirds of the women for whom we have this information named themselves. In addition, when each respondent was asked to rate the extent of worries, problems, or upset that she experienced about her own mental health, the ratings on this question were highly correlated with the extent of self-reported depressive symptoms ($r = .52$, $p < .001$). Many of the women do worry about their mental health, especially when they experience many symptoms of depression.

This chapter considers the ways in which the low-income mothers we interviewed conceptualized emotional problems, their experiences with mental health professionals when they did seek help for their emotional problems or those of their children, and the barriers which deter women, especially those who are seriously concerned about their own mental health, from reaching out for help. The results of interviews on these topics suggest that many traditional therapeutic approaches are counter-productive for low-income mothers. The most successful treatment approaches would seem to be those which recognize that for low-income mothers, mental health problems are inextricably bound to life circumstances.

CONCEPTIONS OF MENTAL HEALTH PROBLEMS

To find out how the respondents conceptualized mental health problems we reminded them that "people often mean different things when they talk about emotional problems" and asked them: "What kinds of problems would you see as emotional problems?" Some women expressed difficulty in answering the question. For instance, Ms. Jones answered: "I don't know. The only thing I could see is . . . I can't leave this apartment, and it bothers me emotionally because I want to get out, and the worries I have with my kids being in here." Ms. Monroe told the interviewer: "I don't know what emotional means. I was depressed, crying all the time." Other respondents answered with assurance, like Ms. Lee who said: "That was me before I got this job."

While many SFP respondents share the traditional conception of emotional problems as internal psychological difficulties and outward behavioral manifestations of those difficulties, they also find it impossible to separate such problems from the disturbing conditions in which people live. Some respondents named *intrapsychic problems* such as anxiety, depression, and excessive worrying as examples of emotional problems. Some cited *behavioral problems* like violence and crying easily. However, the number of references to *concrete life situations* as emotional problems or as precipitating factors in emotional problems was striking. At the core of many of these responses was concern with lack of money and related problems in paying bills, finding a decent place to live, putting food on the table, and getting adequate medical care. As Ms. Norton succinctly stated: "No money or food would cause emotional problems." Ms. Long mentioned "being on welfare," and Ms. Franklin told the interviewer: "Welfare, you know, is emotional strain." Three working mothers named trying to cope with being a mother, a wife, and a wage earner. Other respondents mentioned problems with children, with men, medical worries, and problems at work in response to our question on emotional problems.

Previous researchers have noted that problems which more affluent Americans view as psychological are often considered by low-income persons to relate to the external environment of the troubled individual. Lurie (1974, p. 113), for instance, found that the economically deprived mothers she studied often attributed their children's problems to the "pathogenic conditions of their lives," such as inadequate income, poor health, substandard housing, and run-down and unsafe neighborhoods.

Many clinicians share this view that emotional problems, particularly among poor and oppressed groups, must be considered in the context of environmental problems. One interesting study of clinicians who had worked with black and white families in therapy (Boyd, 1979) discovered that black clinicians (social workers and psychologists) and white social workers were likely to state that socioeconomic or system problems were among "the most common problems" they had seen in the black families with whom they worked. But only 7.7 percent of the white psychologists mentioned such issues in response to the same question. Since the poor themselves consider an environmental, ecological view of mental health problems important, and such a conception is also important to many clinicians familiar with the lives of the impoverished, one must wonder how clinicians without such a perspective can meet their low-income clients halfway in developing a shared conception of the problem and a plan for treatment.

BARRIERS TO TREATMENT

When respondents were asked why people so often avoid getting help with emotional problems, women told us that shame and embarrassment, fear of exposure to others, fear of painful self-discovery, inability to recognize a problem for what it is, cost, lack of time, energy, or commitment, unhelpful and even antagonistic services, and the lack of information prevent people from seeking mental health treatment. Perhaps the most frequently used words in response to this question were "ashamed" and "embarrassed." Ms. Marshall answered,

> I think for one thing because of the stigma that's put on them. People still kind of look down at people going for this kind of help. I think people are a little more open today than they used to be, but the stigma is still there.

Not only is seeking treatment for mental health problems possibly stigmatizing, but it involves exposing one's private self to a therapist. Ms. Long speculates that people who avoid getting help perhaps "just don't like the idea of having someone else know . . . what they think and how they feel."

Sometimes allied to the fear of public exposure is the fear of revealing to oneself the extent of emotional problems. Ms. Newman said: "I think they are ashamed, and if they admit it they might have to accept responsibility. They'd rather blame other people and stay the way they are." Ms. Marcus stated: "They really don't want to think something is wrong with them." Ms. Lewis's statement reflects her own personal experience.

Because they fear it. Because they don't understand what's [wrong] with them. They're scared people will judge them badly. [They think] that psychiatrists are only for crazy people. People also don't like to look at themselves. They are afraid and embarrassed to go to a psychiatrist. From my own experience [I know] it's a difficult thing to do . . . [because] basically it makes you admit . . . what your problems are and that you have to deal with them. I know a few people that would go to see someone a couple of times but then they would get scared and never go again. That's a pity.

Other respondents emphasized the difficulty people may have in recognizing that they actually have a problem. Ms. Lee, whose personal and family history involved a lot of violence said: "It's not that people avoid getting help—it's that they don't know when it's needed. The contrast between normal behavior and sick behavior does not stand out in my particular environment. It just goes on, from one generation to the next." She continued: "Most kinds of people don't think they're crazy till somebody points it out for them."

Ms. Houser stated that a troubled person may simply not want to change. "[They] consider it isn't a problem, [or else] they like the problem. They like [alcohol] like I like my pepsi-cola and coffee." Or people may blame themselves for their problem and not consider treatment appropriate. Ms. Palmer noted: "People think it's their fault so they tend not to want to explore it. They think that they should pull themselves up [by themselves]."

Cost was frequently mentioned as a barrier to treatment. Ms. Patterson mentioned that counseling is often very expensive and that the lack of money could prevent people from seeking help. Ms. Paine noted that good quality help is expensive: "I don't see where they can go. There would be no choice. I would be stuck in State Hospital." Ms. Oliver believes that people who avoid treatment may not want to spend the money. "I've felt that way," she said, "yet I don't feel that way about my children, especially about my son." Ms. Charles, who was herself sent from a prestigious hospital to a city hospital because she is on Medicaid, said: "Maybe they can't afford to pay for it [treatment]." Ms. Hill believes "most people don't go because of money."

Time and energy were also mentioned as factors in the avoidance of treatment. Ms. Patterson said:

If I had money and time, I still don't know if I could get myself to a therapist because it would take so long to get through everything, and that I just couldn't get myself to do it. I think it's a really difficult process—involves a lot of work to get yourself through it and I think a lot of people can't face that.

Problems with mental health services themselves were frequently mentioned as barriers to treatment. Often the respondents spoke of problems with service providers. Ms. Page put it this way:

I've run into mental health workers who have a real bad attitude, and it's not so much an attitude of hostility or anything. . . . They equate being poor with being stupid.

Ms. Hill also spoke from personal experience. "I avoid it [treatment] because they make me feel *more* fucked up." Other respondents spoke of lack of understanding and "bad attitudes" on the part of mental health workers. Ms. Smith mentioned that the fear of being called crazy and locked up could prevent people from seeking help. Ms. Paine felt that the attitude of the mental health system toward a low-income client was punitive. "You behaved outside of society—so into the hospital for punishment." She believes further that "the mind is not understood well enough to give it help."

Perhaps the most alarming barrier to mental health treatment was the fear women expressed that their children would be taken away from them if it became known that the respondents had emotional problems. One woman told us that the therapist she had contacted advised her not to begin treatment with him or anyone. He argued that since her bills would be paid by a public agency, her treatment records would be subject to the scrutiny of other public agencies. He feared that her acknowledgment of parenting problems and her desire for treatment could result in her being seen as an unfit mother. As Ms. Paine, whose child was ultimately taken away from her, said: "If you've had a breakdown, it will follow you faster and further than a prison record."

Ms. Page stressed the importance of finding a therapist who shares her views on important subjects.

I want someone who's a feminist and interested in feminist views or someone like that. It's really amazing to me they don't understand for someone to empathize and help you that their political views have to be somewhat similar. I've met a lot who try to tell you it doesn't matter. As a matter of fact I got into a fight with a therapist because she couldn't understand her political views could color our relationship. I said, "Of course it does. How could you possibly think any differently?"

Similarly, Ms. Taylor discussed the problems she had had with a therapist because of disagreements over views on sexuality and marriage.

Finally, respondents spoke of the lack of information which prevented people from seeking needed treatment. While some respondents believed that appropriate, affordable treatment was hard or impossible to find, other respondents believed that good treatment was available but that many people lacked sufficient information to find it. This was the opinion of Ms. Ross, who said that people "lack knowledge of available services, [feel] a sense of isolation and [feel] . . . as if there is no one who could help." Ms. James stated: "A lot of them don't know where to find the help. The big thing is to know where to go and what to do." Ms. Hampton agrees. "They don't know where to go. They don't know there is free counseling."

It is distressing to learn of so much shame and fear about mental health problems among a group at such high risk for these problems. Particularly upsetting are the reports of "nasty attitudes" among mental health workers, the fear of being called crazy and locked up, and the danger of having one's children taken away. In addition, the association of emotional problems with self-blame, and the assignment of responsibility to the solitary individual to cure herself, must work against appropriate use of mental health services.

WOMEN WHO DO NOT SEEK HELP

We were particularly interested in the six highly depressed respondents who had not sought treatment or support for mental health problems. To understand better what has inhibited these women from seeking help in dealing with their depression, we looked at their definitions of emotional problems, their statements as to why people would avoid seeking treatment for emotional problems, and their knowledge about where treatment could be found.

Ms. Marshall, very depressed according to her CES-Depression Score, defined emotional problems as "worrying over somebody being sick, worrying about kids." Ms. Marshall has a suicidal child. She said about him: "I suppose Joey's problem is hyperactivity. They claim that follows depression. Some people say that it's emotional, but I always thought people just kept kind of to themselves. I really can't understand that because I would think, you know, where he's overactive, how could that be depression?" Ms. Marshall has taken her son to a hospital and a health center but has not sought support or treatment for her own depression. She has much to worry about in her life in addition to her son's problems: her own poor health, her husband's disability, her tense relationship with her mother, the troublemaking of her three sons, the dangers of living in her housing project. Why do people avoid getting help for emotional problems? Ms. Marshall spoke of the stigma that people experience when they seek this kind of help. She named the hospital where she took her son as a "good place to go" if she ever wanted help with emotional problems.

Ms. Jones gave as examples of emotional problems her inability to leave her apartment and her worries about her children. Yet in response to other questions Ms. Jones did not describe herself as having emotional problems. Her depression scores were quite high. People often avoid getting help because "there's some people who just don't let things bother them. And some people in the health center who are embarrassing and have nasty attitudes." When asked where she would turn if she wanted help with emotional problems, she answered, "I wouldn't know that," which is a relatively rare response in our sample.

Ms. Chapman is another highly depressed woman who did not say she had emotional problems and who had not sought treatment for herself. Ms. Chapman's husband frequently beat her and threatened violent revenge against her family if she should leave him. An emotional problem, said Ms. Chapman is "not being able to figure a way out of something that would be a way out of the problem that you may be having, and I would see it as not being able to cope with the problem that you're having, and coping with it unrealistically." Why do people often avoid getting help? "I think first of all they may not admit to themselves that they need help. I think a lot of places are just so impersonal that you don't want to go to them. Some people just don't know where to go." If Ms. Chapman did seek help she might go to a close friend or to the Family Counselling Service whose advertisements she sees. "I think because they don't know you—they can be more objective."

Ms. Rand, who has sought help with emotional problems only through Weight-Watchers, is one of the most depressed women in this sample. She defined emotional problems in these terms: "Many people can't deal with their everyday situation on a normal basis." She also mentioned marital problems and parenting problems as specific emotional problems. While in other interviews she described her own marital and parenting problems in detail, she did not see herself as having emotional problems, and in fact reported resenting the suggestion made by her child's therapist that she seek psychiatric aid herself. When asked why people so often avoid getting help, she replied: "People aren't looking for advice. A group situation would be better. People could hear how others solve the same problems they have." If she did decide to seek help, Ms. Rand is clear about her preferences for treatment: "I would just look for opinions of other people and ask what they'd do. I would not go to a professional place. I don't want anybody to psychoanalyze me."

Two respondents were highly depressed, saw themselves as having emotional problems, but did not seek treatment for themselves. Ms. Webb appeared to believe that nothing could help. "It's always the same thing. The kids are always sick, and my mother is always drunk, and I was just tired of it." Ms. Charles said people often avoid getting help because "maybe they can't afford to pay for it. And then plus the people are just not interested in them." Where would she turn for help if she wanted it? "I ought to work it out for myself, because I don't have nobody to turn to."

Resignation to an unhappy life, inability to admit to having problems that require help, mistrust of the traditional institutions which provide mental health services, and lack of knowledge about where to seek mental health services appear to be deterrents to help-seeking among these highly depressed women who have not sought treatment.

TREATMENT EXPERIENCES

While they have catalogued in detail the reasons why a person might not seek mental health treatment, more than half of the Stress and Families respondents have themselves sought help for emotional problems at some point in their lives, either through conventional mental health services or through mutual aid groups such as Alcoholics Anonymous. Several respondents utilized more than one service provider.

Private practitioners, including psychiatrists, psychologists, and physicians who provided respondents with essentially psychiatric services were the major source of mental health care for the respondents. Of the 25 respondents who received help, 12 (48 percent) were treated by private practitioners who were not associated with community mental health centers. Mutual aid groups, including Alcoholics Anonymous, Weight-Watchers, and parenting groups were the second most common form of treatment or support, serving 10 of the 25 respondents who received help (40 percent). Four respondents utilized community mental health centers, four were hospitalized as psychiatric inpatients, and one respondent visited a drop-in center staffed by volunteers.

Respondents with high depression scores (above 16 points) were more likely to have sought mental health treatment than were respondents with low depression scores. While 41 percent of the low-depression respondents had sought such treatment, 70 percent of the high-depression respondents had done so.

SATISFACTION WITH TREATMENT

In order to determine whether satisfaction with treatment was related to the type of therapy respondents had experienced, we grouped treatment settings into four broad groups: treatment by private practitioners not associated with a community mental health center (psychiatrist, psychologist, or physician), inpatient treatment at a hospital, outpatient treatment at a community mental health center, and participation in a mutual aid group. Table 15.1 shows respondents' satisfaction with these types of treatment.

TABLE 15.1   Percentage of Respondents Satisfied, Dissatisfied, or Unclear about Satisfaction with Treatment at Mental Health Facilities by Type of Facility

	% Satisfied	% Dissatisfied	% Unclear
Private Practitioners (n = 12)	25	42	33
Hospital Inpatient Facilities (n = 4)	25	75	0
Community Mental Health Centers (n = 4)	75	25	0
Mutual Aid Groups (n = 10)	50	10	40
Overall (n = 30)	40	33	27

As this was not a longitudinal study, we cannot assess the effect of precipitating circumstances or severity of emotional problems which led to treatment on the respondents' current satisfaction with their treatment. It may be that the respondents' satisfaction with treatment at different types of mental health services varies with the severity of the problems which led women to these treatment modalities. Nor can we determine whether or not satisfaction with treatment is related to change in the level of depressive symptomatology or related emotional problems. Ideally, we would have liked to see whether these factors affected respondents' satisfaction with treatment.

As can be seen in Table 15.1, while four out of every ten instances of mental health treatment were satisfactory to the respondents, one instance out of three was not satisfactory, and satisfaction could not be determined for over a quarter of the instances of treatment. Community mental health centers had the highest satisfaction rate, although this type of treatment was utilized less frequently than others. Mutual aid groups were frequently utilized, and rarely were they seen as unsatisfactory. However, they were almost as likely to leave respondents unclear about satisfaction as to leave them satisfied. Hospital inpatient treatment was viewed most negatively. Only one respondent who experienced such treatment was satisfied, and the other three women were clearly dissatisfied. Private practitioners present almost as negative a picture, with almost half of the instances of treatment not satisfactory and one-third of the instances unclear.

Looking more closely at the reasons for satisfaction or dissatisfaction, we find that the three respondents who reported satisfaction with their treatment at a community mental health center spoke of a relationship with a helpful counselor. Ms. Trent, who was forced by her social worker to go into therapy through the community mental health center, felt that her case was handled in a manner destructive to herself and her family.

Mutual aid groups were frequently positive experiences but did not always provide help with respondents' initial problems. For instance, through ALANON Ms. Ramsey found very satisfying and therapeutic support in dealing with her abusive husband's and her parents' alcoholism. Ms. James, on the other hand, felt that the parenting group she joined when she felt she "couldn't cope" was supportive but offered "no real help."

In regard to private practitioners, Ms. Lewis felt that her privately contracted therapist helped her over her drug addiction, and Ms. Monroe felt that her private therapist helped her to deal better with her ongoing depression. Other respondents, however, complained that "things didn't click" with their therapists, that drugs were prescribed instead of substantial help in solving problems, or that mental health service providers were just unable to help, for a variety of reasons. Ms. Norton, for instance, said: "They can't solve the problems for you. They can only listen. Eventually you learn that you have to do this for yourself." Ms. Patterson observed: "The therapist just couldn't deal with my problem. He sat there and listened and said almost nothing, really nothing. I think he was overwhelmed." And Ms. Paine was pessimistic. "I don't think I got much help. It generally comes back. Responsibility is taken away for awhile. Relax for awhile, then troubles come again and so do emotional problems."

Only one of the four respondents who had been hospitalized was satisfied with her treatment. Hospitalization followed severe emotional breakdowns in these four women, and the low level of satisfaction may be related to the severity of the problem which precipitated treatment.

While respondents were not specifically asked if they had received drug therapy for emotional problems, seven women mentioned that they had received drug therapy, and all seven felt that this treatment was either inadequate or actually harmful. Ms. Frazier, who went to a psychiatrist, said he was "no help at all." She wanted someone to talk to, but he wanted to hand out pills. Ms. Jackson became pregnant as the result of a rape at age 16, was rejected by her parents, ran out of her house without shoes or a coat, and ended up having a miscarriage and seeing a psychiatrist. When asked about the help she had received, she said she "survived it, but it didn't help" mainly because she was "kept on drugs." Ms. Chapman believes that it would help her to have someone at her clinic who knew her and her family well, because "they wouldn't try to shove a pill at me every time I went."

The most drastic failure of drug treatment occurred for Ms. Sawyer, who told the interviewer that "no professional services have helped." Ms. Sawyer sought help for herself because "I felt like when I was walking I felt like someone was pulling me to the ground." Ms. Sawyer seems to have been suffering from severe depression, but the doctor told her that she felt unbalanced and disturbed because she was nervous. For this he prescribed tranquilizers.

Ms. Sawyer may have a low tolerance for drugs. She indicated that when giving birth to her child she was able to tolerate the pain and did not want anesthetics, which the doctor gave her anyway and which greatly upset her. At any rate, the pills given her for her "nervous condition" seem to have been more than she needed.

> One night someone broke into my house, and because I had taken a tranquilizer before I went to sleep, I could not wake up, even though I heard the noise. I felt the cold air—it was winter—I felt that I was dreaming, I did not wake up until this someone was on top of my chest with a knife.

Ms. Sawyer has determined to avoid medication unless it is absolutely necessary, and she now looks to her church for emotional support.

Ms. Newman also recalled a life-threatening situation. At one hospital where she went for treatment of physical problems she was misdiagnosed and offered pills to deal with her presumed emotional problems. "The doctors were going to send me home with a bottle of pills. They said my sickness was in my head. I demanded to see a psychiatrist. He couldn't come up with anything, said my father took sick at 37 and so I did." Fortunately a friend took Ms. Newman to a different hospital, where doctors found she had severe physical problems. She was told that without treatment for these problems she might have died.

Several respondents were troubled by instances in which they felt they had been blamed for their children's emotional problems. Ms. Ramsey's son has dyslexia "and a lot of emotional fears and anger," and she indicated that his disability has been one of the most stressful situations with which she has had to deal. She began seeking help for David before he was three years old, but she was told his problems were "minor" and that they would straighten out by themselves. The problems, however, did not disappear, and Ms. Ramsey eventually took her son to school for an evaluation, to a social worker, a public school guidance counselor, the Big Brother Association, and a teacher from Head Start. Along the way she was told that her son's problems were "all due to my own fears about him." Eventually his problem was correctly diagnosed, and while much time had been lost in treating the problem, at least Ms. Ramsey is not now being held personally responsible for her son's troubles.

Ms. Rand is another mother who has had difficulty in getting help for a son with emotional problems. She told the interviewer that when her son was four years old his personality changed drastically.

> He began having nightmares and refused to go outside. He started telling stories about a nine year old boy. He said that the boy had a hold of his tongue. He repeated the story over and over but never explained what he meant. He was terrified about the boy. He was outgoing before this and became almost mute and withdrawn.

A psychiatrist "thought my child wasn't disturbed enough and gave me a family counselor. They didn't believe me that his personality had changed so drastically. The psychiatrist said there was nothing wrong with my son, and that I needed to get myself together, and that would help him." Ms. Rand tried to get her son into a school that would help him deal with his emotional problem, but could not do so. "The school they wanted to send him to was more like a rest home for retarded children. He wouldn't have started first grade until he was eight." In this instance, and in one described previously concerning Ms. Ramsey, the respondents perceived the mental health establishment throwing the blame for a child's problems onto his mother while offering little help with the problem itself.

Blaming a child's problem on the mother's attitudes or behavior is so common among mental health professionals (and the general public) that we may not recognize how misguided or harmful this tendency can be (Weisskopf, 1978). "The child is interacting and growing in a complicated and multifaceted environment which extends far beyond the boundaries of the mother-child dyad or even the immediate family. . . . By zeroing in on primarily one aspect of the child's development the clinician is vastly limiting possible outcomes" (Weisskopf, 1978, p. 15). Nor is maternal guilt a desirable starting point in treatment of child or mother.

CONCLUSIONS

Mental health problems cause low-income mothers considerable worry and concern. While a majority of respondents had at some time sought therapy or support from a mental health care service, their experiences had been mixed. Community mental health centers and mutual aid groups received the greatest votes of confidence from women who had used them.

Drug treatment alone, without the opportunity to explore the meaning of emotional problems and without a chance for emotional support, was seen as a particularly negative experience by several respondents. Other women believed that they received no substantial help with their needs. Some women who had sought help with a child's problem believed they were blamed by mental health professionals for the child's suffering, but that no aid to alleviate the problem was forthcoming. Other women were told that their very real physical problems were "all in the head." Such experiences led to cynicism about mental health services, and, in many cases, to reluctance to use them further.

For women who are depressed and who do not see the connection between mental health problems and environmental difficulties there is great potential for self-blame and for the attitude reported by several respondents that a person must not rely on others to solve what is a personal problem. This notion of blame and self-reliance would act as a tremendous barrier to seeking help, and would probably serve to intensify whatever emotional problems already exist, as the woman would add guilt to her other sorrows. This could be particularly damning when depression is accompanied by a deterioration in the capacity to be the kind of mother one wants to be.

Alternatively, a woman who blames herself for her depression and yet retains a belief in the usefulness of therapy may find that such therapy further deepens her self-blame and guilt. If environmental realities are ignored while therapist and patient search for the character flaw at the root of an emotional problem, a woman is liable to sink more deeply into passivity, guilt, and depression while losing the chance to overcome both real-life problems and emotional problems.

While fear of mental health services is a major barrier to treatment for many distressed women, the negative experiences cited by many respondents give credibility to such fear. Because of their economic situation and because they often receive treatment for emotional problems in the general medical system, low-income mothers are often treated at facilities which are overcrowded and understaffed. The dangers of harsh or even incompetent treatment are not small.

It is ironic that a woman's efforts to improve her mental health and her capacity to care for her children by seeking professional help can make her more vulnerable to the charge that she is not a fit mother. When stressed and oppressed mothers experience emotional problems but do not seek help because of the fear that their children will be taken away, both mothers and children suffer. The children suffer if they are forced to leave a parent to whom they are attached for the uncertain fate of foster care, and they suffer if they remain in the home while their mother receives no help. In either case, the mother suffers as well.

Many respondents viewed mental health problems as inextricably bound up in life circumstances. In this, of course, they agree with the empirical findings of the Stress and Families Project, which has found a strong association between mental health status and ongoing life circumstances. We also discovered in conducting the SFP that the respondents found our questions about current life stresses and supports provocative of self-reflection and self-discovery. Some women clearly viewed the interview process as therapeutic, and no woman dropped out of the study. As one woman said: "By being in your study, the questions you've been asking me about myself, I've really found myself out." An orientation to the sources of stress in women's lives and to sources of potential support would seem as promising for therapy as for research (with unintended, though desirable, therapeutic outcomes).

NOTE

Kristine Dever, Elizabeth Neustadt, and Polly Ashley wrote the interview on which this chapter is based.

REFERENCES

Boyd, N. Black families in therapy: A study of clinicians' perceptions. *Sandoz Psychiatric Spectator,* 1979, *11* (7), 21-25.

Lurie, O. R. Parents' attitudes toward children's problems and toward use of mental health services: Socio-economic differences. *American Journal of Orthopsychiatry,* 1974, *44* (1), 109-120.

Weisskopf, S. Maternal guilt and mental health professionals: A reconfirming interaction. *Michigan Occasional Paper* No. V, 1978.

Weissman, M., & Locke, B. Comparison of a self-report symptom rating scale (CES-D) with standardized depression rating scales in a psychiatric population: A preliminary report. Paper presented at the Society for Epidemiologic Research meeting, Albany, New York, 1975.

16

PHYSICAL HEALTH ISSUES

ELIZABETH GREYWOLF, POLLY ASHLEY,
AND MAUREEN FOLEY REESE

Current research has demonstrated that persons undergoing stress or emotional problems are at greater risk for physical diseases (Holmes & Masuda, 1974; Selye, 1978). Stressed individuals are also more likely to seek medical treatment for physical disorders than persons not experiencing emotional problems (Pope, 1979). As a highly stressed group continually facing difficult life dilemmas, low-income mothers are especially vulnerable to health complications.

The Stress and Families Project respondents are no exceptions. They reported an alarming number of chronic health conditions typically associated with stress. (The correlations between the extent of their physical health problems and emotional problems can be seen in Table 16.1.) This chapter explores the self-reported health concerns of the mothers, nutritional inadequacies which exacerbate any tendencies toward chronic health problems, and some of the aspects of the Medicaid system which impede the attainment of adequate health care for this income group. The stressful and unremitting life conditions of this sample have been amply discussed in previous chapters. This chapter highlights what the cumulative effect of continual coping with those life conditions can do in terms of physical damage.

The average woman in this study was only thirty years of age, yet many of the women seemed to have medical histories more likely to be found in the middle-aged. Over one-third of the sample described their health over the preceding two years as fair to very poor; over one-quarter reported experiencing an illness, injury, or condition requiring hospitalization or surgery within that period. Almost one-fourth of the women were also thinking about or waiting to have a minor operation. An alarming 42 percent reported that they have a problem which requires regular treatment, while 22 percent had two or more problems requiring regular treatment.

TABLE 16.1   Correlations Between Extent of Physical Health Problems (Life Conditions Health Stressor Score) and Extent of Emotional Problems

Depressive symptoms	.36**
Anxiety	.43**
Mastery	−.002
Self-esteem	.45**
Stability of self-esteem	.40**

* p < .05
** p < .01

Many of the conditions the women reported are typically associated with stress, including chronic asthma, ulcers, pneumonia, alcoholism, psoriasis, colitis, tuberculosis, migraines, hypertension, arthritis, and weight problems. Almost one-quarter of the women reported moderate to severe menstrual problems, and several mentioned chronic gynecological problems such as endometriosis. In addition to the problems which had been diagnosed and treated, six women experienced undiagnosed or untreated problems, and nearly half said they were in need of two or more treatments or checkups from a doctor, dentist, or eye doctor.

Not surprisingly, these health problems took a toll on the women's abilities to lead normal lives. Forty percent reported that in the previous two years they had been prevented from doing certain kinds of work or housework because of their health problems. Poor health restricted nearly half of the women from engaging in other activities during those two years. Nearly one woman in five indicated she had had to remain in bed all day for 25 or more days, while one-third had to spend 10 or more days in bed. These figures are particularly alarming when one considers that most of the respondents are the primary caretakers of their young children.

To add to the picture, 33 women reported health problems with someone in their extended families, and 23 of them indicated that this caused them additional stress. Anxiety over their children's health can sometimes be the "final straw," triggering a mother's health breakdown, as was the case with Ms. Bradley. A single mother, Ms. Bradley reported what happened when her son had a bad accident: "My son tried to climb the fence in front of the house. He got his arm caught on the top part of the fence and ripped it . . . had to get 15 stitches in his arm." Immediately following that episode Ms. Bradley became ill. She said "the stress from his situation brought on my asthma attack."

DIETARY DEFICIENCY

The need for an investigation of nutrition within a study of low-income mothers who are at high risk for depression is well documented. While poor nutrition can be found at all income levels, the poor are more often the victims of inadequate nutrient intake and malnutrition. According to the National Council of Organizations for Children and Youth (Garetz, 1976), pregnant women on food stamps get less than two-thirds of the calories and protein needed for normal fetal development.

Eighty percent of the women in the sample were using food stamps at the time of the study. One-third reported they did not have an adequate amount of money to spend on food in the week prior to being questioned about their nutritional intake. While this program provides some assistance, it does not ensure that sufficient food for one's family can be provided in a consistent fashion.

Mothers attempted to cope with money shortages in a number of ways. Some shopped at larger supermarkets or food co-ops. Some used community gardens and grew their own vegetables. One woman managed to save an estimated 25 percent on her summer food bills in this way. For another, however, there were times when the community garden provided the only food available to her family.

Food preparation and maintenance were often made difficult by inadequate storage and cooking facilities. Nearly one-fourth of the women indicated they had inadequate storage facilities and refrigeration problems. This means they must shop more often if they want to include fresh food in their families' diets, an undertaking made more difficult for the majority of women who must use public transportation.

The nutritional status of the respondents was measured through use of the 24-hour dietary recall, a method commonly used in nutritional surveys (for example, Boek, 1956), often by nonnutritionist interviewers. It is a fast method of learning about dietary intake and does not require specialized knowledge to use properly. This method requires that an interviewer ask the respondent to list the things she ate in the last 24 hours, after making sure that the food intake of this period was typical for the respondent. The interviewer asks about everything put into the mouth and swallowed, including water and all beverages and vitamin and mineral supplements.

Interviewers were instructed to probe for information about the size of all food portions and the specific methods of preparations. The 24-hour recall method relies on the respondent's memory and willingness to report accurately as well as on the skill of the interviewer. The method assesses dietary adequacy for a given day, but of course cannot capture the fluctuations in dietary adequacy which might be associated with fluctuations in depressive mood or available money to buy food.

The data from the dietary recalls were analyzed by two trained nutritionists, each with a master's degree in nutrition from a recognized school of public health. Adequacy of dietary intake for the sample was computed using the tables from *Nutritive Value of Foods* (U.S. Department of Agriculture, 1971). These tables detail minimum daily requirements for a variety of dietary elements; they do not take into account individual differences in metabolism.

Using the 24-hour recall method of assessing dietary adequacy it was determined that few of the women interviewed were free from serious dietary deficiencies. The dietary adequacy achieved by the sample as a whole is

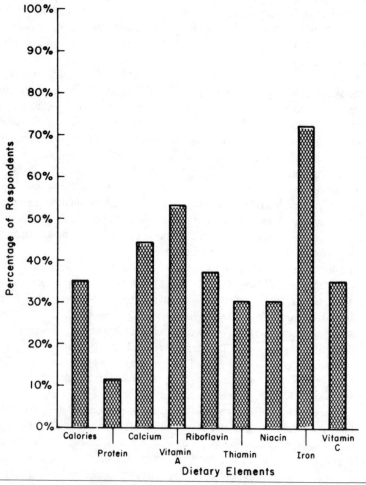

FIGURE 16.1   Percentage of Respondents with Less
Than 80% of USRDA for Each of
Several Dietary Elements

TABLE 16.2   Correlations Between Intake of Dietary Elements and Per Capita Household Income, Per Capita Weekly Food Expenditures, Respondent's Educational Level, and Respondent's Depressive Symptom Score

	Income n = 39	Food Expenditures n = 40	Education n = 42	Depressive Symptoms n = 39
Calories	.25†	.40**	.14	−.14
Protein	−.09	.10	.12	−.05
Calcium	.05	−.05	.14	−.34*
Vitamin A	.21†	−.13	.35*	−.26†
Riboflavin	.07	−.01	.27*	−.19
Thiamin	.09	.05	.38**	−.34*
Niacin	.07	−.04	.22†	.06
Iron	.17	.28*	.11	.04
Vitamin C	.14	−.04	.25†	−.12

†p < .10
* p < .05
** p < .01

illustrated in Figure 16.1. The percentage of women who received less than 80 percent of the U.S. Recommended Daily allowance of each of the ten important dietary elements is shown on this graph.

Deficiencies are most apparent in the intake of iron (vital to red cell development), vitamin A (essential for normal skeletal and teeth development), and calcium (important for blood clotting and for assuring the proper hardness of bones and teeth). Deficits of calcium and thiamin have been related (with other dietary elements) to depression and depression-like symptoms. Considering the sample as mothers of young children, the high level of calcium deficiency is a special concern. Also alarming is the fact that over one-third of the women indicated a deficiency in caloric intake.

Associations were calculated between nutrient intake and the following variables: per capita household income, per capita weekly food expenditure, attained educational level, and depressive symptoms. On the basis of previous research we expected that income, food expenditures, and educational level would be associated positively with dietary adequacy, while depressive symptom score would be negatively correlated with the adequacy of diets. As can be seen in Table 16.2, women with higher incomes had marginally higher intake of calories and of vitamin A. Weekly food expenditure was strongly correlated with caloric intake: the higher the expenditure, the higher the caloric intake. Weekly food expenditure was also associated positively with the intake of iron.

Educational attainment was even more strongly associated with diet than were the income and expenditure variables. As educational level increased, women reported greater intake of vitamin A, riboflavin, and thiamin and marginally greater intake of niacin and vitamin C. Finally, with increased depressive symptoms, women reported reduced intake of calcium and thiamin and marginally reduced intake of Vitamin A. Of the four correlates of nutrient intake, education appeared to be the best predictor of diet.

While the findings suggest that income limitations per se do not always necessitate poor diet in this sample of women, it obviously is less easy to provide well-balanced family meals on a low income. While the nutrients most frequently lacking in the diets of the women studied can be found in inexpensive food, a number of factors associated with low-income lifestyles exacerbate the tendency toward inadequate diets.

In view of the numerous money-related problems encountered by the sample, lack of information and education become even more important factors. Additional time, nutritional information, and energy are needed to plan adequate meals around inexpensive but nutritious foods such as peanut butter, soybeans, and inexpensive cuts of meat, fish, or poultry.

The findings also show a relationship between deficient nutrient intake and the experience of depressive symptoms. From our data, it is impossible to tell if the depression preceded the inadequate diet or if the inadequate diet preceded the depression. Nor can our data reveal whether a more adequate diet would alleviate the depressive symptoms, or whether the depressive symptoms must first be cured before the women will have the energy, initiative, and necessary interest in food to make a healthy diet possible. These results demand further investigation with a longitudinal design.

THE LIMITATIONS OF MEDICAID

While Medicaid is highly valued by the respondents, this program was reported to have many drawbacks. The majority of women were receiving Medicaid assistance at the time of the study. Half of these women reported being unable to obtain one or more medicines which had been prescribed by physicians. Antihistamines, cough medicines, and varied cold preparations, including two mild preparations frequently prescribed for children's ear problems, were reported to be unobtainable through Medicaid. Women reported being able to obtain only certain rather obscure vitamins for adults, even when they were pregnant. Penicillin was unavailable to one woman because her pharmacist said Medicaid had not paid some earlier bills.

Of those receiving Medicaid assistance, 69 percent have reported being unable to procure one or more dental services, such as dentures, fillings, extractions of less than seven teeth, root canal work, and even sodium pentothal for painful dental procedures. In addition, respondents reported not being able to obtain the services of a nutritionist, orthopedic shoes with braces, and intrauterine devices. One respondent's doctor said that Medicaid would not cover the intrauterine device she wanted to use. He gave her, instead, a prescription for birth control pills, which she was afraid—for health reasons—to use. Half of the respondents who use Medicaid services thought their treatment would be of better quality if they had the money to pay for services themselves.

LIMITED CHOICES

Another concern for women who could not afford private health insurance was that of finding doctors willing to accept Medicaid patients. Unlike those financially secure enough to be able to pay cash or purchase third-party insurance coverage, such as Blue Cross/Blue Shield, those women receiving Medicaid coverage are limited in their choice of doctors. Although there may be other motivating factors for doctors excluding Medicaid recipients from their practices, most respondents felt there is an unwillingness on the part of doctors to deal with the payment delays frequently associated with Medicaid bureaucracy.

Sometimes Medicaid patients are initially unaware that a doctor they have chosen has limited his/her practice. At times they are forced to cope with the frustration and humiliation of being turned away without receiving treatment. Ms. Richards, for example, made an appointment for her daughter with a specialist located some distance from her apartment. Upon arriving at the physician's office she found that her daughter could not be treated.

> I went all the way there. I didn't tell them when I made the appointment that I was on Medicaid, just assumed that they would take it. I started to fill out the form and the receptionist said, "What kind of health insurance do you have?" so I told her Medicaid and she said, "We don't take Medicaid."

> I learned my lesson. Now I always ask because I'm not going to get all the way there and have them say no, we won't take you. Adrienne [her seven-year-old daughter] was right there and she said, "Aren't I going to see the doctor?" And I said, "No honey, they won't take us here." We had to leave.

Transportation difficulties can exacerbate situations like Ms. Richards' and also situations that require immediate care. When questioned as to why the women had chosen the health facility they were currently using, the most frequent response (33 percent) was the facility's closeness to home. Having to rely on public transportation rather than private automobiles, many women feel more secure when they can locate a health facility within walking distance.

In addition to frustration, embarrassment, and time loss, a major impact on women can be the feeling that their children end up receiving less than optimal care. Some mothers feel that the necessity of relying on government-supported health insurance gives them not only fewer options but less satisfactory options. As Ms. Richards said:

> It just bothers me when I really would like to go to some doctor that won't take Adrienne. Like before the pediatrician that I have for her [now], I heard about this pediatrician that was very, very good; he was supposed to be one of the best. And I called him up and he says, no, they wouldn't take me. It set me off because I knew he was very good; I had heard through a nurse who took her children there. But I couldn't take Adrienne there because they wouldn't accept it [Medicaid].

Because of the difficulties mentioned, finding a facility where they can feel comfortable is very important to the women. Perhaps the most telling comment summing up the choice of her health facility came from the woman who said: "They treat me like I'm normal there, even with a Medicaid card."

ADMINISTRATIVE FAILINGS

The government backlog of payments to drugstores can create problems for those who rely on Medicaid. Some women have indicated that pharmacists refused to fill prescriptions for them because of the money owed by the government from previous Medicaid purchases. Because of the attendant red tape which causes delayed payments, many women experience the stress associated with being unable to secure needed pharmaceutical items for themselves and their families. Ms. M. told of her experience with one drugstore where "they threw the pills at me once. Said 'Don't come back here no more, we don't get our money.'"

Similar difficulties with payment reimbursement were mentioned for doctors as well. One woman said she looked for doctors with large practices. Those doctors, she felt, were more likely to accept Medicaid patients because they could more easily absorb the cost of temporarily delayed reimbursements. As was mentioned previously, many doctors refuse to deal with the red tape and Medicaid restrictions.

Not all the women were aware of what is and is not covered by Medicaid, and they found the confusion created by the continual updating of these items very upsetting. As Ms. K. explained: "You never know from week to week if they're going to stop paying for antibiotics or you can't get your teeth fixed anymore . . . and you're afraid." One woman indicated she had to have a hearing because she had believed caps for her son's teeth would be paid for when this was not the case. Another woman reported both she and her social worker were reprimanded by her social worker's supervisor when a humidifier, recommended for treatment of a medical problem, was purchased and approved for payment. A third woman talked about her problem procuring glasses because she didn't realize Medicaid only approves payment for specific types of frames. This item was mentioned by several women who complained that the choice of frames was limited to only the least attractive.

Lack of Medicaid coverage for dental care has been a problem for most of the respondents at some point in their lives. Time and again women mentioned that having been able to get dental work for themselves and their children would have prevented the loss of teeth which eventually became so decayed they were extracted. Many women said they simply do not go for checkups they know they need because of limited coverage. The familiar answers to the needs for root canals, caps, and teeth replacements were, "I didn't get the caps," "I didn't have the work done," or, less frequently, "I used other money to pay and got behind in my bills."

DELAYED TREATMENT

The respondents' health problems are often exacerbated by delayed treatment. This is true of women who are on Medicaid but do not have full coverage of problem areas like dental care, and especially for those women like Ms. Gillens who are not covered by Medicaid and cannot easily pay for treatment because of lack of funds. Those individuals who cannot afford private medical insurance but whose incomes are too high for Medicaid eligibility may be the hardest hit. They do not have the security of Medicaid since their incomes are not quite low enough, yet they are not able to purchase private coverage. Other families have some coverage but no extra money to pay for anything insurance does not cover. What happens to these women in times of crisis?

Even though the warning signs of pain and discomfort appear, some women ignore them until the last possible minute because they know that attending to their health needs will mean financial upheaval in the long run. Ms. Gillens is only one of many examples.

Ms. Gillens's children are covered by Medicaid, but she and her husband pay for Blue Cross coverage for themselves. Blue Cross will pay for visits to a hospital but not a clinic, and the family usually has only enough money "to either pay for the doctor or pay for the medicine." Ms. Gillens's health care problems "usually wait until I figure we can't wait any longer." For example, she once let a severe backache go unattended until she "had a terrible chill and found I had a 104 degree fever." Her coverage extends to emergency room care, so she waited until what was eventually diagnosed as a kidney infection was so advanced it could no longer be ignored. In this way Blue Cross will pay for the emergency room treatment and she usually has the money to pay for any medicine prescribed. This either/or (either a doctor or medicine) approach may be used by many women in similar circumstances and certainly decreases the chances for speedy and full recovery.

CONTINUING THE CYCLE

Not only are the health risks of low-income mothers increased by stressful life conditions and events, it appears their children are also at higher risk. Tessler et al. (1976) found that children are more likely to see a physician on those days their mothers are experiencing stress episodes. At those times, children are 2.5 times more likely to experience illness than would be expected by chance (Roghmann & Haggerty, 1972). Children's accident rates also increase in relation to mothers' stress and psychological disorders. Brown and Davidson (1978) found that when women experienced a serious, long-term, difficult or threatening life event their young children had increased risk of accident.

Regardless of the cause or causes, this close connection between a mother's mental state and her own and her children's physical states strongly suggests that a mother might be considered as a health barometer for her family. As she fares, so do her children to a considerable extent. This interrelationship precludes the possibility of maintaining optimal health care for children without also providing preventive care and/or treatment for their mothers.

As health care costs continue to soar, Medicaid coverage becomes more and more essential to disadvantaged segments of our society. Regarding families with no access to proper family health care, questions such as how to develop mental and emotional resources remain academic, unresolvable dilemmas.

NOTE

Polly Ashley conducted the analyses of dietary adequacy for this chapter. Elizabeth Greywolf and Maureen Reese are responsible for the remainder of the chapter.

REFERENCES

Boek, J. Dietary intake and social characteristics. *American Journal of Clinical Nutrition*, 1956, *4* (3), 239-45.

Brown, G., & Davidson, S. Social class and psychiatric disorder of mother and accidents to children. *Lancet*, February 18, 1978, pp. 378-80.

Garetz, F. K. Breaking the dangerous cycle of depression and faulty nutrition. *Geriatrics*, 1976, June, 73-75.

Holmes, T. H., & Masuda, M. Life change and illness susceptibility. In B. S. Dohrenwend & B. P. Dohrenwend (Eds.) *Stressful life events: Their nature and effects*. New York: John Wiley, 1974.

Mechanic, D. Stress, illness and illness behavior. *Journal of Human Stress*, 1976, *2* (2), 2-6.

Pope, C. Illness with a high emotional component and the use of Medical services. *Medical Care*, 1979, *17* (12), 1182-95.

Roghmann, K., & Haggerty, R. J. Family stress and the use of health services. *International Journal of Epidemiology,* 1972, *1,* 279-86.

Selye, H. *The stress of life* (revised paperback edition). New York: McGraw-Hill, 1978.

Tessler, R., Mechanic, D., & Dimond, M. The effect of psychological distress on physician utilization: A prospective study. *Journal of Health and Social Behavior,* 1976, *17,* 353-63.

U.S. Department of Agriculture, Nutritive Value of Foods, Home and Garden Bulletin #72. Washington, DC: Government Printing Office, 1971.

**PART VI
CONCLUSION**

17

FAMILIES REVISITED

MAUREEN FOLEY REESE

During the initial effort to recruit families for this study a promise was made to each respondent that they would be made aware of the study findings. By the time analyses were completed, one year (and in some cases two years) had gone by. However, when the time came to return to each respondent it proved to be a more complicated undertaking than could have been anticipated. Three main issues were raised by the staff, and these had to be resolved in a series of meetings before revisits could be arranged: (1) What was the best way to summarize the study results for the women? This issue was especially problematic because the main findings of the study might prove emotionally disturbing to women already coping with severe life stresses. (2) Should we attempt to determine the women's retrospective feelings about participation in the study to see if there were any long-term effects? (3) It was also suggested that revisits to the respondents would provide an opportunity to add longitudinal data to our data base. By "catching up" on intervening life events in the women's lives we could assess what had altered over time. This chapter describes the dilemma of summarizing the findings, the women's retrospective feelings about their participation in the study, and an overview of the major changes which had taken place in their lives.

SUMMARIZING THE FINDINGS AND
PREPARING FOR REVISITS

Preparing a summary of the findings proved a difficult ethical undertaking. The findings of the study were not optimistic for the women as a group.

225

Many of the respondents were already stressed and highly depressed; others were at high risk. We feared that divulging some of the information, such as the increased vulnerability of their children, would only increase their anxiety. We wondered if the element of trust which had been established during the lengthy interviewing process would be impaired by returning with a negative summation and no suggestions for resolving any of the myriad problems they already faced. This quandary is an all too common research issue; the dilemma of truth versus potential emotional and psychic harm. It has been discussed by other researchers, such as William Foote Whyte. Whyte, after gaining access to the private lives of streetcorner gangs in the North End of Boston, decided openly to discourage the people in that community from reading any analyses of his work with them (Glazer, 1977). He reasoned that his informants might be embarrassed or otherwise damaged by his portrayal of them, and this might lead to feelings of betrayal and losing face in their community. While the Stress and Families Project respondents were not likely to feel endangered by losing face in their communities, we were all too aware that they were in need of positive events in their lives, and that our summary of findings could not offer them much hope of positive outcomes. Without question, we had a responsibility to return to the women: denying them information might be protective of their feelings, but it could also mean denying them potential power through knowledge that could be utilized in any number of ways. At the same time, what could we offer as solutions to help mitigate the stresses they experienced, and how were we to minimize any anxiety which the report might generate? Depending on the individual woman's mental health and her interpretation of the findings, we could anticipate several different affective reactions.

It was decided a personal approach, provided by two former field-workers, would help. Although a manuscript had been completed, staff sentiment was that it should not be given to the respondents as it was technical in nature and might easily overwhelm or alarm them. It was decided a simpler, more easily understandable summary would be prepared, stressing an ecological perspective. It was believed that the women who were not content with this summary would request more information, which we could then provide. Two women, in fact, eventually did request additional information.

Writing the summary was a delicate task. We attempted to write a brief summary of the study's findings which would be grounded in fact yet presented in such a way as to minimize its threat. We also tried to write it so that it was not confusing to the less educated women, yet not condescending to the better educated. It attempted to attack stereotypes about poor women that even some poor women had come to believe about themselves. Above all, there was an attempt to convey that we had come to understand the pain and hardship inherent in their life circumstances, that we appreciated the wealth of information they had provided, and that we planned to continue dissemination of the information gained. It was decided that the two returning interviewers (one white, one black) should discuss the results informally with the women and leave a copy of the prepared summary. They would also gather longitudinal information at the same time.

At the end of the field study, most women had made comments suggesting that their involvement in the research had been a rewarding, even therapeutic, experience. Now that the women had had time to reflect on their experiences, we were interested in assessing whether there was any long-term impact of that process. We decided to ask the women to tell us what they remembered as the best and worst things about the study, hoping to isolate troubling aspects of working with low-income families and those that might enhance further experiences of field work.

In addition, to gather longitudinal data and discover what had happened in the major areas of the women's lives, we decided to also use a briefer interview schedule to chart any changes that had taken place in the 11 life conditions areas we had previously investigated.

RETURN VISITS

The task of contacting the respondents proved to be more complicated than anticipated. A high rate of inner-city mobility made it necessary for us to canvas neighborhoods and telephone books in order to trace the whereabouts of many of the respondents. Several expeditions were made to follow up leads that were provided by former neighbors. We were finally able to contact 34 of the original 43 respondents. However, it was virtually impossible to locate some of the women who had moved because they had left no forwarding addresses and had had their phone numbers changed or unlisted. We decided against using any official channels, such as welfare offices, to trace the remaining nine women because we believed it would be a violation of the anonymity we had promised them.

All of the women we contacted (except two, who were experiencing medical problems) readily agreed to meet with us. We were heartened by this initial response. Although both of the interviewers were well acquainted with the data, they refamiliarized themselves with the particulars of each woman's life up until the last time she had been interviewed. This proved to be a wise strategy because it helped to establish rapport with the women much more quickly. At times the women indicated that they were pleased to learn we knew of things they had said during an interview a year or two before. However, each encounter was an emotional experience; the interviewers were apprehensive about causing the women further anxiety, and the women appeared uneasy as well. Even though we cautioned the women to remember that the findings were not about one particular woman but what the women shared in common, it became apparent that each woman was comparing her life situation to the things we were saying. Some single mothers sighed when they heard that women who lived with husbands or boyfriends were not on the average less depressed than women who did not live with a partner. One woman without any family living near her said it helped to know that often having relatives nearby brought its own set of problems. But, despite all the precautions taken to minimize the emotional impact of the revisits, it was not unusual to see tears. Many of the women sat quietly, glancing downward, and inward, nodding their heads as if to confirm our findings. Perhaps the major part of the affective reaction seemed related to their understanding that "someone had really heard" what their lives were all about. There were also the women who said they felt sorry for those "unfortunate women" we had interviewed. A similar reaction was noted by Lillian Rubin (1976) when she returned to the working-class families she had studied. This suggested to her that these individuals were protecting themselves from further pain by denying that the findings had any connection to their lives. Other women exhibited indignation as they talked about the need for social action to ameliorate these stressful life conditions. In general, the women expressed relief at hearing that they were not alone; other low-income mothers also had a difficult time.

At the end of the field study they had made comments suggesting that involvement in the research had been a rewarding, even therapeutic experience for most of them. This indicated that while we were interviewing them we were not only collecting data but simultaneously intervening in their lives. Now that the women had had time to reflect on their experiences we were interested in assessing whether there was any long-term impact of that process. What remained as the most powerful and/or least liked aspects of their involvement? Would they attribute any change in their mental health to their participation in the study? In retrospect, did any of the women feel that we had exploited them—taken advantage of their trust, insight, and willingness to help others? Our hope was to isolate salient aspects of working with low-income families that would enhance the experience of fieldwork for both respondents and researchers.

RETROSPECTIVE FEELINGS

It took little encouragement from the interviewers to get the women to discuss their feelings about being respondents. There was a striking consistency between what the women had said about their involvement a year or

two earlier and their responses on the open-ended and forced-choice questions during the revisits. Women mentioned such things as having the opportunity to talk about their problems, gaining self-awareness, and having a
meaningful relationship with the interviewer and observer as the best aspects
of the study.

One-third of the women mentioned that being in the study was an experience in self-awareness. The questions that were asked during the field study
stimulated the women to reflect on their experiences, feelings, and attitudes.
As one woman said: "It made me aware of some of the forces in my life that
affected it. . . . It was like she was showing me who I really was." This
prompted them to look at things they had never really looked at before.
Another woman said she "never thought about stuff till you started asking
me, then I realized I was an important person, too." It also made them
consider new ways of looking at old problems. In some cases, the questions
made them realize that they were not alone because we had identified feelings they had never shared with anyone else. While they were being interviewed, they had listened to the things they were telling the interviewers.
Patterns emerged; as they did, the women were able to see their lives more
clearly.

Overwhelmingly, the women talked about the interviewing process as if
it had been a cathartic experience. Rather than saying that they resented
being asked questions about the pain and stress they were under, most
women said it was a relief to talk about such things. "It felt good to be able to
talk your problems out to someone who understands," said one woman.
Another said: "I felt to myself, well, here's a woman that wants to know how
it is to deal with stress and low income . . . and before that nobody wanted to
know. And that was what I needed to tell somebody."

These reactions seem to contradict the widespread notion that if one asks
people about the disappointments in their lives one will exacerbate their
distress. Interviewers always made it a point to ask the women about their
problems and experiences in a direct manner. It seems there were important
benefits from doing that—in terms of emotional relief for the respondents
and rich data for the study. One woman described how this directness
affected her: "She would ask me a personal question about my family, my
husband . . . what it was like to be a low-income family without much
money, for me to be under stress with the hospital bills, just actually what it
was like to cope. Everything was an honest trip. Say how you really felt, so
I'd tell what I really felt."

Half of the women said that meeting the interviewer or child observer was
one of the best things about being in the study. They talked about how they
had looked forward to the interviewer's arrival every week, about how they
had enjoyed the hours they spent talking, and about the trust they had built.
Some women indicated it was difficult for them, and in some instances for

the children, when it all ended because the process had been a rewarding exchange. This termination had a painful effect on the women who were most isolated and depressed, although interviewers had attempted to prepare women by periodically reminding them that completion of the interview schedules was approaching. We now found that some women still expressed feelings of abandonment.

Only when we presented them with a list of positive aspects of the study did any of them (three women) choose receiving money for one's work. Given their financial situations, $150 was a good sum of money. While it probably facilitated the recruitment of most women, money became less significant in relation to the intrinsic benefits the women felt they received during the course of interviewing.

Similarly, the interviewers asked the women to tell us about what they saw as the worst aspects of the study. Overall, they had very few criticisms to make. A review of the negative remarks made at the end of the field study revealed that there was a reduction in criticisms. This may be because the original criticisms were minor and with the passage of time faded from the women's memories. Only two women showed any resentment toward the study. One black woman mentioned that she thought "the questions were too white oriented." The other woman said: "It made you feel like you were selling part of yourself so your kids could have Christmas." On a more positive note this same woman said: "I liked the people I worked with. . . . If it's going to help others by all means."

When we pressed the women by presenting them with a list of negative aspects to choose from, four women declined to say anything negative about the study. For the remaining women particular types of questions were seen as the most disliked aspect of the study, such as those that asked for specific information (dates which were hard to remember) and questions that asked for yes or no answers and did not allow them the chance to indicate their true sentiments.

It is worth noting that not one woman said that the interviews took up too much time. In fact, several women felt that the study was not long enough. This is surprising, considering that the interviews took four or five hours a week for several months. It appears to speak to the pressing need these women have to talk about their experiences.

As a staff we had worked hard at ensuring worthwhile relationships between the fieldworkers and the respondents. At staff meetings we had discussed our relationships with the women and brought up ethical concerns. This way we always kept a check on our attitudes and feelings toward the women. This process sensitized us to see the subtle ways in which cultural differences clouded our understanding of other people's experiences. This aided us in empathizing with the women and finally coming to a close understanding of their lives. Overall, however, it was now apparent

that the women had viewed the process as one which was mutually beneficial. Their long-term, as well as short-term, feelings were overwhelmingly
positive.

CATCHING UP

We were eager to find out what changes had occurred in the lives of the
women since we had last seen them. Would we find that many of them had
higher incomes, safer housing, better jobs, and less stress-filled relationships with their families and friends? While we hoped to find such changes
had taken place, we feared that worsening economic conditions in the country may have made life even more difficult for many of them.

As usual, the interviews were varied. Some of them were very disturbing,
some were pleasant but uneventful and left us wondering how some women
retained a positive approach in the face of poverty. Others—far fewer—
were filled with news about positive accomplishments and improved mental
health.

Analysis of the findings from the return visits corroborate the findings of
the field study. Women who reported concern over their mental health also
reported a staggering number of problems in the areas of physical health,
intimate relations, housing, parenting, and support networks. Change and
disruption in all major life conditions areas had continued for many of the
women since the time they had been interviewed. While 44 percent of the
women reported no change at all in income, 28 percent now indicated they
had even less money and, not surprisingly, saw life as more difficult. Another 28 percent said their incomes had increased somewhat and overall they
found things easier and their mental health improved.

A good deal of change had occurred in family composition and neighborhood residences during this intervening period. Of the 32 women, 20 reported changes in the number of persons living in their households, four of
the recontacted women had moved from their neighborhoods, and four were
in the process of moving. Six women said they had been victims of neighborhood crimes such as breaking and entering and vandalism. One woman
talked about finding her friend half beaten to death on her doorstep.

Health concerns continued to plague the women, as might be expected.
Seventeen women talked of physical health problems which bothered them;
two women had attempted suicide, and two had been hospitalized because of
emotional problems.

Twelve women also talked about problems with their children, and eight
of these were women who had experienced a drop in income.

We decided to compare the scores the women had previously obtained on
the CES-D Scale (using 16 and above as the depression indicator) to the

comments they made regarding their mental health during the interview. The women were grouped into four categories: those who had been depressed and said they still felt depressed; those who had been depressed and indicated they were feeling more positive mental health; those who had not been depressed and indicated continued well-being; and those who had not been depressed but were experiencing poorer mental health. By identifying these groups we were able to differentiate women according to whether they were suffering from recent onset of or long-term emotional problems. It also gave us some insight into how much movement there was in mental health status and what may have led to improvement and deterioration.

LONG-TERM DEPRESSION

Of the eighteen women who had originally scored high on the CES-D Scale during the field study, 18 talked about the fact that they were still experiencing poor mental health. In fact, some of them said they were more depressed than ever. As we had found earlier, these women were more likely to report poor physical health, difficulties over housing, and problems in their relationships with their husbands/boyfriends, children, other relatives and friends. They were also more likely to report a drop in income, especially devastating during current rapid inflationary years. These women were, as we had suspected, the most vulnerable in the sample, experiencing unabated stressful conditions year after year. Two of the twelve women had attempted suicide, and another had experienced the attempted suicide of her forty-year-old mother, who lived in the same building; two women were hospitalized for depression; two marriages ended; ten women reported a serious health problem; one child was made a ward of the state and institutionalized because of his destructive behavior; another mother reported that her sons had been lighting fires.

LIFTING DEPRESSION

Compared to the group experiencing sustained depression, six women who had previously scored high on the depressive symptomatology scale were feeling better about themselves and were more confident about their ability to handle the stress in their lives. While it would be impossible to say if the mental health of these women would continue to improve after our visit with them (because they still remained at high risk for depression), it did give us an opportunity to consider the facts surrounding their improved outlook. In each case there appeared to be interrelationships among several factors in the woman's life (increased income, improved relationships, better housing, and so on), and it would be impossible to speculate about what had occurred first.

It is noteworthy that all six women said they had gained an overview of their lives from participating in the study and they all attached therapeutic value to the relationship they had with their interviewer. It is not unreasonable to speculate that this experience opened the way for other positive experiences. A brief review of their improved circumstances illustrates how one positive experience may lead to others.

One woman had become involved with a religious group and was actively studying the Bible. She said that "it might not be the answer for everyone, but it's helping me." Consequently, she broke off her relationship with a man who was beating her and she lessened her contacts with her alcoholic parents. Much to her surprise, her social network evolved into a group of people she had once felt were "way above me." Her continued efforts to have her five-year-old son's disabilities properly diagnosed finally came to fruition during this time, and she reported feeling relieved to know that a special program was being designed to help him overcome his birth defect. At the time of the interview she was working as a housekeeper a few days a week and hoping to move her family out of project housing. She said that although "things are getting harder, I'm feeling better about my ability to handle things."

Another woman, who had dropped out of school at sixteen, returned to school to get her GED (General Education Diploma) after the interviewer stopped visiting her. The director of the community program she attended took an interest in her and helped her to make a transition to a nearby community college. The positive reinforcement she was receiving from her teachers was greatly improving her self-image. In fact, she was considering a transfer to a four-year school to major in biology. Meanwhile, she found a doctor who is able to treat her daughter's hearing problem, and the child's school work improved almost immediately. Of her relationship with the man she was living with, she said, "it's getting better." So were the other relationships in her life because, she explained, "where I do know myself better I can listen from the outside instead of getting into everything."

Ms. S, who was a shy, almost timid woman when we first started interviewing her one and a half years before, said that she had become "less nervous, more friendly and open." This she attributed to the self-confidence she gained from attending a community college and working at a field placement related to her course of study. She had been offered full-time employment upon completion of her associate of arts degree and was delighted at the prospect of becoming self-sufficient. At the age of sixteen she had become pregnant, dropped out of school, and gotten married. By the time she was twenty-one, she was divorced and was receiving welfare for herself and her two children. Acquiring a GED and an associate of arts degree were important factors affecting her future outlook. Although she had been receiving obscene phone calls from the landlord and had received an eviction notice a few days prior to the revisit interview, she was managing to cope with things quite well.

Ms. J said that before she was in the study she had "no hope at all." Now that has changed. While having someone to talk with had helped to improve her outlook, other pleasant things have happened to her. The apartment she lives in and once felt so badly about has been remodeled. This had a significant impact on her mental health; she no longer felt like moving and was proud to "show the apartment off." Ms. J also had a stroke of good luck in winning a large sum of money in the state lottery. At least for the present, things were looking better.

Ms. C had given birth just prior to the return visit. When the baby was born she had a tubal ligation; as a result, she said she was feeling more relaxed, more confident, and less worried. Her relationship to the baby's father had strengthened. "Somehow we are closer now—babies bring families together." It is clear that Ms. C felt she had more control over her life now that her family was complete. She was even entertaining ideas about eventual career directions that she would like to pursue.

These experiences illustrate the powerful rippling effect that occurred when these women experienced some hopeful changes and/or received some positive reinforcement. The women mention deriving a sense of self-worth from these positive experiences and an increased sense of agency over their lives as well. This, in turn, paved the way for more positive experiences.

RECENT DOWNTURN IN MENTAL HEALTH

To our surprise, there were four women who had been enjoying good mental health but who, during the revisit, reported a negative change. Two of the women, however, seemed to be experiencing life cycle depression; one had turned forty-four and was going through a process of reevaluation; the other woman had just graduated from college and had been accepted into a Ph.D. program, which spurred an examination of values and life direction.

The remaining two women were trying to cope with an accumulation of life stress. One single mother, who was extremely dependent on her family, was trying to cope with the fact that her mother and her brother had serious health problems and her nephew had had a nervous breakdown. The other woman had been trying desperately to escape the ghetto. A new baby, rising inflation, the rats, and closed-in space of her apartment were all taking a toll on her mental health.

NONDEPRESSED WOMEN

Ten women who had previously scored low on the CES-D scale indicated they were enjoying good mental health. In fact, five of these women said they were feeling more positive about their own abilities. There seems to be no one unifying characteristic among these women, except that they reported fewer negative events during the intervening period. All but one woman, who was overweight, said they had *no* health problems. Seeing these women was a reminder that not all low-income mothers experience the specific stressors which this study has found to be threatening to mental health, such as extremely low and unreliable income, poor physical health, and nonsupportive relationships. Other women manage to retain good mental health in the face of difficult life circumstances. While our book has emphasized the risks to which low-income mothers and their children are subject, it is heartening to remember that some fortunate families do not experience these troubles.

CONCLUSION

When we began our fieldwork, the issue of returning to families was a straightforward one. We would tell the women what we learned about the stress-depression link among low-income mothers. However, as time passed we became increasingly aware of the complexity of the issues involved. In the end, we were satisfied with our resolution of these issues, and we felt the women were satisfied with our attempt to thank them for participation as well.

The revisits aroused mixed emotions. On one hand, it was alarming to learn that unaltered stressful life circumstances had taken a toll on many of the respondents' lives in the form of attempted suicides, mental breakdowns, health problems, and children's adjustment problems. On the other hand, it was encouraging to learn that participation in the study had been a positive experience. It was not unusual for women to link their improved mental health to the process of being interviewed and to relationships with the interviewers. Piotrowski (1978) and Rubin and Mitchell (1976) also noted the ways in which their research was a process of self-reflection and personal growth and, hence, an intervention into their respondents' lives. This points to the need for more discussion in the scientific community about the respondent-researcher relationship and the effect of research methods on the lives of respondents.

REFERENCES

Glazer, M. *The research adventure: Promise and problems of field work.* New York: Random House, 1972.

Piotrowski, C. *Work and the family system.* New York: Free Press, 1978.

Rubin, L. *Worlds of pain: Life in the working class family.* New York: Basic Books, 1976.

Rubin, Z., & Mitchell, C. Couples research as couples counseling. *American Psychologist,* 1976, *31,* 17-25.

18

SUMMARY AND CONCLUSIONS

DEBORAH BELLE

SUMMARY

The Stress and Families Project was begun to investigate the life context of low-income mothers in order to learn why this group is at such high risk for depression. The study found that for many low-income mothers this context includes unpredictable income, unrelieved child care responsibilities, poor housing, inadequate employment opportunities, dependence on social agencies for the necessities of life, and the experience of discrimination and violent crime. Many mothers have no time in the day for themselves, and many are forced to deal continuously with emergencies in an attempt to maintain family stability. The study respondents experienced a high rate of depressive symptoms and frequently were without a sense of mastery over their lives.

Among the women who were interviewed, however, there were wide variations in the difficulty of life circumstances and in emotional well-being. Some women reported virtually no symptoms of poor mental health, while others reported almost as many symptoms as the scales allowed. The life circumstances of the respondents—their economic resources, housing, work experiences and health, for instance—also differed enormously. Those women who experienced more stressful and less supportive environments also experienced more symptoms of depression.

The respondents experienced stressful life events with much greater frequency than has been found for the general population. Yet the experience of stressful life events, even major tragedies and emergencies, was not as powerfully related to poor mental health as were chronic or slowly changing conditions of life. Events appear to affect the mental health of low-income mothers insofar as they alter the enduring conditions of life.

For the women who were interviewed, money was the most problematic issue of life. Money problems affected all areas of life, beginning with the most basic. One-third of the respondents said they did not have enough money to buy adequate food for their families. Respondents with lower incomes reported significantly more depressive symptoms and symptoms of anxiety than did respondents with higher incomes. Even when women had similar income levels, difficulties concerning money, such as unpredictability of income and lack of control over income, were related to worries in many areas of life.

There was great variation in the ways the respondents spent their days. Some women were most often at home caring for children, while others held jobs outside the home or attended school. Some women spent much of their time with adults, while others rarely saw adults in the course of the day. Such differences in daily routine were not generally associated with differential risk of depression. However, the extent to which women had time to themselves and the extent to which they were able to arrange their daily schedules to suit themselves, rather than to meet external demands, did appear to differentiate women with few depressive symptoms from those with many such symptoms.

Variation was also apparent in the respondents' early childhood experiences. There were women who had grown up in middle-class homes but become poor in adulthood, and others who had grown up in extreme poverty or foster homes. The women also varied in the extent to which their childhoods had been marked by important losses and disruptions, such as the divorce or remarriage of parents. Women who had experienced deprived and disrupted childhoods were more likely to experience stressful life conditions in adulthood than were women with more stable and secure childhoods. Childhood stress factors were also related to poor psychological health in adulthood, although such factors did not explain as much of the variance in current adult mental health as did the stressfulness of current life conditions.

While low-income mothers are frequently stereotyped as too lazy to work, the study found that most of the women have extensive work histories, expect to work during their future lives, and expect to derive considerable satisfaction from working. Many women, however, reported difficulties in finding employment compatible with their responsibilities as parents. In order to work while still caring for young children, some women took part-time work, home-based work, and work with flexible, evening, or nighttime hours. These jobs, however, were generally very poorly paid and did not provide benefits or opportunities for advancement. For many women who wanted to work and stop receiving welfare benefits, the cost of child care and the threat of losing Medicaid benefits without being able to afford private health insurance destroyed the economic rationale for work. Women in the study who were not working but who wanted to work reported much higher levels of depressive symptoms than did employed women, and women with extensive work histories reported fewer depressive symptoms than did women with shorter work histories. The respondents, as a group, were firmly committed to the work ethic.

Women were, however, forced to turn to public welfare programs when they were unable to work because of their responsibility for infants and small children, or unable to support their families fully through earnings from employment, and unable to rely on the earnings of a husband. For women forced to rely on welfare benefits, inadequate information about the benefits to which they were entitled was a frequent source of worry and frustration. Women also feared the control the welfare system exercised over their lives, the loss of privacy, and the stigma attached to being a welfare recipient. Women coped with the regulation and dehumanization of the welfare experience in different ways. Some amassed as much information as they could from others who had received welfare benefits and from written materials; some learned to meet the expectations of those with power to affect their lives; and some sought advocates to help them achieve the benefits to which they and their children were entitled.

Women reported that discrimination prevented them from getting many of the things they wanted in life, from jobs and promotions to respect. Black respondents rated racial discrimination the most harmful in preventing them from attaining such things. Both black and white women agreed that, excluding racial discrimination, discrimination because of one's low income was the most harmful type of discrimination experienced. Respondents reported incidents of discrimination at all of the familiar and important institutions of urban life, from restaurants to welfare offices. Most violent acts of discrimination were directed against blacks. Respondents reacted to discrimination by direct confrontation of the discriminator, by active protest to an outside agency or community group, and sometimes by deciding to ignore the incident. Women reported that discrimination had severe emotional consequences, the pain often lasting for months and even years. Discrimination also affected the respondents' children and their own child-rearing strategies.

Although serious discontents were voiced about the political system of our country, over half of the women in the study usually vote in national, state, and city elections, and 10 of the 43 respondents had at some time tried to solve problems with the aid of their political representatives. However, many of these attempts had not been successful and made women more pessimistic and cynical about working through the political system. Most women expressed distrust of politicians, whom they believe ignore the needs of the poor while perverting political institutions for their own ends and in the interests of more powerful individuals. A majority of the respondents opposed Medicaid restrictions on abortion. While many respondents were favorably disposed to government work programs for those on welfare, many appeared to lack crucial information about these programs. Their favorable comments appeared to reflect their belief in the value of work, along with the hope that such programs would help them to find decent employment.

Women who received help with tasks, especially child care, and women who had someone to confide in were less depressed than women without such help and emotional support. This kind of assistance often came from relatives and friends. Yet social ties often brought additional stress. Friends and relatives experienced difficulties similar to those which troubled the respondents themselves, and many women told us they suffered through these problems along with their own. Women also provided assistance to those close to them, and sometimes the demands of friends and relatives were draining. Overall, women who had large social networks, lived in close proximity to network members, and interacted frequently with network members were not immune to stress or depression. Their mental health was similar to that of women who were less social involved. Thus, while social support was associated with good mental health, social *involvement* was not.

While half of the women in the study shared a household with a husband or boyfriend, these men differed greatly in the extent to which they provided financial support, emotional support, and child care and housekeeping assistance to their families. The more support a woman received from her partner, the better her mental health and the more her children reported that they turned to their father for nurturance and support. The mere presence of a man in the household was, however, no guarantee of such support.

The mother-child relationship appeared to suffer under the influence of stress and particularly under the influence of depression. Women reported that parenting was one of their most difficult tasks when they were depressed. Women who were stressed, depressed, or anxious spoke about their child-rearing beliefs and practices in distinctive ways: they stated they were more demanding of their children, less tolerant of disobedience, and used more shouting and physical punishment when confronted by a child's disobedience. Observations of mothers and children together in their homes indicated that mothers who experienced more depressive symptoms were less responsive and nurturant, more restricting and hostile to their children, than less depressed mothers. Children whose mothers were more depressed were more likely to report themselves unhappy at home than were children of less depressed mothers.

The respondents were often frustrated in their attempts to cope with stressful life circumstances. These stressful situations were often both unexpected and of relatively long duration, a combination which presents severe challenges to coping capacity. In addition, the respondents were generally restricted in the options available to them for responding to such threatening situations. Even after they enacted resourceful coping strategies, many women were not successful in their efforts to cope. The severe threats facing the respondents, their limited options for coping, and the poor rate of success in coping with life problems eroded the belief that the world is consistent and responsive to one's efforts. Repeated experiences of this kind can be said to overdetermine symptoms of poor mental health.

Most of the respondents had personal experiences with mental health services. While some of these experiences were helpful, many were not satisfactory and left the respondents distrustful of the mental health care system. Several respondents received only drug therapy when they wanted a chance to discuss their problems with a therapist. Other respondents reported that they were blamed by therapists for their children's problems and not aided in solving these problems. Many women were reluctant to seek therapy because of the fear they would be judged too "unstable" to retain custody of their children. Some women found that their physical health problems were interpreted as emotional problems, with the result that needed physical treatment was denied. Such experiences contributed to the women's pessimism about the usefulness of treatment for mental health problems. In discussing their own conceptions of emotional problems, many of the respondents revealed that they view such problems as inseparable from the difficult circumstances of their lives.

Poor physical health as well as poor mental health reflected the difficulties of women's lives. The respondents experienced severe health problems such as colitis, recurrent pneumonia, hypertension, and ulcers, many conditions which have been found to be stress-related. Women's daily diets were generally not adequate in essential nutrients, and women reported many difficulties in serving their families proper meals. Inadequate incomes, inadequate storage and refrigeration facilities, and the lack of specialized knowledge required to prepare nutritious foods on a limited budget appeared to be important barriers to balanced diets. Women reported many difficulties in finding good medical care for themselves and their children. Medicaid benefits did not cover many crucial services, and bureaucratic confusion further reduced the usefulness of this program. Women whose incomes were too high for Medicaid benefits often found they simply could not afford needed health care. Some women eschewed preventive care entirely, in favor of waiting until medical problems had reached crisis proportions because emergency care was reimbursable while routine care was not.

Return visits to families one year after the end of fieldwork indicated that women still viewed their participation in the study positively. Several women credited their improved mental health to the self-reflection and self-discovery stimulated by the interviewing process and to their relationships with the interviewers. Respondents whose highly stressful life circumstances had not improved during the year following the study reported many severe problems at the time of the return visits. Unabated problems had taken their toll in the form of attempted suicides, mental breakdowns, health problems, and children's adjustment problems.

CONCLUSION

Seen in the context of human lives, depression appears an almost unavoidable response to an environment that allows women little control over most of the important things in life and little hope that life will improve. The long-term problems of poverty, burdensome responsibilities, and foreclosed opportunity contribute more heavily to the depression of low-income mothers than a single crisis or tragic event. Women's mental health, in turn, is crucial to the mother-child relationship. The findings of the study suggest several strategies for protecting the mental health of low-income mothers and their family functioning as well.

Interventions should be aimed at those low-income mothers who experience the most stressful and the least supportive environments, since these women are most at risk for depression and other mental health problems. Among low-income mothers, those with particularly low or unreliable incomes, those who have been unable to secure the kind of paid employment they have sought, those without confidantes and child care help, and those with a history of change and loss in childhood appear to be at high risk. Black women appear to face more severe discrimination in many areas of life than do white women. This study found no reason to believe that a woman with a small social network is at greater risk than a woman with a relatively large social network. In determining risk one must instead ask whether the social network provides emotional and instrumental support, or whether the social ties actually create more burdens than they lift.

This study also suggests that parenting education is not needed to make depressed women aware of their difficulties in the mother-child relationship. Interventions which limit attention to that relationship and leave other aspects of the mother's life unchanged should be less successful in improving parenting than those which recognize the connections among life stresses, depression, and parenting. Interventions which help women overcome the stresses of their lives would almost certainly also improve women's mental health, their maternal behavior, and the quality of the mother-child relationship.

Since money problems are particularly central to depression in low-income women, and since many women regard decent paid employment as a potential route out of poverty and depression, programs which help women to find and keep such employment could have a powerful impact on mental health. Affordable and acceptable child care is essential to many women who would like to work. A long overdue upgrading of pay scales for much traditional "women's work" is also needed to enable women to support their families when they do work at such jobs as waitressing, factory work, and human service work. Training for women in nontraditional, well-paying jobs is also crucial. Public policies must address the dilemma many women face of losing Medicaid benefits when they work and yet receiving no health benefits at work and such low pay for that work that they cannot afford a private insurance plan.

Therapy for low-income mothers must address the context in which they live. If mental health professionals are knowledgeable about the relationship between women's psychological well-being and environmental circumstances, they can incorporate this perspective into their treatment efforts. If therapy is properly oriented, in combating depression women can also gain control over other areas of their lives. However, if environmental realities are ignored while therapist and patient search for the personality defect at the root of an emotional problem, a woman is liable to sink more deeply into passivity, guilt, and depression while losing the chance to overcome both real-life problems and emotional problems.

Mutual help groups can be particularly powerful resources for women in emotional distress and in the midst of oppressive life conditions. In such groups women meet with others who have similar experiences, provide and receive emotional support, and work together toward solutions to problems. Advocacy efforts to help women resolve legal problems, gain the welfare benefits to which they are entitled, or secure job training can be a wonderful adjunct to other therapy or a therapy in itself.

Women who are having problems with their children must not be kept away from professional help by the very real threat that they will be judged unstable and have their children taken away from them. Supportive services should be available to mothers to enable them to resolve their problems and keep their families together. Families that can be helped should not be torn apart.

Since many women attempt and fail to find appropriate mental health treatment through the general health system, changes in the types of treatment available, removal of the financial barriers to treatment elsewhere, and improved referral mechanisms are needed. The provision of drug therapy alone will not satisfy women's needs to explore the connections in their lives between their emotional problems and the stressful conditions in which they live. Consciousness-raising to make clear the stress-related nature of depression and of undesired types of maternal behavior would help to remove the stigma which now surrounds emotional problems and "poor parenting."

The consciousness-raising must also extend to the larger society, and particularly to those who come in contact with low-income mothers at the major institutions which affect their lives, such as the welfare office, children's schools, and mental health and general health services. It is time we stopped blaming the victims of overwhelming life circumstances and instead worked together to remove some of the stresses from their lives.

ABOUT THE CONTRIBUTORS

Polly Ashley earned her B.S./B.A. degrees from Bennett College in 1975 and her M.S. from Harvard in 1977. She is currently employed as a biochemist at Dupont's Haskell Laboratory for toxicology and industrial medicine, where she is engaged in biochemical toxicology research.

Deborah Belle is research associate and lecturer at the Harvard Graduate School of Education, where she is also Director of the Stress and Families Project. She earned her Ed. D. degree at the Laboratory of Human Development at the Harvard Graduate School of Education in 1976. She is co-editor of *The Mental Health of Women*.

Weining C. Chang is Associate Professor at the Department of Psychology, Texas Southern University and is also a lecturer at the University of Houston. She has been associated with the Stress and Families Project since 1977. She received her Ph.D. in psychology in 1973 from the University of Houston. Her current interests include cross-cultural studies in human organization and issues related to women and children.

Diana Dill is a doctoral student in Human Development and Counseling at the Harvard Graduate School of Education.

Ellen Feld is a doctoral candidate in Human Development at the Harvard Graduate School of Education. She is currently co-director of a study of women's coping strategies and staff development consultant for the Children's Hospital Medical Center in Boston, Massachusetts.

Elizabeth Greywolf is a writer and a staff member of the Stress and Families Project. She is especially interested in the dynamics of intimacy and alienation. Her latest publication is "Stressed Mothers Syndrome" in the November 1980 issue of *Behavioral Medicine*.

Cynthia Longfellow is a research fellow at the Harvard School of Education, where she received her Ed.D. in human development in 1979. Her current research investigates how children are affected by and cope with stress.

Vivian Parker Makosky is Associate Professor of Psychology and Department Chair at St. Lawrence University, where she has taught since 1970. She earned her Ph.D. in experimental-social psychology at Ohio University in 1971. She was a research associate with the Stress and Families Project during 1976-77.

Nancy Marshall is a doctoral student in human development at Harvard University and a staff member of the Somerville Women's Center. Her research interests include the impact of welfare, employment, and child care policies and practices on women's lives, and the availability and effectiveness of informal and formal support networks for women and their families.

Jacquelyn Mitchell is Assistant Professor of Afro-American Studies and Applied Behavioral Science at the University of California at Davis. She received her Ed.D. from Harvard Graduate School of Education in 1979. Her most recent article, "Reflections of a Black Social Scientist," will appear in the winter 1982 issue of the *Harvard Educational Review*.

Maureen Foley Reese is an Ed.D. candidate in human development at the Harvard Graduate School of Education. Her research interests concern the ways in which social structural forces impede or facilitate adult development, especially among women. She is co-author of the article, "Stressed Mothers Syndrome: How to Short-Circuit the Stress-Depression Cycle."

Elisabeth Saunders is staff psychologist at the Family Court Clinic, Clarke Institute of Psychiatry, Toronto, Ontario. She earned her Ed.D. degree at the Laboratory of Human Development, Harvard Graduate School of Education, in 1979. She has collaborated with Dr. R. Selman in developing a description of children's conceptions of the parent-child relationship.

Ronna Schuller is a doctoral student in clinical psychology at Temple University, where she received her M.A. degree in 1980. She is currently investigating qualitative and structural dimensions of self and object representations in bulimic women.

Emilie Steele is Assistant Professor at the College of Public and Community Service at the University of Massachusetts/Boston. She is an Ed.D. candidate at the Harvard Graduate School of Education in the areas of teaching, curriculum, and learning environments. Her research interests focus on how adults construct reality and how this construction affects choices they make.

Ruth F. Tebbets is currently a postdoctoral fellow at the University of California, Berkeley. She received her Ph.D. in social psychology from Harvard University in 1981.

Phyllis Zelkowitz received her M.A. in applied psychology from the University of Toronto and is currently completing her doctorate in human development at Harvard University. She teaches in the Department of Education at Concordia University. Her research interests include the study of children's social networks and the effects of social change on the family.

Susan Zur-Szpiro received her M.Ed. at the Harvard Graduate School of Education in 1979. She is currently working as a therapist at a child guidance clinic in Cambridge. Her research and professional interests include studying families in stress and helping them to gain the control needed to deal with problems in their lives.